THE IDEA OF THE CHURCH

MERCER UNIVERSITY

MERCER UNIVERSITY PRESS

Endowed by

TOM WATSON BROWN

and

THE WATSON-BROWN FOUNDATION, INC.

THE IDEA OF THE CHURCH

Historical and Theological Perspectives

FREDERICK J. PARRELLA

MERCER UNIVERSITY PRESS | Macon, Georgia

MUP/ P686

Published by Mercer University Press
1501 Mercer University Drive
Macon, Georgia 31207

27 26 25 24 23 5 4 3 2 1

Books published by Mercer University Press are printed on acid-free paper that meets the requirements of the American National Standard for Information Sciences—Permanence of Paper for Printed Library Materials.

Printed and bound in the United States.

This book is set in Adobe Caslon.

Cover/jacket design by Burt&Burt.

ISBN 978-0-88146-915-8

Cataloging-in-Publication Data is available from the Library of Congress

CONTENTS

To Gina, With All My Love

PREFACE

In 1983, when the Graduate Program Pastoral Ministries was established in the Religious Studies Department of Santa Clara University, I was asked by Anne Marie Mongoven, O.P, to teach a course in ecclesiology. I did so for many years until my retirement in 2020. My early lecture notes were handwritten. When computers entered our world, I typed some of the notes on that ancient Apple desktop in my office. Fast-forward, I now have nine chapters on the idea of the church, beginning with an introduction on the nature of theology, the origins of the church in the preaching of Jesus, the development of ecclesiology as a discipline, and the two-thousand-year history of ecclesiology. Of particular note are the six chapters that present and explore this history—not the history of the church, but the history of the church's own self-understanding: put differently, how the church defined itself as church through the ages.

This book is intended for advanced undergraduates and first level graduate students. I want to thank all of my own graduate students through the decades for their ideas and questions in the ecclesiology class and for the wonderful work they submitted in their papers and reports. I am very grateful to Ramon Duran and Sammy Pulos for their assistance in formatting the manuscript. Finally, I want specially to thank Marc Jolley, the Director, and Marsha Luttrell, Publishing Assistant, of Mercer University Press for their support for this book and for making it available to a wider audience.

1.

INTRODUCTION: THEOLOGY, ECCLESIOLOGY, AND HISTORY

1.1 The Situation of the Church Today

The pre-Socratic philosopher Heraclitus is famous for his dictum that "all things are in flux; nothing remains the same (παντα ρει, ουδεν μενει)." For him, the only permanent reality is change itself because everything is in the state of becoming. This is as true of our personal lives as it is of our major political, cultural, and educational institutions. It is just as true of the great world religions, including Christianity. Or is it? Is there something that endures and transcends the passage of time and remains the same? Is there something eternal hidden in the flux of time?

Let me illustrate this with a story. On a reunion of my elementary school class about a decade ago, I was shocked to see how everyone had changed in appearance. We had left school in the late 1950s as children and almost overnight, it seemed, we had grown old and passed the fullness of our lives. Some of us were hardly recognizable in features and voice. While I could examine my own picture as a boy of thirteen and be quite surprised by the toll of the years, still I was the same person, the same consciousness, five decades earlier. From the "outside in," I could see the changes—education, profession, marriage, the onset of old age, etc.—yet from the "inside out," I was one continuous flow of growth in experience and consciousness. While I had changed, I simultaneously sensed changelessness within. Our lives comprise a history of what the poet T. S. Eliot calls a pattern of "timeless moments"—of change, growth, death, and rebirth. Even these timeless moments exist *in* time. There is no timelessness without time as its framework of both confinement and freedom. As Eliot says, "only through time time is conquered."[1]

Has the Church of Jesus Christ failed to take history seriously? Some Catholics, including the last two popes before Pope Francis, John Paul II and Benedict XVI, seemed to prefer a timeless church. The romantic nineteenth-century view of the church as "Christ in time" continues to appeal to many. Yet, even the enduring presence of Christ takes place in a clear and distinctive temporal pattern. Without this pattern, without history, the whole mystery of the church as the "divine self-gift" is unintelligible.[2] Just as my classmates and I at the reunion shared our histories to understand our present selves, Christians must examine the church in its historical context and, more important theologically, from its historical sense of itself. Whatever the church is today, its present reality is the result of two millennia of growth and decline, of action and failure to act, of right action and sinful action in response to political, social, and economic forces within and without. Like our lives, the church reflects the pattern of death and resurrection and their intimate connection. The church today is a sum of all those steps and missteps of the past centuries. Just as I understand myself after many decades as an ever-changing continuum of consciousness, the community of Christ embraces this continuum of the church's self-awareness. In doing so, we will see an enormously varied pattern: a small community of Jews who proclaimed Jesus as the messiah; a leaven of truth and civility in an unraveling civilization; the most powerful institution of the Western world; a community fragmented and split by theological and political hostilities; a community, in response, that turned inward to become Roman Catholic rather than truly "catholic"; a Roman Church split between the authentic Gospel of Jesus and the preservation of the post-Tridentine church, each wrestling with the problems of the modern and postmodern world in radically different ways.[3] Add to this picture the current sinful and scandalous behavior of some clergy, both priests and bishops, guilty of

[1] T. S. Eliot, "Little Gidding," *The Four Quartets* (New York: Harcourt, Brace and World, 1943), 58; T. S. Eliot, "Burnt Norton," *The Four Quartets* (New York: Harcourt, Brace and World, 1943), 16.

[2] Avery Dulles, *Models of the Church,* rev. ed. (Garden City, NY: Doubleday, 1987), 9.

[3] On postmodern culture, see Paul Lakeland, *Postmodernity: Christian Identity in a Fragmented Age* (Minneapolis: Fortress Press, 1997).

the sexual abuse that corrupts their power and leaves innocent victims of all ages damaged for a lifetime.

The twenty-first century sees itself as unique, surrounded by theological and ethical issues unimaginable to an earlier time. Add to this the divisiveness of American politics, the Covid pandemic, and climate change and it is no wonder so many people feel adrift and unmoored. For these and other reasons, perhaps people seem justified in their perception of a certain historical uniqueness. The objective world, with its extraordinary size and technological complexity, has made the microcosmic worlds of individuals' own spiritual selves both powerful and insignificant, isolated yet intimately linked with others, enormously precious yet appallingly small at the same time. Many persons today are more aware of the depth and power of their own experience along with their solidarity with others; at the same time, they are also disillusioned about their individual lives making any real difference in the context of a global world. People in the third millennium ask different questions than the medieval or the modern individual: what is the meaning of *my* life? Is there really a reality called God to whom I can turn in times of need? Does my individual life make any real difference in the life of the world as a whole? What can I turn to beyond myself for a norm for choice and action? What is my responsibility to those less fortunate—the poor, the marginalized, the refugees? Am I my brother's and sister's keeper and, if I am, how should I act, what should I do? What are my needs for community, family, and a place to share my being? All these questions are the raw material of a broader theological foundation of church and ecclesiology in the third decade of the twenty-first century.

In addition, the institutional church has lost great credibility with numerous charges of sexual abuse on the part of some clergy—priests, bishop, and cardinals of the church. In the words of Kevin O'Brien, S.J.:

> In recent months, the Catholic Church in the United States has again reckoned with the scourge of sexual abuse of minors and vulnerable adults. Revelations of systematic abuse of authority by individual priests and by bishops have stirred a variety of emotions within us and those we serve: anger, sadness, compassion for the victims and their families, disgust, disillusionment, and frustration, to name a few. Senseless infighting among factions in the Church and the scapegoating of gay and lesbian Catholics have only compounded these

reactions.[4]

The Catholic world's news reminds us that the scandal, crime, and sin of sexual abuse is not an American or ecclesial problem alone. At the same time, the church must ask itself many questions, including these: how do we interpret Scripture in light of sexual violence, the suffering of victims, and abuse of power? How can twenty-first-century Scripture, theology, and ecclesiology offer hope to those in despair? Moreover, can we rely on our ministerial formation programs to teach students the responsible and ethical exercise of their authority? Do our formation programs cultivate the skills to heal the abused and disheartened by scandal and betrayal of sacred trust? In our study, work, and prayer, we must be attentive to the abuse of power and shameful actions within the church. This awareness is essential to the much-needed healing process. The church's theological, biblical, and spiritual resources offer a way forward to necessary reform and reconciliation. Ultimately, ecclesial hope is in the One who founded and still guides the church. It is vital that the church have ministers that are not only competent but also holy men and women, deeply committed to the mission of Christ and the community.

This personal situation of historical uniqueness in the culture, characterized by both individual freedom and power on one side and collective frustration and weakness on the other, also applies to the Catholic Church. Catholics are correct to see this historical moment as special, a place and time of promise but also of challenges and dangers. The Catholic Church in this new millennium is at a watershed of its own self-understanding and its relationship to the world. The Church has witnessed more ferment within its inner spiritual and structural fabric since the Reformation. The world view of the papacy and Church authority changed very little from the imposition of the Tridentine reforms at the end of the sixteenth century to the Second Vatican Council in 1962. Liturgy, doctrine, morality, and Catholic practice and devotion, remained fundamentally frozen in time in what Yves Congar has called Tridentinism, "an all-embracing system of theology, ethics, Christian behavior, religious practices, liturgy, organization and Roman centralization brought about by the reforms of the Council of Trent."[5] The institutional framework of isolation and legalism triumphed convincingly over individuality and personal choice during this period. By contrast, today—at least in the

[4] Edited response of Father O'Brien to a question I posed to him in a conversation in the spring of 2020 when he was president of Santa Clara University.

[5] Yves Congar, *Fifty Years of Catholic Theology*, ed. Bernard Lauret (Philadelphia: Fortress Press, 1988), 3–4.

Western world but increasingly so elsewhere—the objective institution of the Church and the social, political, and spiritual lives of individual Catholics stand in conflict with each other, with each side struggling to be the dominant and exclusive source and norm of faith and truth. Both the personal and the institutional are at the crossroads of a new relationship. Many Catholics have confronted the recent revelations of sex abuse by the clergy and the blind eye of bishops with horror, embarrassment, and a call for fundamental changes in the church.[6] The Catholic tradition that has nourished the majority of Western people for nearly two millennia needs a re-definition of its identity, a renewed understanding of the relationship between the individual and the community, a more humane interpretation of authority, a more imaginative view of its moral and doctrinal tradition, and a more expansive interpretation of its role in the world of the future, especially its relation to other Christian churches and religious traditions. Pope Francis has made a genuine effort to confront these challenges and eliminate the last vestiges of the Tridentine church.

The chapters that follow will present a theological and historical sketch of the church's self-understanding. Theologically, it is the story of the origins of the church in the life, ministry, death, and resurrection of Jesus; the story continues with a history of ecclesiology or the doctrine of the church, from the first cry of the disciples, "He is alive," down to twenty-first-century history and society. The story that follows is a kind of family album, so that our pictures of the church today can be contextualized and nourished by the myriad of pictures from the two millennia before, especially those of Jesus himself in the Gospels and the earliest community of faith in his message of eternal life. "Family album" is an apt metaphor for what a history of ecclesiology is. In spite of its profound institutional flaws, it is the history of God's family, God's people united in the Holy Spirit.

This book is divided into sections: first, some simple definitions of theology and ecclesiology; second, an exploration into the historical and theological foundations of the church in the life and death of Jesus; third, the emergence of the community in the first century; fourth, the period of the Fathers

---

[6] On this situation, see these books by Donald Cozzens: *The Changing Face of the Priesthood. A Reflection on the Priest's Crisis of Soul* (Collegeville, MN: The Liturgical Press, 2000); *Sacred Silence: Denial and the Crisis in the Church* (Collegeville, MN: The Liturgical Press, 2002); *Faith That Dares to Speak* (Collegeville, MN: The Liturgical Press, 2004). See also Mark D. Jordan, *The Silence of Sodom: Homosexuality in Modern Catholicism* (Chicago: University of Chicago Press, 2000).

of the Church; fifth, the church in medieval times; sixth, the decline of the Renaissance church; seventh, the Protestant and Catholic reformations; eighth, the church in the modern world; ninth, the ecclesiology of the Reformation and two great twentieth-century theologians of the Reformation; finally, the church and the papacy of the post-Vatican II era and the new millennium.

The ecclesiology of the Second Vatican Council (1962–1965) marked not only the end of one era but the beginning of a new period of ecclesiological history: one of self-doubt and self-exploration by the various communities who proclaim Jesus as their Lord. New questions, unimaginable to Christians of other centuries, emerged: how can we understand the church vis-à-vis other great religious traditions and world cultures? What does it mean to understand the church, as Karl Rahner calls it, as a "world church"? What is the role of the church in a primarily secular and Western environment? How can the Christian tradition be translated for people in a postmodern culture? What does it mean to call the church "catholic," and what is the relationship between a catholic church and "Roman Catholicism"? How can the church remain one and holy given so many distinct and diverse historical churches? Are the churches, or is *the* church, faithful to the mission of the Gospels? These questions and challenges, among many others, that the new millennium brings to the church are daunting.

1.2 Definition of Theology

First, one must first understand the nature and goal of theology. The words of Evagrios of Pontus in the fourth century present an ideal introduction to theology: "And if you pray truly, you are a theologian."[7] Theology has something to do with the search for the ultimate meaning of life, a quest for God, not only in the knowing but also, primarily, in the doing. Theology ought not to be intellectual hair-splitting, drowned in a sea of abstractions; it is also not the repetition of eternal truths or submission to a finite authority. Jesus reminds us that those who are blessed are not the ones who say "Lord, Lord…" but those who know the will of his Father and do as his Father wishes (Mt 7:21). The words of Evagrios are a constant reminder to theologians of any

[7] See Evagrios the Solitary, also known as Evagrios Pontikos (345–399 CE), "On Prayer: 153 Texts," no. 61, in *The Philokalia: The Complete Text*, compiled by St. Nikodimos of the Holy Mountain and St. Makarios of Corinth, trans. and eds. G. E. H. Palmer, Philip Sherrard, and Kallistos Ware, 5 vols. (London: Faber and Faber, 1979–95), 1:62.

era that faith must come before understanding. To paraphrase Martin Buber, all words spoken *about* God are all right as long as they are also words spoken *to* God.[8] Or, as American philosopher John Dewey has said of philosophy in words also true of theology, "philosophy is the mind in service of the heart. It is an adventure in making life whole."[9]

Theology, as twentieth-century Protestant theologian Paul Tillich states, is the "function of the Christian church" and must serve the church.[10] Theology can have both a broad and narrow meaning: narrowly, theology is a cognitive exercise in understanding faith in statements of truth and moral norms passed down from one generation to another. In the famous phrase of Saint Anselm in the thirteenth century, theology is *fidens quaerens intellectum* or faith seeking understanding.

All religions have a theology, regardless of their cultural differences in form and expression. Some religions, such as Buddhism, might refuse to call the discipline "theology," but it is theology nonetheless, even if the *Theos* or the "God part" has no verbal counterpart in the Buddhist tradition and the *Logos* aspect is based on a radically different philosophy of knowledge. Western theologies—Jewish, Christian, and Muslim—strive to explain the core of faith through rational discourse based on God's revelatory Word. This word can be found in the Hebrew Scriptures, the New Testament, and the Qur'an, as well as the writings of peoples that have interpreted these sacred texts. Unfortunately, sometimes a particular theology makes the mistake of thinking that its tradition possesses the only real and authentic truth in the same way that it possesses the only true salvific faith. In a world of fundamentalisms—whether they be Roman Catholic restorationism, conservative evangelical Protestantism, or Islamic fundamentalism—these narrow-minded and sometimes fanatical expressions of faith disgrace the work of theology. These expressions of faith create idols of finite thoughts and words, equating human words with the divine Word. As an old adage says, "the safest place to hide from God is in the shadow of the altar."

---

[8] Martin Buber, *I and Thou*, trans. Walter Kaufmann (New York: Charles Scribner's Sons, 1970), 123.

[9] Quoted in Robert O. Johann, *Building the Human*, dedication (New York: Herder and Herder, 1968).

[10] Paul Tillich, *Systematic Theology*, vol. 1 (Chicago: University of Chicago Press, 1957), 3.

1.3 Primordial Faith and Theology

A broader understanding of theology exists beyond its parochial expressions. As Paul Tillich says, theology is the study of one's ultimate concern, of the unconditional meaning of a person's life and their place in the world.[11] All individuals are persons of faith as far as they seek answers to the imponderable questions of life. All individuals seek to articulate this faith and are thus "theologians." Even thoroughly secular people who refuse to acknowledge the reality of a "God," are persons of faith in so far as they encounter the ultimate questions of life and the final significance of human activity. As Tillich reminds us, even if persons deny any ultimate concern, they affirm it at the same time since they would be ultimately concerned about not having any ultimate concern. Catholic theologian Dermot Lane calls this type of faith "primordial faith," an effort to tie one's life together and make sense of the ineffable questions of human existence.[12]

As Tillich further states, the essence of faith is located in the quality of ultimacy in a person's concern. The content of faith, primordial or religious—the belief system that gives shape and form to faith—matters only to particular believers.[13] For example, Islamic truths matter only to Muslims as the teachings of Jesus are of concern only to Christians. Likewise, secular persons of primordial faith, though they would not call it "faith," inevitably possess a content of faith. They may locate this content or system of beliefs in the pattern of daily life—in their homes and families, in their quest for success and the comfortable life, in their desire to help others, in their political or artistic achievements, and the like. Obviously, some beliefs may be noble and worthwhile, that is, worthy of the infinite or ultimate within the person, while other expressions of ultimacy may not. The central issue is not whether persons possess faith but their choice of symbols to express their faith or their ultimate concern in life.

Put differently, religious persons possess a content of faith or a belief system that is passed on to them in the symbols and stories of a particular religious tradition. These symbols and stories—sacred writings, doctrines, rituals, and moral laws—are expressions of what is essential and of ultimate

[11] Paul Tillich invents this popular well-known definition of faith in *Dynamics of Faith* (New York: Harper, 1957).

[12] Dermot Lane, *The Experience of God: An Invitation to Do Theology* (New York: Paulist, 1981), 52–53. This excellent small book was reissued in an expanded form in 2005.

[13] Tillich, *Dynamics of Faith*, 2.

value. For example, Christians and Muslims are both ultimately concerned about the Ultimate itself, but they will express their ultimate concern in the Ultimate in and through a different set of symbols or beliefs. What matters *ultimately* are not the symbols as such but their commitment with their whole mind, heart, and soul to the One present *in* and *through* the symbols of their tradition. Whenever beliefs become more important than the commitment of the whole person to God, then faith becomes idolatry. This is clear in Protestant evangelism and Catholic restorationism, where the words of the Bible or the teachings of the Church assume absolute importance. Robert Johann suggests that such people are "forever confusing limited truth with *the* truth, customary ways of relating to God with the one and only way."[14] The Protestant reformer, Jean Calvin, reminds us that the mind is a "factory of idols"—a temptation of every faith.[15]

In sum, all persons have primordial faith or the drive to make sense of their lives in the context of an ultimate meaning. Many people have religious faith because they express their ultimate concern in explicitly religious symbols. In traditional cultures, of course, faith was always religious since religion and culture were inseparable. This unity existed before the rise of secularism, which was rooted, among other factors, in the breakdown of the medieval world, the Reformation, and the rise of science and technology. Today's culture is witness to the conflict between secular and religious consciousness, between differing answers to the essential human questions: what do I take with unconditional seriousness and without reservation? The conflict is not between faith or lack of faith, but between symbol systems, between genuine religious symbols that unlock the Transcendent and secular symbols that often return us to ourselves and create, in sociologist Peter Berger's phrase, a "world without windows."[16]

1.4 Christian Theology

Theology for the Christian is the systematic effort to understand God cognitively as our origin, our source of life, and our ultimate destiny. This God is the God of Abraham, Isaac, and Jacob, and the one who has revealed Godself

[14] Johann, *Building the Human*, 127.

[15] See Paul Tillich, *The Courage To Be* (New Haven: Yale University Press, 1952), 36.

[16] Peter Berger and Richard John Neuhaus, eds. *Against the World and For the World: The Hartford Appeal and the Future of American Religion* (New York: Seabury, 1976).

to us in the life, mission, and death of Jesus of Nazareth. Theology examines what God has accomplished for us: by God's presence in the life and preaching of Jesus; in God's participation in human suffering, sin, and death on the Cross; in the triumph over death and the darkness of sin in the resurrection of Jesus; in God's continual presence as the Spirit of grace and love through the Christian community.

Since theology is "faith seeking understanding," it presupposes faith; faith is the starting point. Faith presupposes openness to transcendence, a commitment to the infinite reality to which only the name of God applies. In Christian theology, faith is not a structured set of doctrines and moral principles of a specific church, but in the saving power of God in Jesus. Unfortunately, for many Christians, faith has been reduced to the acceptance of beliefs and truths—in the Bible or in church teachings—with a low degree of evidence This understanding of faith reduces faith to a set of cognitive truths. In the Catholic tradition, at least since the seventeenth century, faith has been objectified and transformed into a system of eternal truths. The Second Vatican Council, in the document on Revelation (*Dei Verbum*), rejected so-called propositional revelation, the notion that God "revealed" in statements or propositions. Instead, the Council presented an interpersonal idea of revelation: God did not reveal unchangeable truths. The only thing that God can reveal is God, the divine Self. The words of revelation in Scripture and defined doctrines, the written history of God's presence and human response, are important, of course, but secondary to the encounter with God as Revelation and the human response of faith.[17]

This shift from propositional to interpersonal revelation goes to the heart of the work of theology and, like any important change, it takes time for its full reception by the community. In Catholicism, the reduction of faith to beliefs was due in part to the apologetic and defensive attitude of the Church after the Reformation. Like God who became an object out there, so too faith was reduced to a set of organized beliefs rather than a personal commitment and a relationship with the God of Jesus. This objective way of looking at the world was reinforced in the eighteenth century during the Enlightenment or the age of reason. Ironically—but also predictably—the church that battled rationalism's rejection of divine revelation became rationalist itself in its subsequent theology. As a result of this narrow view of revelation and theological discourse, many "lapsed" Catholics in today's culture are not individuals who have rejected their faith but people who refuse to accept the belief system

[17] See Lane, *The Experience of God*, 32–37, 45–49.

uncritically passed on to them in an authoritarian and often condescending manner.

Thus, we must always distinguish between faith and beliefs. Faith is a gift of God and is universal; faith is commitment, a "setting one's heart on," a personal relationship with God.[18] It involves the whole self in relation to an object outside oneself; thus, it includes both subjective and objective dimensions. While God is the proper "object" of faith, God is also more than an object; the divine embraces the mysterious unity of both subject and object. In this way, faith is like love; it involves both self and the other in a process in which the other becomes more intimate with the self than the self is with itself. This is the authentic meaning of "transcendence."

Beliefs, on the other hand, are the work of theology and are always limited and historically conditioned. Beliefs are symbols of faith, theoretical and propositional expressions of faith, but not faith itself.[19] Nevertheless, beliefs are essential to faith. They thematize, order, and give context to faith. Beliefs are always dependent on a particular time and group of people. One cannot have faith without beliefs because faith, like love, must be expressed in a concrete way. Beliefs include the entire cognitive system upon which faith is grounded: the doctrines that explain the meaning of the faith; moral principles that direct persons to live in faith; liturgy and sacraments that open individuals to celebrate their faith in ritual. One cannot reduce faith to its expression, to its particular form at a given time; this would involve faith in its own self-destruction. The task of theology is to create an acceptable understanding of faith in the context in which people of faith live.

1.5 Theological Method

How does one go about doing theology, and in our context here, ecclesiology? For most people, the question of method in theology is rarely considered. The same method should apply in every aspect of theology, whether it is a theology of Jesus the Christ, church, or a treatment of the sacraments or morality. On the one hand, does one simply open the Scriptures and accept what is written in the book as literal and objective truth? Some preachers, like televangelists, tell people to follow this path. Or do you listen to the statements of the pope, bishops, and ministers as a different sort of "Gospel truth" without examining your own conscience? Catholic and Protestant fundamentalists, followers of

[18] Lane, 56.

[19] Lane, 55–62.

"holy rollers" or "holy fathers," propose this secure path. On the other hand, is religion and theology a matter of subjective feeling, your own "personal thing," as many young people say, regardless of what any bible or church says?

If theology deals with the ultimate meaning of life, how will the objective truths of bible and church stand in relation to this personal and ultimate meaning? The theological method for studying the church that we will follow is the method of correlation of Paul Tillich.[20] This method is not a new method nor is it unique to Tillich; one could safely argue that it goes back as far as Jesus himself in the Gospels. It begins with an analysis of the human situation and attempts to articulate and comprehend the deeply rooted human questions implied in the existential situation. The method of correlation works in this manner: first, theology must answer the precise human question; second, it must answer the question in the form the question is posed. The work of theology, as Tillich says, is mediation "between the eternal criterion of truth as it is manifest in the picture of Jesus as the Christ, and the changing experience of individuals and groups, their varying questions and their categories of experiencing reality."[21] In simple terms, it is the paradox of consistency through change.

Theology has two poles—the eternal message and the human situation—and the method of correlation is a way of uniting the questions implied in the human situation and the answers implied in Christian revelation.[22] On the one hand, the human questions posed in philosophical form must receive an answer faithful to the objective truth and intelligible to the question at the same time. The question cannot be derived from the answer or the answer from the question; yet, both question and answer determine each other and are interdependent. The formulation of the question is a human task; that is, it lies outside the specific work of theology. The substance of the question comes from the theologian's experience of the finite world in philosophy, poetry, psychology, the social sciences, and other disciplines of the human spirit. The question takes form in the context of the culture in which the question arises. In formulating the question, the theologian works as a philosopher. The theological answer, on the other hand, has two sources: its substance is derived from the revelatory experience in the Christian message; its form is

[20] Tillich's method of correlation is best presented in his *Systematic Theology*, 1:59–66.

[21] Paul Tillich, *The Protestant Era*, rev. ed. (Chicago: University of Chicago Press, 1957), ix.

[22] Paul Tillich, *Systematic Theology*, 1:8.

derived from the form of the question in which the philosophical analysis is contained. The theological substance of the message does not exist in suspension; it exists only in cultural and philosophical form, and this form must be correlative with the same form in which the existential question is posed. The substance of these questions is the person him/herself, an individual concerned about his/her being and meaning. This existential question is "the question he asks about himself before any other question has been formulated."[23] For Tillich, the human person is "infinitely concerned about the infinity to which he belongs, from which he is separated, and for which he is longing."[24]

Thus, for example, no absolute and eternal truth about the person of Christ exists in the abstract. The revelatory substance about the meaning of the Christ must be expressed in a form relative to the need of someone asking the question of a savior at a particular time. Put differently, the absolute doctrinal truth of the Christ cannot be separated from the human questions people ask in their timeframe, place, and manner. In an age of existential anxiety about the meaning of life, a theology of the Christ can answer this anxiety. The issue of persons and natures, which was the dominant question of the church of the fourth and fifth centuries, is only tangential to Christian experience today. The inner truth of the doctrine remains the same, but the abstract answer found in the statement of the Council of Chalcedon in 451 CE has to be translated for contemporary minds posing different questions. Indeed, the very meaning of the words in Greek for "person" and "nature" have significantly changed their meanings in a millennium and a half, and failure to take this fact into account is to be unfaithful to the truth of the doctrine.

Likewise, the question of the church in today's culture is very different from the question of the medieval period. No longer is the church the center of culture as it once was; no longer does the ecclesiastical world dominate the political, social, economic, and moral world of the twenty-first century. How can one make sense of the meaning of church today in an individualistic world where community of any kind, never mind a Christian community, is not presumed as it once was? What does church mean in a world of such religious diversity? How can the church be a servant of the Gospels in a time of such social and economic injustice? Any viable ecclesiology must consider the contemporary situation and present a theology of the church accordingly.

As Tillich says of the method of correlation, the method "makes an

---

[23] Tillich, 1:62.

[24] Tillich, 1:14.

analysis of the human situation out of which the existential questions arise, and it demonstrates that the symbols used in the Christian message are the answers to these questions." The substance of these questions is the person him/herself, an individual concerned about his/her being and meaning. This existential question is "the question he asks about himself before any other question has been formulated."[25] For Tillich, the human person is "infinitely concerned about the infinity to which he belongs, from which he is separated, and for which he is longing."[26] Theology cannot speak of reality in purely objective terms. Rather, it addresses the depth of reality that is the ground of both subjectivity and objectivity, and in some mysterious way it speaks *of*—as well as *to*—that ultimate reality more intimate with human beings than they are with themselves. Thus, theology cannot speak about God without also speaking about human persons in their existential condition and vice versa. As Tillich says, "whenever an idea of God is enunciated, it is always in correlation with an interpretation of man, and vice versa."[27] Likewise, the Christ is not only a historical reality, but, in accord with Tillich's method, the absolute answer to the quest in a person's being for salvation and healing, for the conquest of the cleavage that lies at the heart of human existence. So too, the Holy Spirit is not a "third God" but the unity of power and meaning or the heart of God in the very depth of life, the answer to the person's quest for a transcendent union that overcomes life's ambiguities.

The method of correlation has been criticized from persons defending either the autonomy of the question or the transcendence of the answer. The former claim that the method destroys the power and secular independence of philosophy and brings to human experience an answer from Transcendence that such experience neither needs nor desires. In such a situation, God appears as an intruder, a *deus ex machina*, into a world that can do very well on its own. The latter group holds that the method distorts the significance of the Christian message by reducing the Christian answer to whatever human experience requires or finds expedient. This weakens divine Transcendence and the divine cutting edge in human life, transforming God into a projection of human needs and desires.

In contrast to Tillich, the great Protestant theologian Karl Barth (1886–1968) suggested that the theological answers must be considered more

[25] Tillich, 1:62.

[26] Tillich, 1:14.

[27] Paul Tillich, *The Rediscovery of the Prophetic Tradition of the Reformation* (Washington, D.C.: Henderson Services, 1950), 11.

fundamental than the philosophical questions and essentially superior. One should move, as Barth says, "not from a philosophically understood subject to a 'divine object,' but rather from a theologically understood object (as the true Subject) to the human subject, and thus from Spirit to life and the Kingdom of God to history."[28] In reply, Tillich argues that he does not intend the Christian message of revelation to be a product of human experience or that it be reduced to the question and the questioner's needs. As Tillich states, "human existence does not involve answers to the questions of man's relation to God; it involves the *question*...the answer, if it appears, appears in revelation."[29] This answer "cannot be derived from the question. It is said *to* him who asks but cannot be taken *from* him."[30] The answers must be "spoken to human existence from beyond it. Otherwise, they would not be answers for the question is human existence itself."[31] While the form of the answer depends on the structure of the question, the content of the answer comes, in Tillich words, only from the ecstatic event of revelation through the medium of experience. Tillich is careful to place experience between subject and object so that experience is the *medium*, never the *source*, of revelation. In this way, he attempts to preserve the autonomy and transcendence of revelation over human knowledge and personal feelings and desires.

Tillich thus prefigures many of the theological debates in recent decades about the preservation of the distinctly Christian message on one side and its relevance to the forms of modern experience on the other. Since the Second Vatican Council, Catholic theology has espoused human experience as the starting point of theology. In the most famous of conciliar statements, the Council Fathers insist that the church always had the task of "scrutinizing the signs of the times and of interpreting them in the light of the Gospel."[32]

Thus, all human questions should find an answer in the reality of God. It is theology's task to make this reality clear and comprehensible so that faith might successfully seek to understand itself. Faith, according to Catholic

---

[28] Karl Barth, "Introductory Report," *The Systematic Theology of Paul Tillich*, by Alexander McKelway (New York: Delta Books, 1966), 13.

[29] Paul Tillich, "The Present Theological Situation in Light of the Continental European Development," *Theology Today* 6, no. 3 (1949): 305.

[30] Paul Tillich, *Theology of Culture*, ed. Robert Kimball (New York: Oxford University Press, 1959), 49.

[31] Tillich, *Systematic Theology*, 1:64.

[32] *Gaudium et Spes*, The Pastoral Constitution on the Church in Modern World, "Introductory Statement: The Situation of Men in the Modern World," December 7, 1965, 4.

theologian Avery Cardinal Dulles, takes on different forms in different times. He discerns seven major periods or forms of the Judeo-Christian faith from the time of the ancient Israelites to the present, each with its own structure and texture. Faith, in order to be true to itself, must change its form with different historical periods or it will die.[33]

Two obvious dangers exist when the method of correlation fails to work properly: first, an objectification of the Christian message in which theology "hurls the answers at persons like stones"; second, a subjectification of the Christian message in which theology waters down the answer to fit the human question so the objective reality of God's grace is reduced to individual desire. One must go deeper into the real human question and let theology give an answer that is faithful to both the human question and God's revelation. Hence, the objective and the subjective must be correlated. Good theology should always seek to avoid both postmodern subjectivism on one side and an anti-modern reaction in dogmatism and fundamentalism on the other.

1.6 Definition of Ecclesiology

The area of theology that explores the church is called ecclesiology, the study of the Christian community, of those "called out" to be God's people or church. It explores the meaning of divine grace in the historical form of a human community of faith and action. This community affirms its unity with God in Jesus the Christ through the power of the Spirit. From a Catholic perspective, the community of the faithful sees its purpose to become the living sacrament of the Gospel message and the Paschal mystery to the world. Ecclesiology is intimately connected with theology in the narrow sense, an understanding of God; with Christology, an interpretation of Jesus the Christ; with the liturgy and the sacraments as actions not only of the church but also of God; finally, with a theology of grace and eschatology—the presence of God in history and in humanity's corporate destiny.

When Christians use the word "church," they usually refer to the particular church or denomination of their background. Theologically, there is only *one* church of Christ, but given the human condition, this one church has taken many different historical forms. Some theologians make the distinction between the ideal church that is one, holy, catholic, and apostolic, and the many historical churches. Conservative members of a particular church use

---

[33] See Avery Dulles, "The Changing Forms of Faith," in *The Survival of Dogma: Faith, Authority, and Dogma in a Changing World* (New York: Crossroad, 1982), 17–31.

the word "church" to refer exclusively to their particular church, be it Catholic or Baptist. In 1964, the Second Vatican Council, in its document on the church, *Lumen Gentium*, stated that the Church "subsists in," not "is," the Roman Catholic Church, thus implying for that first time that the church as a theological reality is broader than the Roman Catholic tradition.[34]

Historically, the church of Christ can be divided into four major divisions, each with many subdivisions: first, the Catholic tradition of the West or the Roman Catholic Church whose leader is the pope of Rome; second, the Orthodox tradition of the East whose leader is the Patriarch of Constantinople (the West and East separated in 1054); third, the Protestant tradition which emerged in the sixteenth century under the leadership of Luther, Calvin, Zwingli, and others; and, fourth, the Anglican tradition or the Church of England, which separated from Rome at the time of the Reformation and which is known in the United States as the Episcopal Church. These categories are not airtight: many Eastern churches are united with Rome (hence there are Greek and Ukrainian Catholic Churches and Greek and Ukrainian Orthodox Churches); likewise, the Anglican Church is judged Catholic by some, Protestant by others.

As a theological discipline, ecclesiology has both objective and subjective dimensions. Subject and object comprise the basic philosophical division within reality, corresponding to the division of self and world. The subject is the self, the independent center of being and thought; the world is all that is not self, all that stands over and against the self and constitutes the other. Thus, the study of the church consists of both the objective historical community and persons *as subjects*. More specifically, the *objective* pole involves the study of the church as the divine-human community based on the life, death, and resurrection of Jesus Christ. This involves Scripture, the writings of the Church Fathers, the subsequent history of theology, as well as the political and social history of the Christian community. The objective pole answers this question: what is the church, how has the Christian community defined and understood itself through the centuries? The *subjective* pole, on the other hand, involves the search within each human heart for a community grounded in transcendence, one that illumines and embodies our personal and corporate destinies and serves as the societal and cultural locus of our faith in God. The subjective pole attempts to answer this question: what does it mean for me to be a disciple of Jesus the Christ?

---

[34] *Lumen Gentium*, The Dogmatic Constitution on the Church, "Chapter 1: The Mystery of the Church," November 21, 1964, 8.

The church is a theological tradition and a visible society; it is also a personal way of seeing the world and living in faith. Both dimensions must be explored, seeking a point where both dimensions co-inhere in the mystery of faith itself. Ideally, the subjective and the objective, the person and the tradition, individual freedom and communal structure, should exist interdependently and in harmony, creating and nurturing one another. Unfortunately, the historical situation has often been a different matter and the history of ecclesiology exemplifies estrangement between individuals and the institution in their quest to dominate each other.

In the same way that the subjective and the objective dimensions should exist interdependently, other dualisms in the work of theology and ecclesiology must be similarly interconnected. *First*, theology is both theoretical and practical, and one element must not exclude the other. They are, as Robert Imbelli says, more "intimate and reciprocal than an understanding of praxis as 'applied theory' allows."[35] Theology, as the work of the church, cannot be separated from the life of the community; the theologian necessarily lives and breathes the spiritual air of the community. The purpose of theory is always to clarify, purify, and create the forms through which authentic human faith and action can be realized.

Second, systematic theology and spirituality are not two subdivisions of theology but two aspects of one integral whole, united within the faith of the living community. Theology in the last half century has witnessed a "turn to the subject" and human subjectivity, where the individual in faith, as one essential pole in the theological task, is being rediscovered. This has led in recent times to a revival of spirituality in the culture so that spirituality, personal faith, and the life of prayer are rediscovered as constitutive elements in interpreting church. In light of this, contemporary ecclesiology, particularly in the Catholic tradition, should, first, foster an ecclesial, liturgical spirituality, one grounded in Scripture and the community as the Body of Christ and the People of God; second, it should avoid a quietist, individualistic, anti-worldly, anti-cultural, fundamentalist spirituality that often shuns the world or fails to take it seriously; third, it should develop a spirituality that is rooted in transcendence and one that rejects the power of the secular culture to establish norms of human life. Ecclesiology must also avoid the contemporary split between religion and spirituality. Everyone who is searching for his or her own spirituality is, by definition, religious. Likewise, everyone who claims to be

[35] See Robert Imbelli and Thomas Groome, "Signposts towards a Pastoral Theology," *Theological Studies* 53 (1992): 127–37.

religious, if he or she understands religion as more than a social veneer or a "moral club," in Tillich's damning phrase, is also spiritual. Spirituality is as much communal and social as religion is. Religion is as personal and as interior as spirituality is.

Finally, theology, especially ecclesiology, can never be separated from the particular culture in which it lives. The current cultural situation of the Christian churches in this post-Vatican II era is complex and problematic. No longer are churches representatives of a monolithic worldview. Some Protestant churches from the same denomination are pro-gay and strongly feminist; others abhor such movements. Likewise, some Catholic parishes and dioceses are liberal and open to modern ideas and historical change; the next parish or diocese over could not be more different in orientation and approach. Churches are often a mélange of contradictions; they may be theologically pluralistic, ecumenically oriented, secular-minded, and profoundly reactionary. On one extreme, the theological and ecclesial culture comprises the theologically reactionary—in Catholic terms, ultramontane or restorationist, in Protestantism, biblical fundamentalist. At the other extreme are the churches that have let the world rather than the Gospels set their agenda. In many cases, they have become, in Peter Berger's phrase, "bargainers with modernity," reducing the transcendent dimension of faith to the values of the contemporary world.[36]

1.7 Theology and Ecclesiology as Historical Enterprises

Every doctrine in the Christian tradition, including the doctrine of the church, has a long and complex history. In our own century, theologians have come to see that all theology, as Piet Schoonenberg reminds us, "exists in history, not eternity." Theologians who were unaware of the intrinsic historical nature of the Christian faith, those who thought their theology would last for all time, prove the very point they implicitly denied, for they were part of a historical time and a theological enterprise unaware or insufficiently aware of its own historicity.[37] The examination of doctrine historically is essential to the work of theology for two reasons. First, such an examination deepens and enriches our present understanding of the doctrine in question by addressing

[36] Peter Berger, "The Reductive Possibility: Modernizing Tradition," chap. 4 in *The Heretical Imperative: Contemporary Possibilities of Religious Affirmation* (New York: Doubleday, 1979).

[37] Piet Schoonenberg, *Man and Sin: A Theological View* (Notre Dame: University of Notre Dame Press, 1965), 192.

the whole range of possible interpretations in light of the community's historical experience. Second, it serves as a formal principle of criticism for any reigning doctrinal expression because it reveals the relative nature of every historical attempt to express the truth of infinite mystery in a given time and place.

This idea of a doctrine as a historical *attempt* is significant because any doctrinal formulation is always tentative and open to further development. Doctrine is the expression of mystery; mystery is, by nature, infinite—that which is forever revealing itself to us, that toward which we endlessly move. Doctrine resembles poetry as "a raid on the inarticulate," the drive to put into words an ineffable truth, whether it be beauty or holiness.[38] For the theologian, this truth is the inexhaustible reality of God and all that God is for us, with us, and in us. In the tradition of the church, a doctrine functions as a symbol. This means that, on the one hand, any doctrinal formulation points to the mystery of God, self, and world in a manner words cannot fully capture or express. On the other hand, this same formulation expresses and embodies this mystery in a finite, historically conditioned set of words.[39] The theologian Karl Rahner reminds us that the symbols expressing the truth of doctrine evolve, change, and develop; the faith of the community inevitably expresses itself differently at different periods of history. Such a fact does not threaten faith; rather it is essential to the faith's survival. Any faith, he says, which "clings to forms once effective but are now ineffective and meaningless" is a form of faith "which will involve itself in its destruction."[40] Doctrine can and must change as the mystery of faith is experienced in different ways. Never is this mystery frozen or made absolute in the time-conditioned words themselves; rather it is a living reality in the historical community of faith and in its relationship to the God of all ages and seasons.[41]

This pattern clearly applies to ecclesiology. As far as the Christian community is an object of reflection and conceptualization, ecclesiology is as much a historical reality as any other dimension of the Christian faith, and one with its own unique history. The history of the doctrine of the church, however,

---

[38] T. S. Eliot, "East Coker," *The Four Quartets* (New York: Harcourt, Brace and World, 1943), 31.

[39] For a definition of symbol, see Paul Tillich, *Dynamics of Faith*, 42–44.

[40] Karl Rahner, *Belief Today* (New York: Sheed and Ward, 1976), 52. See also Avery Dulles, "The Changing Forms of Faith," 17–31.

[41] On the Origin and Development of Doctrine, see Frederick J. Parrella, "Doctrine Revisited: A Personalistic Interpretation," in *Lumen Vitae* 38 (1982): 396–412.

differs from the history of other doctrines in two ways. First, unlike other doctrines, such as the doctrine of God or Jesus the Christ, ecclesiology is insight of the community into its own inner life and nature. In strict theological order, ecclesiology logically follows and is grounded in an interpretation of God as Trinity, Revelation, and the Incarnation. In a historical sense, however, ecclesiology precedes all other theological reflection since, as the French ecclesiologist M.-J. le Guillou, tells us, "the reality of the Church is presupposed in the proclamation of the Gospel and cannot be separated in the whole dogmatic structure of which it forms the existential foundation."[42] The church is both an object of faith and the communal presupposition and foundation of all reflection on matters of faith. In simple terms, if the church is a family, then like a family, at least some self-understanding of its own life and nature is implicitly present before it can consider the ultimate questions it must confront in the external world.

A second important difference exists between the history of ecclesiology and a historical study of other doctrines. While no doctrine can be isolated from a particular place and culture, the history of ecclesiology is unique in its relationship to church history and to the world outside of the church. For example, when one studies another doctrine—such as the doctrine of grace—one may not need know the complete story of the political history of the Church at the time. With ecclesiology, on the other hand, the Church's self-understanding and self-definition are inseparable from the political and social role of the Christian community at every historical moment. Thus, the history of ecclesiology, while essentially theological, must concern itself with more than just its foundations in the history of ideas. It must also immerse itself in the concrete events of church history. The church's self-understanding, or a formal doctrine of the church, is inevitably grounded in the political, social, and economic world in which the community lived. Thus, in the chapters that follow, theology and history are inextricably—and often not neatly and precisely—interwoven. At the beginning, some ideas on the nature of doctrine are essential for the doctrine of the church that follows.

1.8 Principles of Doctrinal Development

Where do Christian doctrines come from? Does God reveal truths in formal statements or propositions? For many centuries, such a naïve view of truth

[42] M.-J. le Guillou, "History of Ecclesiology," in *Sacramentum Mundi: An Encyclopedia of Theology* (New York: Herder and Herder, 1968), 1:313.

prevailed. Today, theology has its starting point in human experience. This experience is a continuum, from the first disciples who experienced Jesus of Nazareth to Christians today who seek to understand the presence of God in the church. Three principles help to explain the origin and the development of doctrines and moral laws. Christianity is not primarily a system of ideas nor is it a religious philosophy.

1.8.1. Doctrine is the product of the communal experience. After the death of Jesus, his followers experienced the most profound transformation imaginable: from hopelessness to expectation, from death to life, from Cross to Resurrection. The earliest community of Jesus' disciples quickly sought to convey this overwhelming experience to others. The impact of Jesus' Resurrection on their lives was pre-predicative and pre-conceptual, that is, its power seized them before they could explain it in words and concepts. This means that the disciples did not discover in the Resurrection some objective truth about the ordered world or some divine intervention into the normal laws of nature. Rather, they were grasped in the depths of their beings by a truth that, by God's power, profoundly transformed both themselves and all of reality. As soon as they tried to express this absolute meaning of Jesus in their lives, predication, concepts, and judgments arose naturally in the process.

The first attempt at such predication was the oral *kerygma*, or preaching, understandably expressed in the language of Judaism, their faith. Later such predication took the form of teaching, or *didaché*, best exemplified in the Gospels themselves and the writings of the sub-Apostolic fathers like Ignatius of Antioch and others. This suggests that, *first*, experience is deeper and richer than any words about it. Predication—words, concepts, judgments—are an intrinsic part of the experience but always secondary to the experience itself. *Second*, formal doctrines and teachings of the church developed out of the community's need to express the ineffable experience of God in Christ and clarify its relationship with this God of grace and love. Imagine, for example, those deeply felt human experiences that transform our lives in some small or great way. Words fail us as we sit before an empty page trying to express what is too deep for words and yet we are compelled to find the words, the expression, of what paradoxically seems beyond words to us.

1.8.2. Doctrine also is personal in its grounding and import because it is rooted in the personal life of Jesus himself. The concepts of the early community that expressed its experience of Jesus are inseparable from the person of Jesus. Christianity is not a religion *about* Jesus; it is Jesus himself and the complete act of God that takes place in his person. The Gospel of John writes of Jesus: "I am the Way, the Truth, and the Life" (Jn 14:6). With the passage of

Jesus through time, as Gabriel Moran says, "the norm of history was revealed to be not an abstract law but a person."[43] Doctrine is the systematic reflection on the death and Resurrection of one concrete person with implications for all persons at all times.

1.8.3. Can and does doctrine change? The answer is unequivocally yes. The truth of Christianity is not above history or outside the flow of human events and human decisions. Christianity is not a system of ideas, but a historical faith rooted in the concrete acts of God in history. These actions are not merely some extrinsic frame of reference for the truth that God reveals. Rather, God reveals Godself *in* and *through* specific actions and events that constitute the history of the Judeo-Christian people. Doctrine is an intermediate interpretation, which has as its final goal the life and practice of the Christian church. Sometimes Christian doctrines are made absolute in the confusion between the words themselves and the mystery the words convey. The eternal quality of doctrine lies not in its formulation but, as we have considered, its personal grounding. As Alan Richardson says, "Jesus Christ himself remains the same yesterday, today, and forever: the facts of history do not alter: it is our view of his significance which continually needs re-interpretation in the light of fuller knowledge and deeper experience."[44] At its heart, it is a relationship with a historical person, an interpretation of this person's life and meaning.

The historical event of the Cross and Resurrection is once and for all; it cannot lose its concrete character nor be repeated. The understanding of this event and its personal and cosmic implications, however, must be open to change and development as human situations and contexts change. This fact is true of all the doctrines of the church, and any effort to deny this is to create a golden calf of human and transitory truth.

---

[43] Gabriel Moran, *Theology of Revelation* (New York: Herder and Herder, 1966), 76.

[44] Alan Richardson, "The Beginnings of Christian Doctrine," chap. 1 in *Creeds in the Making* (London: SCM Press, 1935).

2.

JESUS AND THE FOUNDATIONS OF THE CHURCH

Before considering the message of Jesus as the foundation of the church, a few words are in order about historical sources. These sources are almost exclusively the Gospels and the other writings of the New Testament. How are the Gospels to be interpreted? Before our contemporary era, Scripture was often taken literally or allegorically. When historiography emerged in the eighteenth century, the same objective tools used to examine the past were also used in exploring the Bible. This was a cause of great concern to many, for example, if we consider the debate between creationism and evolution in Genesis among fundamentalists. Many Evangelical churches still accept the Word of God as literally true.

Mainline Protestant scholars first took the lead in a historical and critical view of the sacred texts in the nineteenth century. The Catholic Church initially saw such an approach to Scripture as a threat to faith, but beginning with church pronouncements from the mid-twentieth century, the Catholic interpretation of Scripture accepted modern historical and literary scholarship.

2.1 A Glance at Catholic Biblical Scholarship[1]

Biblical scholarship offered theologians a new methodology to discover the historical foundations of the church. In Germany and England, the historical-critical approach to the Scriptural evidence evolved in primarily Protestant circles. Catholic theology, with its anti-empirical, *a priori* approach to truth, was slow to catch up with Protestant scholars. The Catholic Modernist period at the turn of the twentieth century, which attempted to place truth in a historical framework, was perceived as a threat to the objective nature of the Catholic faith and the church as the "perfect society." This continued to inhibit Catholic scholarship in its first efforts to establish textual, historical, and form criticism of the New Testament. The Catholic reaction to the new scholarship took place under Pius X and the Pontifical Biblical Commission (1905–1915). Pius X's *Lamemtabile Sane* and *Pascendi Dominici* (1907) were landmark encyclicals against the so-called Modernist movement. At the same time, the liberal Protestant tradition was on the cutting edge of Scripture scholarship in the time before World War I and before the emergence of neoorthodoxy in Protestantism under Karl Barth.

When change came to Catholic scholarship, it came quickly, due in part to World War I. In the 1920s and 1930s, theology witnessed a revival, with a return to the Fathers of the Church, a new emphasis on liturgy, and the Catholic biblical movement. This progress created a significant shift in the way the Catholic tradition was to view its theology and ecclesiology in the coming decades. Four major documents served as the cornerstones of biblical scholarship. First, Pius XII promulgated the encyclical *Divino Afflante Spiritu* in 1943, empowering Catholic Scripture scholars to continue their work in a historical-critical interpretation of the New Testament. Second, the Clarification of the Pontifical Biblical Commission in 1955 was the second major step in Catholic Scripture scholarship. Third, the Instruction on the Historical Truth of the Gospels in 1964 promulgated the long-established scholarly view of three stages of the Gospel tradition: first, the actual words of Jesus, second, the first generation of oral tradition, and finally, the redaction into written form in the second and third generations of the early church. Finally, the constitution *Dei Verbum* of the Second Vatican Council incorporates the 1964 Instruction on the Gospels and changes the post-Tridentine interpretation of the Word of God. More recent twentieth-century Catholic biblical

---

[1] This section is a summary of Frederick J. Cwiekowski, "New Beginnings," chap. 1 in *The Beginnings of the Church* (New York: Paulist, 1988), 5–19.

scholarship has been in the forefront of biblical studies. Two centuries after the first stirrings of modern Scripture scholarship, the historical-critical method, mainstream Protestant and Roman Catholic scholars agree on the nature of Scripture and the historical facts concerning Jesus and the church.[2]

Theologian Richard McBrien suggests five historical approaches to an understanding of the church's origins.[3] The first approach, held by Catholics since the Council of Trent (1545–63), was discredited with the advent of the historical-critical method and the Second Vatican Council.

2.2 Five Approaches to the Foundation of the Church

Non-scholarly conservatism, also called the Catholic "blueprint" approach, holds that Jesus' mission on earth was to establish the church in its visible and institutional form. This approach holds that Jesus instituted the church as a new, divine religion distinct from Judaism. It further accepts Christ's historical establishment of the seven sacraments and the formal appointment of Peter as head of the church. This uncritical view of the church was commonly accepted from the Council of Trent in the sixteenth century until contemporary biblical scholarship. The reforms of the Second Vatican Council were the death knell for this "blueprint" theory. This approach remains popular with Protestant biblical fundamentalists and certain Catholic conservatives who reject the facts of history.

2.2.1. Scholarly conservatism accepts a genuine continuity between Jesus' life and the church that emerged after his resurrection. But Jesus himself did not establish a church independent of Judaism during his lifetime, and the real development of the community takes place during the apostolic and subapostolic generations of Jesus' followers. The second is the most widely held today by Catholic theologians and biblical scholars.

2.2.2. The existential approach of Rudolph Bultmann, one of the greatest Protestant thinkers in the first half of the twentieth century, attempted to preserve the theological importance of the church by rescuing it from the relativities of history and grounding it in the existential acceptance of Jesus in faith. It thus avoids the pitfalls of the scholarly liberal view, but it also rejects any mission to the Gentiles by Jesus and the sacramentalism of Hellenistic

---

[2] On the history of Scripture scholarship, see Stephen Neill, *The Interpretation of the New Testament 1861–1961,* The Firth Lectures (New York: Oxford University Press, 1965).

[3] Richard McBrien, *Catholicism*, 2nd ed (San Francisco: Harper Collins, 1994), 460; originally published in *Horizons* 1 (1974): 38.

Christianity. This view was popular from the 1920s to the 1950s.

2.2.3. In scholarly liberalism, Jesus' imminent expectation of the Kingdom locates the origins of the church in the hearts of the second generation of Christians, not in the action of God in Jesus or in the immediate experience of the disciples after the Resurrection. This interpretation was popular among many liberal Protestants at the end of the nineteenth century and continues today in modified form through the work of liberal Protestant communities.

2.2.4. Non-scholarly liberalism, the opposite of the blueprint model, holds that Jesus was a preacher of the Kingdom but that no continuity exists between Jesus and the community that came after him. What matters is not the Jesus of history but the community of faith. This approach was popular with Protestants at the end of the nineteenth and beginning of the twentieth centuries and remains implicit in many liberal Christologies and ecclesiologies.

Most Roman Catholic and mainstream Protestant biblical scholars and theologians accept the approach of scholarly conservatism. Neoorthodox Catholics still cling to the "blueprint" approach although it has been historically discredited. Some liberal mainstream and Free Church Protestants along with many secular people subscribe to a scholarly or non-scholarly liberalism. For them, the church has made itself too important, and they reject this importance by rejecting its divine origins.

2.3 The Foundation of the Church in the Israelite People

The historical foundation of the church is properly located in God's revelation to Israel and the formation of God's people. The church as the People of God is the continuation of the ancient Israelites who first received divine revelation. Revelation is the mystery of God's presence; God was a participant in the movement of human events. Just as the Jews first experienced the liberating power of God in their escape from Egypt in about 1280 BCE, the church is the new Passover community, freed for all time from the power of sin and death. This community is entrusted with the final revelation of God manifested in the life of Jesus.

2.3.1 God's Revelation in the Judeo-Christian Scriptures. What Christians call the content of Revelation—the Old and New Testaments—is the historical story of divine revelation and human response, of covenant and communion between God and the human family. The Bible is the story of God's revelation in the events of history and the response of human hearts in faith.

While Revelation takes place in history and in human experience, it cannot be reduced to either. God transcends both history and experience and, for this very reason, God is at the same time completely immanent within them. God speaks to us not only from the *outside in* but also from the *inside out.* Divine revelation occurs in two ways: first, through the Logos or the intermediary of another person or event in human experience; second, through what is immediately knowable as Spirit that unites Father and Son. God reveals from the outside in through Word what we know through Spirit from the inside out: that God is our Creator, that we are made in God's image, that God is not an abstract power but a personal being. (This can be compared to what Luke tells us in his twenty-fourth chapter: while the disciples were walking with Jesus to Emmaus they did not recognize him when he was all outside, but knew him as Lord immediately in the breaking of the bread. This is also the point where the Western way of the Logos and the Asian path of Spirit can be seen as complementary.)

2.3.2 What does it mean to say that God's revelation is historical?. The affirmation that God's revelation is historical presupposes a vision of history that Judaism and Christianity have given us. Prior to, or outside of, the Judeo-Christian framework, time was seen negatively, as a burden that demanded escape or release. The time of life and the meaning of life were distinct and antagonistic realities. Time was understood as a circle, a wheel, and salvation meant salvation *from* time, escape from the wheel. The meaning of every human action was to be found not in its uniqueness and its particularity, but only in its capacity to participate in a transtemporal meaning, to reflect the eternal meaning that effectively denied the importance of each historical moment. There was no awareness of history as the movement of one unique and unrepeatable event after another. History was an illusion because the meaning of life was found not in the concrete but in the universal.

Thus, when God revealed Godself to the Jews, God revealed not only the divine life, but also an entirely new and qualitatively different way in which God and humanity would enter a relationship. God the Transcendent was attainable not by release from the burden of time or escape from history. Time itself became God's gift, the place where God was present. Salvation was not salvation *from* time but salvation *in* and *through* time, in the concrete events of human life. History was linear, a straight line from beginning to end, from its creation to its consummation. What is unique about the Judeo-Christian religious tradition is precisely this vision of history. Christianity proclaims that the meaning of all reality, all history, has been crystallized in one unrepeatable historical event, the cross, death, and resurrection of Jesus.

Hence, the church emerges out of the historical experience of the Jewish people portrayed in the Hebrew Bible or subsequently the Old Testament. Jesus himself was a devout Jew, and his own interpretation of his life and mission came from the sacred scriptures of Israel. While Jesus was a "marginal Jew," as Catholic New Testament scholar, John Meier, calls him, his worldview and his sense of mission as the preacher of the Kingdom were thoroughly Jewish and took place in an exclusively Jewish context. The earliest followers of Jesus were all Jews, and the history of the community of Nazarenes or "People of the Way," as they were called in first century, is the history of a sect within Judaism, not a new religion called Christianity. It is impossible to understand the church without first grounding it historically and theologically in the Jewish people and their unique experience of God. As the Gospel of John reminds us: "Salvation is from the Jews" (Jn 4:22).

2.4 Judaism at the Time of Jesus.

The Jewish historical situation from the sixth to the first centuries BCE provides the immediate background for the appearance of Jesus and the world out of which the church eventually emerged. While this background is too broad to be considered in detail, one can highlight a number of important developments in the Jewish world. Judaism in Jesus' time was a mixture of temple ritual and obedience to the law. The age of the prophets and the prophetic spirit, the great soul of the Jewish people, had passed. Since the time of the exile by the Babylonians in 587 BCE and the return of the Jews to Jerusalem in 539 BCE, Judaism was characterized by: first, a decline and virtual disappearance of the prophetic spirit; second, a ritualistic and legal understanding of God's law and the Temple worship; and finally, a time of expectation of change or apocalypse—a sense the world's end was close at hand. ("Apocalyptic" is from the Greek meaning to reveal; the Book of Revelation was called the Apocalypse in older Catholic Bibles.) The Hellenization of the world under Alexander the Great, including Judaism in third century BCE, made profound changes in Jewish culture. Greek became the common language of the Mediterranean world, and the Hebrew bible was translated into Greek by seventy rabbis in 270 BCE. This famous translation was called the *Septuagint*, from the Latin word for seventy. For this reason, the entire corpus of the New Testament was written in Greek, the lingua franca of Jesus' time. Palestine fell to Roman rule in 63 BCE under Pompey, creating the final piece in the mélange of the Mediterranean cultural world at the beginning of the Common Era. Jesus appears in a land under Roman rule, and this fact plays a significant part in the Gospels' stories. Yet, Greek remained the common language on the streets of the Roman Empire, including Rome itself.

The objectivation of laws and beliefs and apocalyptic expectation was in the air and in the spirit of the people when Jesus appeared as an itinerant preacher in the third decade of the first century. The belief in the coming of God's Kingdom was the result of years of political oppression by outside powers as well as the growing separation in the understanding of the Jewish community between the righteous and the sinful. Jesus followed in the footsteps of John the Baptizer and others who were predicting the end of time. In order to understand the world in which Jesus was born, in approximately 4–6 BCE, let us quickly look at the five major groups that existed within first-century BCE Judaism. Each group was divided theologically as well as politically and economically. Three of the five groups—the Sadducees, Pharisees, and the Essenes—were part of a revival of Jewish life and culture under Judas Maccabaeus and his descendants, especially John Hycanus, who ruled as ethnarch and high priest from 134 to 104 BCE.[4] Jesus was related to each of these groups differently.

2.4.1 The Established Order: The Sadducees[5]. The chief priests of the temple, the aristocracy of Jewish life, were members of the Sadducee party. The name "Sadducee" may come from Zadok, the high priests of the temple during King David's reign, or *saddik*, meaning righteous. Three power groups existed among the establishment at the time: first, the high or chief priests, a consistory that held supreme power in both religious and civil matters; second, the elders, the heads of influential aristocratic families who were not part of the sacerdotal class themselves; third, the scribes, who were the jurist theologians, many of whom were Pharisees but were intimately connected to the power base. The Sadducees were profoundly conservative in the interpretation of the Law, allowing no development in its interpretation. At the same time, they were pragmatic and liberal in foreign policy in order not to incur the wrath of the Romans as the occupying power. Jesus had very little to do with the Sadducees, but they are mentioned a number of times in the Gospels. Jesus was not a priest but a layman, and his preaching made him suspect to the ruling class as the instigator of a lay movement. Jesus uses only one example of a priest in his sayings—the Levite in the story of the Good Samaritan

[4] Gerd Theissen and Annette Merz, *The Historical Jesus: A Comprehensive Guide* (Minneapolis: Fortress Press, 1998), 132–33.

[5] For a thorough treatment of the Sadducees, see John Meier, *A Marginal Jew: Rethinking the Historical Jesus*, vol. 3, *Companions and Competitors* (New York: Doubleday, 2001), 389–487.

who neglects the bleeding man because of his need to preserve his ritual purity (Lk 10:31). This story would infuriate the priestly ears of his listeners. Even more, Jesus' message of *metanoia*, a surrender of the self to God, could only bring him into conflict with the Sadducees and their established rules of temple worship and service to the law.[6]

2.4.2 The Zealots or Revolutionaries[7]. The Zealots were revolutionaries who wished to overthrow the Roman army occupying Palestine by violence rather than by obedience to the law, the way of the Sadducees, Pharisees, and the Essenes. Probably descendants of the Maccabees, who were freedom fighters in the second century before Christ, the revolutionaries created some militant opposition to Roman rule after Pompey took control of Palestine in 63 BCE. When Judea and Samaria were placed under direct Roman rule in 6 CE and taxes had to be paid directly to Rome, a teacher called Judas of Galilee refused to pay taxes, claiming that God alone was the ruler of the Jewish people.[8] Disturbances broke out, summoning Sulpicius Quirinius, the supreme Roman commander, to put down the uprising. The Zealots, until the revolution in 66 CE, were responsible for a number of violent incidents in the century between Pompey and the outbreak of hostilities. Some of Jesus' disciples were probably associated with this radical group, for example, Simon, called "the Zealot."

The locus of the revolutionary spirit was Galilee, the home of Jesus and many of his disciples. In 44 CE, when Galilee also came under direct Roman rule, the two sons of Judas of Galilee also refused to pay taxes and caused disturbances. Both sons were crucified by the Roman procurator. Some have suggested that two of Jesus' disciples, James and John, who were called "the sons of thunder," may have had ties with the revolutionary movement. Like modern terrorists, Zealots caused turmoil in the Jewish community. The *sicarii* (from *sica*, dagger) were knife-wielding guerrilla fighters who murdered people in crowded streets, especially on festival days, in order to foment revolution. Pontius Pilate, the procurator of Judea from 26 to 36 CE, left Caesarea to take control of Jerusalem in order to maintain civil order at the time of the Passover when Jesus was crucified. While other Roman states were granted self-rule in some form, Judea, the small piece of land including Jerusalem and its environs, came under the direct rule of a Roman military official. Few people were as tenacious in opposition to Roman rule as the Jews.

---

[6] Hans Küng, *On Being Christian* (New York: Doubleday, 1976), 177–83.

[7] See Meier, *A Marginal Jew*, 205–8, 565–69.

[8] Theissen and Merz, *The Historical Jesus*, 142–43.

A more serious revolt against the Romans developed in 66 CE under John of Gischala, also from Galilee, after Christianity had reached Rome itself. This final outbreak brought Vespasian, the future Roman Emperor, to Judea in 68 CE to put down the revolt. When he returned to Rome later that year to become emperor, his son Titus took over the army. In 70 CE, Titus sacked Jerusalem and destroyed the temple so that no stone was left upon stone. This event was described as the "abomination of desolation" for the Jews portrayed in the Gospel of Matthew (Mt 24:15). A small group of Jews continued the fight against the Romans, but they were conquered at the fortress of Masada in 73 CE. This marks the end of ancient Judaism. In 132 CE, the final revolt took place under the Zealot leader Bar Kokhba, "Son of the Star," resulting in the second destruction of Jerusalem and the closing of the city for centuries to Jews.

The national expectation of a liberator and a messiah played a considerable part in the revolutionary movement. Jesus sharply criticized the landowners and the ruling classes, and something in Jesus' message made him attractive to the Zealots. Yet, the Gospels also make it clear that Jesus' revolution was not political and that his purpose was not to work for the downfall of the government but to preach the Kingdom of God. Jesus was concerned about a revolution at the heart of the human person's relation to God.[9]

2.4.3 The Essenes[10]. The Essenes were a type of monastic movement within Judaism. They obeyed the law strictly and established small communities in the desert, believing that they could bring about the Kingdom of God by abandoning the world and devoting their lives to prayer and fasting; they renounced worldly life and pleasures. The Essenes (from "devout" or "pious," *Hasidim* in Hebrew) originated in the latter part of the second century BCE. Early followers of the Maccabean revolt, they quickly broke away and followed an anonymous "Teacher of Righteousness." He was probably a Zadokide high priest forced out by a Maccabean high priest, perhaps Jonathan (ruled 160–143 BCE), called the "Wicked Priest" in the Qumran writings. The "Teacher of Righteousness" joined himself with fundamentalist Jews who had existed before him and transformed this community into an alternate temple for the community in Jerusalem.[11]

---

[9] See Küng, *On Being Christian*, 183–89.

[10] See Meier, *A Marginal Jew*, 488–532.

[11] Theissen and Merz, *The Historical Jesus*, 133–34.

The Essenes were strict fundamentalists, interpreting the law in a most rigid and uncompromising way. Their history can be found in the Dead Sea Scrolls that were discovered at Qumran in 1947. John the Baptist was thought to be a member of the Essene community. Unlike the Essenes, Jesus did not preach social or political isolation from the world; nor did he take the law with the fanaticism of this Jewish monastic community. At the same time, much in the seriousness of his message about the Kingdom of God and his criticism of temple worship would appeal to the Essene community. In spite of their profound differences in their attitudes to the law, some resemblances existed between the Essenes and the early church; both understood themselves as the true Israel and both organized themselves in strong communitarian structures. Some scholars have also drawn similarities between the Teacher of Righteousness and Jesus.[12]

2.4.4 The Pharisees[13.] Much debate exists in biblical scholarship as to exactly who Pharisees are. As John Meier says, "the history of 20th century research is strewn with many portraits of the Pharisees, most of which are discarded today."[14] Some saw them as urban Jews, drawing support from the working class, as Judaism moved from an agricultural world to a more urban one where the Law was less relevant to the people and more difficult to follow.[15] Some believe that the Pharisee party was comprised of about six thousand people, mostly from middle class Jews. As W. H. C. Frend says, "they were lay persons and considered themselves a godly elite among their fellow citizens."[16] Jacob Neusner argues that the Pharisees "were driven by an ideal of priestly holiness….The Pharisees sought by strict observance of purity rules to extend the holiness of the temple into the sphere of everyday Jewish living and eating."[17]

The word "Pharisee" means "separated," not "hypocrite," as the adjective "pharisaical" has come to mean in English. Originating in the time of the Maccabees, the Pharisees were first an opposition movement before they came to power under Queen Salome Alexandra (ruled 76–67 BCE). Henceforth they became part of the established power structure and held a seat on the Sanhedrin, the high council of the Jews. They were skeptical of any effort

[12] See Küng, *On Being Christian*, 192–201.

[13] See Meier, *A Marginal Jew*, 289–388.

[14] Meier, 311.

[15] Meier, 311

[16] W. H. C. Frend, *The Rise of Christianity* (Philadelphia: Fortress, 1984).

[17] See Meier, *A Marginal Jew*, 311–12.

to change the situation in Palestine by force against the Romans. Instead, they wished to prepare themselves by prayer, a devout life, and a precise observance of the rules of everyday religious practice. In this way, they believed that they could hasten the Kingdom of God.[18]

In fulfilling the law, ritual purity and tithing were especially important for the Pharisees. Their intentions of helping the people were good and sincere; they wanted to make the many burdens of the law easier for the mass of people. They believed that they could accomplish this by a compromise with the law. Thus, they set up a series of variations within the law, adding interpretations and qualifications to the law to temper the burden of law in its most rigorous form. They believed in a system of supererogation, which means the accumulation of merit in one's relationship to God. Some works were not strictly required by the law but were performed for additional merit; they believed that this merit would count against an individual's offenses in the final encounter with God.

The good intentions of the Pharisees found expression, as W. H. C. Frend says, in their "systematized works of mercy and charity toward the poor." They believed that "almsgiving and deeds of loving kindness are equal to all the commandments of the law."[19] Some of the social outlook of the early church was undoubtedly based on their behavior. Their emphasis, however, on merit and the pursuit of good deeds to enhance one's righteousness came into immediate conflict with Jesus. His concern was not external obedience to the law and accumulation of merit but setting one's heart wholeheartedly on God. As Jesus pointedly tells us, "the Sabbath was made for humankind not humankind for the Sabbath" (Mk 2:27).

Historically, the Pharisees are portrayed more negatively in the Gospels than they deserved. Early followers of Christ were condemned for abandoning the tradition and the Law. The antagonism of Jesus to the Pharisees should be understood in light of the situation in the church of the 80s and 90s CE. Jesus' attitude toward the Pharisees was the Jesus of the early church, not the historical Jesus. Ironically, some scholars believe that Jesus himself was probably a Pharisee of a liberal kind. All modern Judaism has been handed down from the tradition of the Pharisee party after the destruction of the Temple under Titus in 70 CE.[20]

2.4.5 The People of the Land. Average Jews were not members of the

[18] Theissen and Merz, *The Historical Jesus*, 135–36.

[19] Frend, *The Rise of Christianity*, 137.

[20] See Küng, *On Being Christian*, 201–7.

Sadducee or the Pharisee party. Neither revolutionaries like the Zealots, nor monastics like the Essenes, the people of the land were the common folk, mostly farmers and tradesmen, who formed the majority of the Jewish population. While many of these people were religious in spirit, fidelity to the law demanded by the Pharisees or Sadducees was often beyond their reach. Since much of their livelihood depended upon contact with the Gentiles, they were ritually impure and thus barred from temple worship and other social functions. They were unable to make great shows of almsgiving as the Pharisees and Sadducees often did, and, since they were unwelcome in the temple, they were treated with condescension and sometimes derision. Many were considered sinners. The widow in Mark 12:38–44 who only had a few pennies to put in the basket was surely one of the "people of the land." One notices how Jesus praises her at the expense of the Pharisees and elders who make a big show of their charity. Life—politically, religiously, and economically—was often difficult for the people of the land. In Jesus, they saw an immediate advocate and one sympathetic to their plight. Jesus showed great understanding of their situation and showered compassion upon them. From this group of common people most of Jesus' followers came—perhaps Jesus himself if he were not a Pharisee.[21]

2.5 The Jesus of History and the Christ of Faith.

What can we know of the actual Jesus of history? In what sense are the Gospels records of history? In answering this question, we must avoid, on the one hand, a literal, historicist view in which the Gospels are an actual reenactment of Jesus' life and mission. On the other, we must reject the Gospels as legends with little historical content. John Meier calls these two positions "history remembered" versus "prophecy historicized."[22] The quest for the historical Jesus is one of the most controversial parts of biblical studies and theology. Beginning with scholars like Reimarus, Lessing, Herder, and Strauss three and four centuries ago, the quest has passed through a number of stages: the liberal quest of the nineteenth century, the collapse of the liberal quest in the early twentieth century, the new or second quest beginning in the 1950s, and finally, the more recent third quest. The present quest emphasizes the social history of Jesus' time, his place within Judaism, and an attention to non-canonical sources.[23]

---

[21] Cwiekowski, *The Beginnings of the Church*, 34–35.

[22] John Meier, *A Marginal Jew*, 312.

[23] Theissen and Merz, *The Historical Jesus*, 10–11.

Most mainstream Scripture scholars generally agree on a historical minimum—that is, facts we can be certain of historically—for a life of Jesus. The following is Dermot Lane's interpretation of such a historical minimum.

> Jesus was a man and "appeared externally around him in exactly the same way as any other human individual appears." Jesus was born between 4 and 7 BCE and most likely died in 30 CE at around the age of thirty-five. If 30 CE is the correct year, the first "Good Friday" took place on 7 April. (The person who was to change the calendar and introduce the "Common Era" was ironically born "before" the acknowledged year of his birth. Apparently, Dionysius the Little, a sixth-century Syrian monk, miscounted by four to seven years when he remade the calendar.)
>
> Jesus was a rabbi, one who proclaims the divine law. Unlike other rabbis, he taught in fields and on lakeshores, not just in synagogues; he appealed to people that other rabbis would avoid such as women and children, sinners and tax collectors.
>
> Jesus was understood and accepted as a prophet, and he understood himself in the same way. A prophet was a messenger of God, one called to proclaim God's will, not one who predicted the future. The fact that Jesus was a prophet was the generally accepted opinion, and this fact was made known to the leaders of the Jews. Jesus himself says that it is not fitting for a prophet to die outside of Jerusalem.
>
> Jesus preached the Kingdom of God, an eschatological time of fulfillment and the completion of the Jewish people's liberation from sinfulness and oppression. While this Kingdom was a future reality, it appears that Jesus understood that the Kingdom was also breaking in on the world in and through his preaching and ministry.
>
> Jesus tried to change Jewish ideas about the Kingdom—from a political, materialistic understanding to a spiritual, universal, and personal one.
>
> Jesus made a radical call for repentance, for *metanoia* or change of heart. Jesus announced that God wants more than simple obedience to the law and requires personal faith and trust.
>
> Jesus was a miracle worker but he was not alone; there were many other miracle workers of his day. What made Jesus different was that his miracles were a direct response to faith, and often Jesus' praise of faith was the climactic moment of the miracle story. For Jesus, the primary purpose of miracles was a sign of the breaking in of the Kingdom of God.
>
> Jesus spoke with authority. Normally, a rabbi would conclude his

> prayer with the expression "Amen." Jesus began praying with "Amen," suggesting a prior rapport with God now present in his words. Jesus emphasized this authority by claiming the power to forgive sins. The sinner in the Judaism of Jesus' day was an individual to be shunned by others. On the contrary, Jesus reaches out to sinners and befriends them.
>
> Jesus was received by the people as one who preached and promised salvation. This salvation was based on an interior relationship with God rather than the external obedience of the law.
>
> Most of all, Jesus appears as one who assumed a unique personal closeness to God; his whole view of life was radically theocentric, that is, one in which God was the center of all life.[24]

Given this historical minimum, the question remains: can we discover the real Jesus of history? Or is the Jesus in the Gospels the Christ of faith, the person seen in the light of faith in the Resurrection? On the one hand, it is naïve to think the Gospels are history as we know history today. The Gospels were written as confessional documents, from persons of faith to others of faith. Their purpose was not to inspire faith (preaching, *kerygma*), but to explain the faith to people who already accepted Jesus in their hearts (teaching, *didaché*). On the other hand, it would also be an error to believe that there is no history in the Gospels or that our knowledge of Jesus is only a product of the later faith of the community. History must be seen as both objective and subjective. There is no reenactment of history as it *actually* was; this was the error of Leopold van Ranke and the school of historicism at the beginning of the twentieth century. But there are objective facts, events, and data to be studied and considered carefully. These facts make little sense, however, without their reception by an analytical and interpretative mind. For example, given the abundance of objective evidence from forensics, audiotapes, film, and eyewitnesses, the assassination of John F. Kennedy in 1962 is still a matter of interpretation. Was there a lone assassin or a conspiracy? Was the official final report without flaws? The same can be said of the tragedy of September 11, 2001.

In examining the story of any individual, whether it is Plato, Jesus, George Washington, or Jamie Dimon, the question remains: how do we really know the mind and heart of another? According to Avery Dulles, it is only

---

[24] See Dermot Lane, *The Reality of Jesus: An Essay in Christology* (New York: Paulist, 1975), 32–39.

through an individual's friends, those who shared the intimate stuff of life, that we can know another person as the individual really is. Communication, loyalty, and trust, knowledge of the person from the inside out as well as from the outside in, are essential. The goal of such knowledge is not the objective facts of another's life but an intersubjective understanding of the other. This kind of knowing another is knowledge by participation, one that transforms the knower in the process of knowing. This is the knowledge that wives and husbands, brothers and sisters, and lifelong friends have of each other. Who better knew Jesus than his friends and disciples, those who gave up their lives for him and had their own lives transformed by what God accomplished in him?[25] Hence, one can say that in the Gospels there exists an accurate, albeit, subjective, view of Jesus. This means that the Jesus of history has been passed down to us through the subjective eyes of faith in a faithful and loving manner. What is truly the objective history of Jesus is hidden in the depths of the subjective response to Jesus. Surely the evangelists did not fabricate the historical life of Jesus, but they gave us much more of a theological interpretation of Jesus than a historical portrait. They described Jesus through their eyes and the eyes of the community and painted a portrait of Jesus relevant to the theological questions of their particular time and place.

2.5.1 Jesus and the Church: Christology and Ecclesiology. As we have already considered, Jesus was born between 4 and 6 BCE, and he died in 30 CE. We know that he certainly was executed between 26 and 36 CE because, from Roman records, Pontius Pilate was procurator of Judea during these years. The first historical evidence of the community of Jesus begins to appear about 50 CE in the writings of Saint Paul and later in the Acts of the Apostles of Luke. The earliest writing of the New Testament is 1 Thessalonians by Saint Paul, written about 50 CE.

Whatever the church today, it has its roots in the historical life and preaching of Jesus. Jesus' message was the coming of God's Kingdom. If God was present in Christ, as Saint Paul tells us, then Jesus' actions reveal the actions of God. The church has its foundation, then, in Jesus' life, ministry, death, and resurrection, and the faith of his earliest followers. Likewise, if the church is the church of Jesus Christ, it must present the portrait of Jesus that its earliest members have passed down to us. A church that does not take the words and deeds of Jesus in the Gospels as its foundation has rejected its cornerstone. Unfortunately, this has been the frequent pattern of church history.

---

[25] See Avery Dulles, *Apologetics and the Biblical Christ* (Westminster, MD: The Newman Press, 1966), 34–35.

In other words, there is no theology of the church without a historical and theological understanding of Jesus the Christ; there is no ecclesiology without Christology. Understanding the church today as the church must be founded on an understanding of Jesus the Jew, his Jewish heritage, and the disciples, both men and women, who first saw him as the Messiah or the Christ.

2.6 The Theological Origins of Church: Jesus and the Kingdom of God

Jesus certainly does not preach a "church," a word that appears only twice in the four Gospels, in Matthew 16 and 18, written in the 80s CE. The word "kingdom" is found 104 times in the Synoptic Gospels, "kingdom of God" in Mark and Luke and "kingdom of heaven" in Matthew (Matthew, writing for a Jewish audience, did not wish to use the word "God"). In the Gospel of John, eternal life is often employed as the spiritual counterpart of the kingdom. There are serious problems with the term "kingdom," because it has no simple referent in today's experience. (A young child who hears the word "kingdom" might first think of Disneyland or Disneyworld.). For the Gospel writers, the Kingdom of God is the powerful rule of God in human life and history, the reality of God's presence in all of the created order. Perhaps an analogy of "kingdom" can be found in the commitment of marriage. When two people marry, they freely surrender their individual lives to share in all of life and love; they enter each other's "kingdom," so to speak, given the intense mutual life that husband and wife share.

Whatever the church of Christ has become in two millennia, it must be intimately related to Jesus' preaching and God's works of healing and grace in Jesus. Sometimes, the church forgets that only God is the true object of faith, that only God is of ultimate importance. Like the Grand Inquisitor in the *Brothers Karamazov*, the church has asked Jesus: "Why have you come back to disturb us?" Sometimes the church is guilty of domesticating God, making adherence to its own structures and doctrines the final goal of Christian life, rather than the Kingdom that it preaches and embodies.[26]

What is this Kingdom of God like? Since we rarely use the word today in a political sense, we need to recall its original meaning. Some have translated the Greek *basileia* (whence the English "basilica") as "Reign of God,"

---

[26] See Hans Küng, "The Coming Reign of God," part B in *The Church* (New York: Sheed and Ward, 1968), 43–45.

but this too has its own difficulties. (Americans, for example, talk not of the reign of a president but his term of office). "Kingdom" or "reign," as the Gospels use the word, is a political metaphor for the presence of God, for the actuality of God in human experience. Jesus announces an intimacy of God *within* human history; indeed, Jesus *is* this intimacy. As essential as the Kingdom is to Jesus' message, after the resurrection, the earliest community does not preach the Kingdom of God, their Lord's central message. Rather, they preach Jesus himself as the one in whom the Kingdom has become flesh, the personal and historical realization of this Kingdom. A profound unity between Jesus as the Kingdom of God in history and the church is essential to ecclesiology. Saint Paul called this unity of the Christ and his followers one "body," the first and most vivid image of the church in the New Testament. If Jesus is the Kingdom of God and we are intimately connected to him as one body, then we too are bearers of God's Kingdom within; we too, as God's image or as children of God, make the Kingdom visible. As Zooey tells Franny in J. D. Salinger's two stories, *Franny and Zooey*: "But most of all, who besides Jesus knew—*knew*—that we're carrying the Kingdom of Heaven around with us, *inside*, where we're all too goddam stupid and sentimental and unimaginative to look?"[27] The following characteristics of the Kingdom, according to Hans Küng, will elucidate this symbol of the power and the love of God in our midst.

2.6.1 The Kingdom of God is Eschatological. The Jewish people in Jesus' time lived in a period of expectation, a sense of the coming end of time or the end times in some apocalyptic event. When Jesus proclaimed that the Kingdom of God was near (Mk 1:15), his listeners were not surprised. Other prophets besides Jesus had preached the coming of the Kingdom as well as a gospel of repentance. Jesus was preaching the end of the age, in Greek, the *eschaton.* The formal study of the end of time is called eschatology, in Latin, the study of the *novissimis*, the newest or last things.

Eschatology in twentieth-century biblical scholarship has been understood in three ways: (1) realized eschatology holds that the Kingdom is complete in Jesus himself; (2) futurist eschatology believes that the Kingdom is still to come and Jesus is the preacher and sign of its coming; (3) dialectical eschatology posits that the Kingdom is here already in Jesus and in the Gospel message but is not yet complete.

The meaning of the word *eschaton* or the "end times" should be

---

[27] J. D. Salinger, *Franny and Zooey* (Boston: Little Brown and Company, 1961), 172.

understood in a two-fold manner: a *terminus ad quem*, a specific point of ending; and the directedness or the movement towards this end. Likewise, eschatology can be studied, first, as the historical end of the world, time, and history; second, as the personal destiny of the individual in death. The New Testament treats the end times primarily in a communal and historical perspective, but the personal dimension is also present in different language. For example, in the Gospel of John, Jesus does not preach the Kingdom entering history but eternal life. This poses the question: what is the relationship between the communal end of history and the personal quest for eternal life? What does Jesus mean by eternal life and what does eternity mean ontologically and personally?

2.6.2 Time and Eternity. The mystery of time and eternity lies at the heart of our relationship with God as well as our own self-understanding. Eternity, in Saint Paul's words, means that "Christ is all and in all" (Col 3:11). Paul Tillich remarks that "eternity is not the extinction of time; it is the creative unity of all times and cycles of time, of past and future."[28] Likewise, Tillich posits this profound truth: "One could never grasp the eternal, but one could be grasped by it."[29] The preaching of Jesus can be interpreted as eternity grasping us; put differently, eternal life is what Jesus preaches when he preaches the Kingdom of God. If, as Tillich says, "eternity is the unity of all the consecutive moments of time,"[30] then eternity both embraces time and is the hidden secret of every moment of time. Jesus, in preaching the Kingdom of God, brings the eternal into time. So in addition to the previous two, to understand the Kingdom or Reign of God, Hans Küng suggests these five following characteristics.

2.6.3 The Kingdom is an Act of God. Jesus preaches the Kingdom as an act of God, not the product of human effort or human piety. The crux of the disagreement between Jesus and the leaders of the Jews was precisely this point: obeying the law perfectly would not bring about God's Kingdom because it is God's action, God's free gift, not something merited by human action, intention, or ritual. Two famous Gospel stories exemplify this truth: the parable of the Laborers in the Vineyard (Mt 20:1–16), and the Parable of

---

[28] Paul Tillich, "On the Transitoriness of Life," chap. 8 in *The Shaking of the Foundations* (New York: Charles Scribner's Sons, 1948), 68.

[29] Paul Tillich, "The Paradox of the Beatitudes," chap. 3 in *The Shaking of the Foundations*, 27.

[30] Paul Tillich, "Symbols of Eternal Life," *Harvard Divinity Bulletin* 26, no. 3 (1962), 2.

the Prodigal Son.

In the first story, the landowner or the "good employer," as one commentator suggests, is God. Yet, even with this fact, and an understanding of the parable in the context of Jesus' listeners at the time, Jesus reveals an image of God that causes some concern.[31] For most people who have worked in the vineyard since dawn, why is God so generous to the latecomers? Why do they receive as much? For the student who does poorly on an exam after hours of intense study or the mother who is dying of cancer and will never see her children grown and married, the question is the same: why am I given less although I have worked as hard, and perhaps harder, than others? Why must I suffer while others are spared? These questions force individuals into a deeper and not always satisfying or appealing understanding of God. God does *not* make life equal for all nor is there some deep-down abstract equality or justice invisible to our human eyes now but which we must accept naïvely as "God's will." Nothing makes the situation different; no amount of prayer or sacrifice will necessarily change what some think is fate and others the capricious will of the creator.

The church misses the point whenever it believes that God can be manipulated and shaped by the human idea of justice. Church people, trapped into a *quid pro quo* understanding of the divine-human relationship, often become disillusioned when their hours in the vineyard are not rewarded according to their expectations; or negatively, when they are not spared loss and anxiety, sickness, and pain, given their beliefs that they are undeserving of such treatment. Even in the inequality of their work, all the laborers are equal in the eyes of the landowner. This was a shock to the people who first heard Jesus' parable, just as the story shocks many pious people today. Nothing we do can merit God's favor, nor can we build up merit; it is all grace, it is all God's gift.

In the famous story of the Father with two sons, Jesus once again reveals an idea of God that contradicts our expectations. For the younger son, who has spent his last penny on pleasure, receives in return much more than he deserves, while the older son, who works dutifully on his father's land, receives only his due and never knows the great mercy and generosity of his father. The father and the two sons represent two kinds of response to the call of the Kingdom. Many people, on first reading the story, identify with the younger son and are delighted to hear of God's great mercy. Most people, however,

---

[31] See Daniel Harrington, *The Gospel According to Matthew*, The Collegeville Bible Commentary (Collegeville, MN: The Liturgical Press, 1983), 80–81.

are older sons. They see the truth that should make them free as a secret burden, wallowing in their own hard work, piety, and self-righteousness, furious when one of their less-deserving brothers has the "fatted calf" of today's world slain for them. They want a just world, a world where the just and righteous are rewarded with the Kingdom and the wicked are excluded. The Lucan parable presents us with a very different picture of God: of a father awaiting the return of his lost son, prodigal with mercy, forgiveness, and unconditional acceptance. A relationship with God based on unquestioned fulfillment of the law is not enough. God wants more, the heart of the human person in trust and humility, and God rewards those accordingly. No wonder Jesus' relationships with known "sinners" were such a scandal to the Pharisees and the Scribes. No wonder their strict obedience to the law was not enough to merit them the Kingdom in Jesus' eyes.

2.6.4 The Kingdom is Universal and Spiritual. The Kingdom is universal and spiritual, not political and earthly. Unlike some Jews who believed that the Kingdom of God meant the restoration of the throne of David in Jerusalem, Jesus' vision was far beyond this. He preached a radical message, one that touched the roots of the person's relationship with God. (The word *radix* in Latin means root; hence the vegetable radish, rooted in the earth.) Jesus did not preach a message in which religion was confined to the social and political boundaries of Israel, but a proclamation that was open to all. In the famous story of the Samaritan woman at the well, he tells her this: "Believe me, woman, that the hour is coming...when true worshippers will worship the Father in Spirit and truth...God is Spirit, and those who worship him must worship him in Spirit and truth" (Jn 4:21–24).

In Jesus' time, Israel was a theocracy; to be part of God's Kingdom was identical to the political reality of the Jewish State. Jesus gives ample evidence of the universality of the Kingdom: he refuses to identify the Kingdom with things exclusively Jewish (e.g., his curing the Roman centurion's servant in Luke 7:1–10 and the story of the Samaritan woman in John). In a contemporary context, this frees the church as the sacrament of the Kingdom of God to work *through* political structures but not to identify itself *with* any political form in an uncritical and absolutist manner. The Kingdom of God transcends all human political forms and is present, in fragmentary form, in all of them.

2.6.5 The Kingdom Announces Joy and Forgiveness. The Kingdom is a message of joy and forgiveness, not a judgment or vengeance on sinners. In the story of the Prodigal Son (Luke 15), Jesus reveals a God who is always waiting for a person's return, a God who is unconditionally accepting and loving *in spite of* sinfulness. It appears that Jesus is almost more concerned with sinners than with the righteous, revealing a God who loves sinners more than the just and the religious. The only sin that cannot be forgiven is the sin against the Holy Spirit, a sin that rejects one's sinfulness and the need for forgiveness.

This image of an unconditionally forgiving God is a disturbing one for many Christians who consider themselves justified and righteous. For these people, the reality of God is placed within the confines of a system of merit in which the good must be rewarded and the evil punished. And yet, the Gospels clearly state that those who were perceived as good and righteous in Jesus' time were not rewarded; instead, it was the sinners and the marginalized of his society who were invited to the everlasting banquet. Likewise, we can witness this same system of merit today in the often-heard phrase, "what goes around comes around." This concept does not capture the spirit of the Gospels because it implies certain inevitable consequences to human actions, limiting both the power of grace and the dynamics of human freedom. Rather the truth of God's Kingdom can be clearly captured in the remarkable phrase of the American philosopher, Robert Johann: "Being takes care of its own."[32]

2.6.6 A Kingdom of Metanoia or Change of Heart. The Kingdom is a call for *metanoia*, a change of heart, a reform of one's whole life. Jesus does not call for new commandments or moral laws, only that one give everything back to God with his or her whole heart. Even the commandment of love is not a commandment; no one can command love since love must emerge as the result of human freedom. Entering into communion with God is not possible without first entering into the inner layers of one's self; one must deal with ego, the small, petty part of the self that differentiates and discriminates. When one tames the ego, one gets closer to the dimension of the self that is also divine—that point that the mystics describe where God is our other and true self. This divine self is the image and likeness of God in which we were created. It is the child of God that we are, but self-centeredness and sinfulness get in the way. One must die to the ego-self so to be alive to the image of God within.

Jesus' message in the Gospels is the path of finding life through death, that is, through surrendering one's absolute self-importance, letting go of oneself for the sake of the other. As Jesus says, "he who seeks only himself brings himself to ruin whereas he who brings himself to naught for me discovers who he is" (Mt 10:39). (This theme is repeated frequently in the Gospel—see also Mt 16:25, Mk 8:34–35, Lk 9:23–24, and Jn 12:24.) Jesus proclaims *metanoia* at the beginning of his public preaching according to Mark:

---

[32] Johann, *Building the Human*, 122.

"This is the time of fulfillment. The reign of God is at hand! Reform your lives and believe in the gospel" (Mk 1:15). Likewise, the word "time" in the Greek text is not *chronos* or the normal passage of time measurable on a wristwatch or chronometer. Rather the word used is *kairos*, or a special time, a time of crisis, a time of decision, the right time. Jesus' message of the Kingdom or Reign of God is the time of fulfillment, the time of decision. Failure to change one's heart or reform one's life is the very essence of the sin of *hybris*, the human flaw of pride in Greek tragedy. Pride places the self at the center of the universe in the individual's mind. Thus deceived, the individuals can act like God and inordinately desire to draw all things to themselves, or the sin of concupiscence.

Jesus' message of surrendering one's ego or false self and discovering the child of God within is not dissimilar to the spirit of Zen Buddhism where the self must deny its own self, that is, its ego self, in order to enter into Nirvana. For Jesus, the forgotten self is the ego, while the self that remains is the child of God. No wonder Jesus says to the crowds in Capernaum, "I assure you, unless you change and become like little children, you will not enter the Kingdom of God. Whoever makes himself lowly, becoming like this child, is of greatest importance in that heavenly reign" (Mt 18: 3–4).

2.7 Jesus and the Message of Love

The Kingdom of God is a Kingdom of love, and this is the message of Jesus in the two great commandments (see Mt 22:37–40). It is about God's tender love for all of God's creation, especially the human person. Jesus' strength and faith manifests this love in its perfect form. What is the love that Jesus preaches like? *First*, the love of God and love of neighbor is inseparable. This is clear from all of Jesus' preaching and healing. The famous stylized account of the last judgment in Matthew 25: 31–46 advises that the only way to love God is to love one's brothers and sisters. As John tells us: "Let us love God in deed and in truth and not merely talk about it" (1 Jn 3:16). *Second*, the meaning of neighbor is the "one who needs me now," the person we encounter right before us. Jesus insists that the individual in need is one's neighbor—for example, in the story of the Good Samaritan (Lk 10:25–37), or of the woman with the hemorrhage (Lk 8:43–49).

Finally, Jesus adds a special dimension to love: love of enemies, which appears to be the unique feature of Christianity. "Love your enemies, do good to those who hate you" (Lk 6:27; see also Mt 5:44). Jesus reveals a God who asks us to love *as God has loved us*. "This is my commandment: love one another as I have loved you" (Jn 15:12). Thus, Jesus preaches a love that surpasses the Golden Rule. Followers of Jesus must do more than love another as they are loved—this is a merely a *quid pro quo* situation. One must love others as God loves, even to the point of loving those who hate you and revile you.[33]

Love, of course, takes different forms in the pattern of life, yet love in its essence is always the same. Love means a caring for another, of placing oneself and one's needs and desires second to the other's. At the core of love is sacrifice, of giving up of oneself for another. The joy of love comes from a "reunion" with another as well as a reunion with oneself and the divine as the ground of both self and other. This is why people who love always feel, paradoxically, most themselves in the process of loving, even though the focus of their being is on the other, not themselves. Through each other, lovers begin to discover, or preferably, re-discover, "their other and true selves," hidden under layers of self-centeredness, fear, anxiety, and a failure to trust. Jesus' message of love is a call to trust God in and through loving God's children.[34]

According to a number of different thinkers, human love takes three classical forms: *epithymia*, sexual love; *eros*, the drive to universal beauty and goodness; and *philia*, the love of friendship (recall Philadelphia as the City of Brotherly Love). Divine love or *agape* is the unconditional element that informs all human love. It is not a separate type of love but that to which all human love strives. All of these elements come together in the life, ministry, preaching, and death of Jesus. Jesus is the incarnation of agape, God's perfect love in a human life. Agape embraces all human expressions of love and serves as both their judgment and their fulfillment. Agape raises every form of human love to the level of divine possibility.[35]

Theologian Zachary Hayes summarizes Jesus preaching on the Kingdom this way:

> [The Kingdom] symbolizes, principally, a liberation from the limitations of human self-centeredness. God's rule can become actualized only where human beings are open to such love and be responsive to it. In so far as God's gift is accepted and responded to in human life and all human relations, there God's love comes to rule in human life and shape human relations in a decisive way. The conversion to which Jesus

[33] See Küng, *On Being Christian*, 255–62.

[34] See Paul Tillich, *Love, Power and Justice* (New York: Oxford University Press, 1959), 23, where love is defined as "the reunion of the separated."

[35] Tillich, 18–34.

calls us is, in essence, a conversion from self-centered existence to a God-centered existence. The meaning of a God-centered existence is expressed in the mystery of the indiscriminate love of God [that] is the model after which human life is to be lived.[36]

2.8 The Relation of Church to Kingdom

The relation of the church to the Kingdom of God is a debated theological question: how much of the Kingdom of God is embodied in the life of the church? How much does the Kingdom transcend any earthly expression or embodiment? Two polar interpretations of the relationship between the church and the Kingdom exist. First, Jesus in his lifetime intended to found the church as a natural historical continuation of the Kingdom of God in history. Second, at the opposite pole, the church and Kingdom are related only by human circumstances and human decision after the death of Jesus. The Kingdom of God is a purely eschatological concept, and it is the function of the church to simply announce its presence.

Against both positions, most scholars accept the following historical scenario of the church's emergence.[37] *First*, in his lifetime, Jesus did not intend to establish a church as a religious community distinct from Israel. No evidence in the Gospels suggests the establishment of a religious community separate from the Jews. There is no "public announcement by Jesus of his intention to found a church or a new covenant or any programmatic call to join a community of the elect."[38] The references to "church" in Matthew 16 and 18 are the only two such uses of the term *ecclesia* or church in all four Gospels. *Second*, Jesus laid the foundations during his public ministry for a church to emerge after his death and resurrection. His message was divisive; the Jews who accepted his message were clearly distinguished from those who did not. He proclaimed not only "the dawning of God's Kingdom [but] the emergence of an eschatological messianic people, to which he claimed his disciples belonged."[39] *Third*, the church has existed from the time of faith in the resurrection. There is no resurrection without its reception in faith by Jesus' earliest disciples who believed in Jesus and his message. *Fourth*, the foundation of the church does not lie solely in the intention or message of Jesus but

---

[36] Zachary Hayes, *Visions of a Future: A Study of Christian Eschatology* (Wilmington: Michael Glazier Books, 1989), 50.

[37] See Küng, *The Church*, 72–79.

[38] Küng, 73

[39] Küng, 75.

in the whole action of God in Christ from incarnation, preaching and ministry, and death and resurrection.[40] No church could exist before Jesus' passage through death and resurrection because the church is not simply a human community established historically by Jesus' individual will but a mysterious and spiritual unity created by the Spirit. Not until Jesus' death and transformation could the essence of the church emerge historically. No grace can exist before its origin; no Spirit can be present until Jesus himself leaves history and resides "at the right hand of the Father." Only Jesus' death validates his preaching of the Reign of God; only his resurrection can establish this reign as more than any earthly Kingdom. Only with his passage through death to eternal life can the life-giving Spirit, the heart of the church, dwell in the community of faith as its source of life, hope, unity, and holiness.

[40] Küng, 80–81.

3.

JESUS' DEATH AND TRANSFORMATION

3.1 The Paschal Mystery

Every church in the Christian world has a cross as its central symbol, and some churches are cruciform in shape. The Cross makes Christianity precisely what it is: a way of death and resurrection, the symbol of the path of transformation from old to new life. For the Christian, the Cross of Jesus marks the central event of history, the moment of complete interpenetration of the human and the divine, the meeting place of the temporal and the eternal. One might say that the church was born on the Cross. For with Jesus' death, he is no longer present to the world physically but henceforth in the Spirit, the personal Spirit called "Holy" and the foundation of the church. There is no resurrection without the death of Jesus on the cross, and the Cross would be meaningless without the resurrection hidden within Jesus' death. Understanding the meaning of the Cross and resurrection, the Paschal mystery, is essential to understanding the meaning of church.

3.2 A Historical Approach to the Cross

The radical dimension of Jesus' message inevitably led Jesus to his death. Jesus was the great scandal to the Jews who heard him preach and saw him heal the suffering and the needy. Apparently unmarried and without visible means of support, Jesus was an itinerant preacher who traveled throughout Judea, Galilee, and the environs of Tyre and Sidon, announcing the Kingdom of God. First, he gathered a group of twelve around him. His message appealed to many devout Jews expecting the messiah, the person who would bring the end times they had long awaited. The people of the land—the poor and struggling Jews who were not able to obey the law in all its strictness—were especially attracted to his message. The Sadducees and the elders were alarmed that he would incite the people to armed revolution, bringing the wrath of the Romans upon them all. (Their worst fears were ultimately realized with the outbreak of violence in 66–67 CE.) Perhaps the Essenes saw a man who would bring about the Kingdom. Yet unlike the Essenes, Jesus was no monk and did not reject life in the world. Likewise, the Zealots may have thought initially that a new revolutionary hero had come, but they too were disappointed when Jesus refused any political office and avoided confrontation with the political authorities. Finally, the Pharisees, mostly good people, were quickly disillusioned with Jesus' message. They feared that Jesus would destroy their agenda of caution, compromise, and devotion to the Mosaic Law.

The source of the scandal to the devout Jews was evident: he associated with the sick, the lame, the poor, and the oppressed. In Judaism, a physical ailment or infirmity was a sign of sinfulness, either in one's self or in one parents and lineage. The cripples and the lepers sought him out as a sign of hope in their hopeless world. Even worse, he associated with women, who were inferior to men in Jewish culture. "Better to burn the Torah than teach it to a woman," was a saying of Rabbi Eliezer in ca. 90 CE. For Jesus, the sexes were equal. He forbade divorce, except for in cases of adultery, to prevent Jewish men from putting their wives away without redress. Jesus treated women with compassion and equality, and women accompanied him on his journeys. Three of his closest friends in the Gospels were women—Mary Magdalene and Martha and Mary—sisters of Lazarus. Perhaps this revolutionary attitude towards women was the cause of his final break with the Pharisees.

The last abomination was his involvement with moral failures. The most serious charge against Jesus was that he was a "friend of tax collectors and sinners" (Mt 11:9). He often shared table with these people; this was a profound gesture of acceptance and equality. To the righteous Jews, Jesus was in very "bad company." In Jesus' words, "truly I say to you, the tax collectors and the prostitutes are going into the Kingdom of God before you. For John came to you preaching a way of holiness, but you did not believe him, but the tax collectors and the prostitutes did believe him" (Mt 21:31–32).

Jesus took religion and seemed to turn it upside down. In Jesus' confrontation with the Pharisees and the scribes, it is clear that he did not take their laws of ritual purity seriously. Jesus revealed a God who was not so concerned with religious observance as loving one's neighbor, a God who forgave sinners and expected others to do likewise, a God for whom sacrifice was less important than forgiveness and reconciliation, a God who wanted nothing less than the inner heart of the human being. Jesus revealed a God who seemed to love sinners more than the righteous; sinners do not conceal their sinfulness and hide it behind their devotion and ritual piety. In Jesus' preaching and ministry, the foundation of the Jewish religion was shaken to its core. At the same time, as a devout Jew, Jesus did not reject Judaism, for he made it clear that he came "not to abolish the law and the prophets but to fulfill it" (Mt 5:17). The three Synoptic Gospels distinguish Jesus' opponents by the particular groups or parties to which they belonged. The collective term, "the Jews," appears only eleven times in Matthew, Mark, and Luke. Only in the Gospel of John, written about 90–95 CE, is the term "the Jews" consistently used seventy-one times.

In questioning Jewish law, Jesus undermined its power by insisting that the law existed for human beings, not the other way around. In Mt 5:21–48, Jesus makes the law intensely personal. He questioned the importance of temple worship and ritual purity, putting human beings, not visible rituals, first in the eyes of God. Finally, he claimed authority for himself, unlike any other rabbi. He identifies himself with God's cause and speaks with the authority greater than Moses and the prophets. Jesus' words of contrast in many New Testament passages of "but I say to you..." suggest his own sense of God's mission within him and his faith in God's cause that he had accepted as his own.[1]

3.2 A Theology of the Cross

At the center of the church's faith is the saving power of the Cross. What does it mean to call the Cross of Jesus a saving event? How does the death of one man offer eternal life to all human beings? According to theologian John Dwyer, there is no simple explanation in the New Testament of just how the Cross effects salvation. In fact, there is little in Matthew, Luke, or John on the saving event of the cross. In "Q" (from the German word, Quelle or "Source") a document that contained most of the spoken words of Jesus and was used by Matthew and Luke, no reference to the Cross as a saving event exists.[2] Only Paul and Mark regard the Cross as salvific. Even here, ambiguity

[1] See Küng, *On Being Christian*, 251–77. My comments are a summary based on these pages.

[2] The document called "Q" is a construction of major German and English Scripture scholars; it has never been discovered. This is part of the "Two Source" Theory, that all of Matthew and Luke are based on the Gospel of Mark and "Q." Very little material is unique to Matthew and Luke, with a few exceptions such as the famous Infancy Narrative of Jesus' birth in Bethlehem.

exists because Paul uses language from his Epistle to the Romans that is legal and cultic: "Through his blood, God made him the means of expiation for all who believe" (Rom 3:25). Is salvation to be understood as only a juridical reality? Dwyer believes that Paul's answer to this question was a resounding no and that Paul's purpose was not to present a fully developed theology of redemption or soteriology in the spirit of St. Anselm more than a millennium later. Rather, Paul uses the language of expiation or satisfaction because he wished "to affirm that what the sacrificial worship of the Old Testament sought to achieve was actually accomplished in and through the death of Jesus Christ."[3]

3.3 Theories of Salvation

There is a basic distinction in doctrinal theology between the "that" and the "how" a truth of faith is interpreted. Faith requires that Christians believe in the "that," the fact of something; the "how," the manner in which this "that" is interpreted, is open to theological speculation through the centuries and is subject to change as the culture changes. This is true of all doctrines: the Incarnation of Jesus and the confession of the fifth-century Church of his full humanity and full divinity; the existence of an afterlife and the classical four last things; finally, for our purposes here, Jesus' death as a saving event. Often the "that" of a truth of faith becomes so attached to the particular "how" that the "how" becomes part of the content of faith itself. This, as we shall see, is true of St. Anselm's classical theory of satisfaction—a splendid "how" for its time but not a workable theory today.[4]

Without a clear treatment in the New Testament of how the Cross truly saved humanity from their sins and justified them in the eyes of God, a number of theories have been suggested by post-New Testament theologians on the saving power of the Cross. *First,* during the patristic era, Jesus' life and mission were understood by some Fathers of the Church as the completion of the Incarnation. In this approach, the Cross is not so much a saving event as proof that Jesus is really human and participated in the entire human situation. This theory emphasized the solidarity of Jesus with every human person and the solidarity of the divine and human through Jesus. Yet, it was unable

[3] John Dwyer, *Son of Man, Son of God: A New Language for Faith* (New York: Paulist, 1983), 157.

[4] This distinction can be found in Alan Richardson's *Creeds in the Making* (London: SCM, 1935), chap. 4.

to take fully into account the Pauline idea of salvation.[5] This idea of the Christ as the completion of creation is still prominent in many Eastern Orthodox Churches that place the emphasis on divinization of the person rather than redemption or a "buying back" from sin.[6]

Second, the devil's trick, the somewhat bizarre theory of certain Fathers, proposed that Jesus' divinity was kept secret from the devil so that Satan would share in the plot to kill Jesus. Because the prince of darkness dared to raise a hand against the Son of God, he fell into a trap and lost all his power, not only over Jesus, but also over all other human beings since the time of Adam and Eve. *Third*, the redemption theory suggested that the human race was literally "bought back" from sin—redemption as *in caveat emptor* (let the buyer beware). Some suggest the ransom was paid to God, others that the devil was bought off. The metaphorical meaning of this theory, taken from economics—redemption or buying back—remained in the theological language in order to explain the mystery of salvation. Fortunately, the literal meaning of redemption in an economic sense has virtually disappeared.[7]

Finally, the satisfaction theory of Anselm of Canterbury in the twelfth century became the most popular and famous of interpretations of the saving or salvific value of the Cross up until our own time. Virtually every Christian was raised with some knowledge of this theory as normative in explaining the Cross. Anselm's idea was this: the offense against the divine dignity in the sin of Adam required restitution. Finite and sinful humanity could not make this restitution for an offense of such magnitude. Only the Son of God, by his death, was capable of the reparation the divine honor demanded. Since God is infinite requiring infinite satisfaction, only Jesus, as the Son of God, could offer infinite satisfaction to the Father. No finite expression would be equal and compelling to the infinite God. Unfortunately, the satisfaction theory has dominated Western theology for eight hundred years, and Dwyer claims that the "satisfaction theory" has done enormous harm to the church throughout the centuries.

The principal complaint against St Anselm's theory of the Cross is that God appears as a feudal lord—and rightly so, since Anselm was writing in feudal times—demanding a *quid pro quo* for the loss of divine honor. It makes the Incarnation necessary because without it, restitution to God for the sin of

[5] Dwyer, *Son of Man, Son of God*, 158–59.

[6] Redemption is an economic metaphor. Redemption comes from the Latin word *redimere*, a combination of *re(d)-*, meaning "back," and *emere*, meaning "buy."

[7] Dwyer, *Son of Man, Son of God*, 159–60.

Adam could not be made. God is revealed not as the generous and loving Father in the New Testament, but almost sadistic, pleased by the suffering and punishment inflicted upon Jesus, regardless of whether he was innocent or guilty. This is not the God Jesus presents in the New Testament, a God who awaits his sinful younger son with longing and forgiveness, a God who is concerned about the poor, the crippled, the sinner. Dwyer's contention is that St. Paul presents us with a very different God than St. Anselm does. As Paul writes, "God was in Christ, reconciling the world to himself" (2 Cor 5:19). In Paul's mind, God is not the *object* of reconciliation but the *subject*; God is not passive awaiting satisfaction from his creatures. Rather, God is active, instigating and effecting reconciliation. God accomplishes this reconciliation by uniting us to the divine life of grace through divine participation in the human situation in Jesus.[8]

3.4 The "Crucified God"

If one rejects Anselm's satisfaction theory, what remains? Paul Tillich and Jürgen Moltmann propose a rich theory of redemption, as John Dwyer summarizes. "The man on the cross is the person whom the eternal God has chosen as his counterpart forever."[9] The Cross signifies God's unconditional acceptance of each human being and the entire human race, sinful, selfish, and unable to change. In the Cross of Jesus, salvation is present because God is present: God participates in the most extreme of human conditions. Thus, estrangement, sinfulness, despair, suffering, and death—all embodied in the face of the Crucified One—no longer indicate God's absence, where God has abandoned the human condition, but reveal instead, like everything else human, God's loving presence. The Cross is the place where God is most alive and most truly God in our midst, from the place where it appears God is least visible to the place where God is most present to us. Suffering and death are transformed, not only in time but also in eternity.[10]

The Cross presents us with a picture of the true God, a God of unconditional love and acceptance, not a God of conditions or stipulations, a God of rules and rituals. God requires nothing from us except our trust in God's unconditional love for us and acceptance. Because Jesus could live and die in the way he did, his death on the Cross redefines who God is for us. For if Jesus is the one whom God has selected from all eternity to be his counterpart,

[8] Dwyer, 160–64.

[9] Dwyer, 182.

[10] Dwyer, 182–83.

the one through whom God has chosen to communicate the fullness of divine life, then the God who is present in the Crucified One is radically different from the God of all human expectations. This God is different from a God who asks us to merit forgiveness. The Cross of the Christ tells us that God not only participates in human suffering; God also accepts it and transforms it. The Cross reveals the paradox at the heart of life: there is meaning in meaninglessness, hope in hopelessness, and joy hidden in the depths of despair. In the famous story of Elie Wiesel, Jewish survivor of the Holocaust, this presence of God in the blackest of human situations is made clear.

> The SS hung two Jewish men and a boy before the assembled inhabitants of the camp. The men died quickly but the death struggle of the boy lasted half an hour. "Where is God? Where is he? A man behind me asked."...I heard the man cry again "Where is God now?" and I heard a voice within me answer, "Here he is—he is hanging on the gallows."[11]

In a famous sermon written late in his life, Paul Tillich captures the same idea.

> It is the greatness and heart of the Christian message that God, as manifest in the Christ on the Cross, totally participates in the dying of a child, in the condemnation of a criminal, in the disintegration of a mind, in starvation and famine, even in the human rejection of Himself. There is no human condition into which the divine presence does not penetrate...[12]

Every life contains its own time of Calvary, moments of shame and sinfulness, physical and spiritual pain, estrangement and death. The Cross reveals a God who is present to persons in their darkest hours, up unto the hour of death itself. One theologian has gone so far as to suggest that the crucifixion of Jesus reveals "the eternal cross at the heart of God."[13] In a sermon written during World War I, Paul Tillich says that all suffering is reflected in the heart of God. There is a "holy necessity," or the law: "Through suffering to

---

[11] Elie Wiesel, *Night* (London: Penguin, 1981), 76–77.

[12] Paul Tillich, *The Eternal Now* (New York: Charles Scribner's Sons 1963), 46.

[13] H. Wheeler Robinson, *The Cross in the Old Testament* (London: SCM Press, 1955), 185.

joy, through death to life." This "holy necessity" is in God as it is within us.[14] The Cross is thus a two-edged reality. As theologian Dermot Lane writes, "on the one hand the cross reveals the dark side of history, disclosing the enormous potential for evil that is latent in all of us individually and collectively—a kind of cosmic hatred. On the other hand, by allowing the 'transfiguring breath of evil,' depicted at Calvary to shake our lives once again, we begin to experience the power of the cross."[15]

In addition, the Cross is "a judgment on us which affirms what is true and rejects what is false."[16] As Maximus the Confessor, a Christian monk, theologian, and scholar who lived in the seventh century writes,

> In the crucified Christ forgiveness is offered and life is given. For humanity it is no longer a matter of fearing judgment or of meriting salvation, but of welcoming love in trust and humility. For God has allowed himself to be murdered to offer his life even to the murderers. Christ's death on the cross is a judgment of judgment.[17]

It is a judgment "not in the sense of punishment inflicted but rather in the sense that it is God's assertion about what is false and what is true in us."[18] The Cross is a judgment of the ego-self as a human creation, of individuals on their own, unwilling to trust and unable to hope. The Cross is a judgment against all human institutions, including the church and all religions, whenever it makes absolute claims and makes the finite the infinite. Finally, the Cross is a judgment against barriers between the sacred and the secular. The Cross suggests that finite reality stand on its proper ground, a ground that is sacred, God's ground, not our creation. The paradox of the Cross is manifest in the world itself: what is truly of God is also most truly itself. Put differently, the Cross frees the world to be itself.[19]

If the church sees itself as a community under the Cross of the Christ, both empowered and judged by the cross, a theology of the Church becomes

---

[14] Quoted in Erdmann Sturm, "Between Apologetics and Pastoral Care: Paul Tillich's Early Sermons," trans. Doris Lax, *The Newsletter of the North American Paul Tillich Society* 26, no. 1 (2000), 17.

[15] Dermot Lane, *Christ at the Centre: Selected Issues in Christology* (New York: Paulist, 1991), 77.

[16] Dwyer, *Son of Man, Son of God*, 184–85

[17] Maximus the Confessor, *Questions to Thalassius* 43 (PG 90:408), *Patrologia Graeca*, ed. J. -P. Migne, 162 vols. (Paris, 1856–1887).

[18] Dwyer, *Son of Man, Son of God*, 184–85.

[19] Dwyer, 185–87.

placed on its "proper ground." Ecclesiology is transformed into something very different from what much of the history of ecclesiology reveals. In the high Middle Ages when Christendom reigned, the message of the Cross as judgment on all of the finite order was lost in the growth of institutional and papal power. Later, the Reformers rediscovered the Cross only to forget its message of divine judgment again. A theology of the church without the Cross loses its transcendent foundation and becomes another human construct seeking its own preservation. The history of the church's self-understanding and interpretation is two-edged: it portrays both the church's courage and its lack of courage to accept the Cross of Christ. When people read in church documents that the church is founded in the Paschal mystery, they must remember that there is no Resurrection without the Cross. Perhaps the sign on some Baptist churches captures the heart of the Christian message simply and perfectly: "We preach Jesus of Nazareth, crucified, risen, and coming."

3.5 Human Suffering

If God participates in human suffering manifest in the face of the Crucified One, then the meaning of human suffering also changes. Two basic approaches to suffering—and the great riddle of why some apparently suffer so much more than others—are popular in the minds of many. The *first* approach is rationalization, the effort to explain away the unexplainable and mysterious reality of suffering. Whenever I hear the phrase, "it was God's will," I know either someone has access to the mind of God in a way that I, nor anyone else for that matter, do not, or that this individual has put faith in a God that I cannot love and respect. God does not "will" the death of a child in an automobile accident or the passing of a young adult by some disease or by suicide at the prime of life. It cannot be God's "will" that the young are maimed or starved or filled with crack cocaine or fentanyl or damaged for a lifetime by sexual molestation or abuse. If God actively wills suffering and death, then God is a monster, a capricious, arbitrary God who plays with creation for divine pleasure and sport. Nothing, it seems, can be further from the God whom Jesus reveals to us in the Gospels as both his Father and ours.

A second popular approach to suffering says that it is absurd, devoid of meaning. Yet, if suffering is part of life and suffering is meaningless, then life itself must also be absurd and without meaning. Since suffering is without meaning, no reasons exist to placate the divine, only to enhance the human and to live as free of suffering as possible. Not unlike those who try to find the hidden reason in suffering in God's will, those who deny any meaning in suffering have a profoundly diminished view of God, finding it impossible to believe in a personal and loving God in the light of the absurdity and pain of the human situation.

Over and against those who either rationalize suffering or see suffering as meaningless, a meaning of suffering exists that can only be understood as paradoxical. In the depths of the most horrendous examples of human suffering, meaning is hidden and waiting to be revealed. The absurdists must discover that even their denial of any meaning is, in itself, meaningful. Likewise, the rationalizers must learn that the meaning of suffering cannot be discovered by reason. Suffering is neither sensible nor the result of divine will; it cannot be contained in the categories of human reason. Searching for an explanation to suffering, as if the wisdom of God were something we could attain on our own, is useless. Rather the meaning of suffering grasps us with its inner meaning and significance. Suffering is a mystery, and in the ancient meaning of the term in Saint Paul, mystery is also a sacrament.[20] Suffering is a kind of sacrament of the inevitable truth that individuals in their own way must come to understand. Like all sacraments, on the one hand, suffering embodies this truth in the most concrete of ways during those days and hours of physical pain or spiritual anguish; on the other hand, it reveals the infinite and ungraspable nature of truth itself. Suffering is also an essential window into the primal truth of reality itself. In suffering, a person no longer sees life from the outside in but from the inside out. One who suffers understands, in the poet Ranier Maria Rilke's words, "the cycle of the whole going on."[21]

Suffering has a revelatory character, unlocking the inner mystery of God. One who explores the depths of the self enters more deeply the divine mystery, both terrifying and earthshaking, alluring and fascinating.[22] In the depths of ourselves, we confront God both as one infinitely beyond us yet infinitely close, or, in Rudolph Otto's words, "wholly same and wholly other." When could one encounter God more completely than in suffering? Where does God most fully encounter individuals, where could the divine be more present and accessible, than in suffering? Likewise, it follows that if persons

[20] See Col 1:24–29.

[21] Ranier Maria Rilke, *Duino Elegies*, The Fourth Elegy, ll., the German text, with an English translation, introduction, and commentary by J. B. Leishman and Stephen Spender (New York: W. W. Norton & Co., 1963), 60–61.

[22] See Rudolph Otto, *The Idea of the Holy* (New York: Oxford University Press, 1960), chapters 1–7.

discover God in the depth of themselves, then in suffering they discover the real God, a God who suffers with us. Imagine a mother helpless, in pain on her deathbed hearing the news of her teenage son's serious accident and death. At this moment, this woman may see a God suffering with her, a God, as she said, "who had to suffer and learn…how it feels to suffer like I am now." This is the final message of the Cross. If our image of God is not only of a transcendent God, but also immanent God, close to us, one who dwells within us, then suffering becomes comprehensible as part of the mystery of God's love, human sinfulness, and the limits of the finite mind. The church should give up Anselm's satisfaction theory and teach the Cross as God suffering with all people.

3.7 The Mystery of the Resurrection

The church's historical origin is in the Resurrection of Jesus. The Cross and Resurrection are inseparable events historically and ontologically, that is, in the order of being. The central mystery of Christianity, which constitutes and informs the church, is the transformation of Jesus from death to life. Saint Paul reminds the early community of Jesus' followers, the *ecclesia* at Corinth, "and if Christ has not been raised, then our proclamation has been in vain and your faith has been in vain" (1 Cor 15:14). The Cross and the Resurrection are inseparable because Jesus was raised in glory. The Resurrection of Jesus was intrinsic to a death of unconditional love and openness to God, his Father. The word "resurrection," a rising up or "being raised up," is a spatial metaphor; of course, there is literally no "up." Resurrection means the all-powerful, all-inclusive transformation of life, nature, and history, by the ineffable and loving power of God.

The idea of resurrection existed in Jewish thought before Jesus. Some of the Jews, such as the Pharisees, accepted a general resurrection of the dead, but the Sadducees, denied it.[23] The Gospels tell us that Jesus not only agreed with the Pharisees in affirming the reality of the resurrection, he also rejected any materialistic element attached to it in Jewish thinking. Jesus insisted that the risen "neither marry nor are given in marriage but are like angels in heaven" (Mk 12:25). Nothing of significance in our earthly life remains with us after the resurrection—whether one had married or not, was rich or poor, young or old.

Paul put the individual resurrection of Jesus in this context of the general

[23] See Mk 12:18.

Resurrection. He understood and interpreted the resurrection of Jesus as part of the apocalyptic expectation that all the dead would rise—hence Jesus is "the first born from the dead" (Col 1:18). As Jesus' ministry proceeded, it is likely that Jesus, as an eschatological minister of God, saw his own life as mysteriously connected with the realization of the widely held apocalyptic expectation of a general resurrection. At the same time, it is unlikely that Jesus foresaw his own resurrection as a separate event before the general resurrection at the end of time.[24]

What happened at the Resurrection of Jesus? Two days after Jesus' death, the disciples heard strange stories that Jesus was alive and that some of the twelve he had gathered around him had seen him. After the Passover festival, returning to their hometown of Emmaus, a little town about seven miles from Jerusalem, two of his followers, Cleopas and perhaps his wife, met a stranger on the road who asked why they seemed so troubled and unhappy. They told this man all about Jesus, his preaching, their hope for the Kingdom, and finally about his execution that destroyed their hopes. The stranger seemed to read their minds and know the deepest secrets of their hearts. He spoke of the Law and the prophets, and explained Jesus to them in a way they had never understood before. When they arrived at Emmaus, they asked him to dine with them. As they broke bread together, they recognized the man was Jesus himself. They had not recognized him until that moment, but as soon as they realized who he was, he disappeared, leaving a powerful presence of the Spirit of God with them.[25]

This popular story from the Gospel of Luke serves as a window into the origins of the nature and mission of the church. Early followers of Jesus experienced a transformation of both Jesus and themselves. The appearances of Jesus after his resurrection have a number of characteristics in common. At first, the disciples do not recognize Jesus. There is a discontinuity between the Jesus they knew and the risen Christ; he walks through walls, he speaks with them yet they do not recognize him because he is different in some strange way. Saint Paul, in describing how the dead will be raised, says: "What is sown is perishable, what is raised is imperishable. [The body] is sown in dishonor, it is raised in glory. It is sown in weakness, it is raised in power. It is sown a physical body, it is raised a spiritual body" (1 Cor 15:42–44). This "spiritual" body of Jesus is not simply the resuscitation of Jesus' earthly body. Otherwise, Jesus would be known immediately by his followers, and he would be subject

[24] Lane, *The Reality of Jesus*, 70.

[25] See Luke 24:13–35.

to death again.

At the same time, a real continuity exists between the Jesus of history and the risen Christ. The apparition stories are clear on this point. For this reason, he eats with them on the shore of the Sea of Tiberius in John, chapter 21. Likewise, Jesus lets Thomas put his hands in his wounds so that he might have faith that Jesus is truly alive (Jn 20:24–29). Jesus remains the Crucified One even in his glory. This point is essential: the disciples could see Jesus alive and transformed in the objective order *only when* they themselves also experienced a subjective transformation. Its mystery can be found only in the transcendent union of subjectivity and objectivity, of the self and the world, through the power of the divine Spirit.[26]

Under the impetus of the Spirit, the small community went out, first, to preach the message of Jesus, and then to preach Jesus himself. What did they preach? The first message of these early disciples is probably found in the Acts of the Apostles (Acts 3:12–26). According to scholars, it most likely contains the earliest Christology of the community. For example, this text does not call Jesus the Son of God. This truth only emerged later from the church's reflection on the life and preaching of Jesus in light of its experience of the risen Christ—in much the same way as in the Emmaus story: the slow and deliberate movement from doubt to faith until at last, "their eyes were open before them."

Another important element in the apparition stories is the exclusive nature of Jesus' appearances. Jesus made himself known only to those who had faith in him before his death. There were no appearances to Pilate or to the Sanhedrin, for Jesus' Resurrection was much more than merely one historical event among others. Even the people on the road to Emmaus (one can presume many others were traveling on the day after the Passover holiday) probably did not see Jesus. Because they did not have faith in Jesus during his ministry, they could not have recognized the risen Jesus. This suggests that the essential event of Christianity is not only in the life of Jesus but its fulfillment in his death and resurrection. Paul himself, the greatest of the apostles, did not know Jesus during his lifetime. The experience of Jesus as alive means more than the encounter with an objective event in time and space; it means seeing Jesus, and therefore all of reality, including oneself, transformed by the power of God. This is the Good News that the disciples went forth to preach—God's action in raising Jesus from the dead because God is the God of life and death. The disappearance of Jesus after forty days marked the end

---

[26] See Lane, *The Reality of Jesus*, 56–62.

of the privileged time in which the disciples who had faith in Jesus in his lifetime could truly see him as glorified after death under the conditions of history. The church celebrates the end of his privileged time as the Ascension of the Lord.

3.8 The Disciples' Response to the Resurrection

In seeing Jesus alive and transformed, the disciples saw, at the same time, themselves transformed. They could see Jesus only through the eyes of faith. No wonder Jesus did not appear to anyone who did not have faith in him beforehand; such a person would not be able to recognize him. The objective approach in itself is often a historicist or scientific interpretation of the Easter event; it takes the Word of God literally and presumes that the Gospels tell us what is scientifically true. The Resurrection is an objective miracle, something that breaks the laws of nature and can be historically discussed and proven. Of course, when such a miraculous event cannot be proven, faith falters. No evidence for the Resurrection at the objective, historical level exists, and it is foolish to try to prove the Resurrection to anyone on the basis of observable data. In contrast, the subjective approach makes the Resurrection an event in the disciples' minds; it is an event projected onto reality out of the disciples' experience and desire, in which the community creates faith instead of faith as a divine gift as the source of the community. Indeed, the church would create itself, instead of its origins in the works of God in and through Christ. The disciples actually encountered Jesus as a person beyond their own imaginations; all the biblical accounts portray both this objective and subjective dimension.

The Resurrection as the fulfillment of God's Revelation could not take place without its reception in faith. Thus, the disciples went forth and preached the Good News of all that God had accomplished through Jesus. They called for repentance—*metanoia*—or a radical change of heart. The early church did not preach the Kingdom of God as Jesus did. Rather, they preached Jesus himself and God's action in him. Very quickly, the preacher of the Kingdom of God was now himself the object of preaching; Jesus the preacher became Jesus the preached. The presence of the Spirit, which comes from Father and Son as the bond of their love, takes the place of the earthly Jesus in those privileged days after Easter. The Ascension and Pentecost mark both absence of Jesus historically and the presence of the church in the Holy Spirit. Through the absence of Jesus, the church is filled with the presence of

God as Spirit, the unity of Father and Son.[27] Inevitably, the Good News of Jesus' life, death, and Resurrection spread outside of the Palestinian Jewish community, first, to Hellenistic Jews and then to Gentiles of the Greek and Roman world. Within a generation after the Cross, Jesus was proclaimed Lord and Christ, and, before the end of the century, God's eternal Word.[28] The church preached that God, present in the Cross of Jesus, is the real God, the One who shares in human suffering, the One who brings life out of death.[29]

In sum, the church has its objective foundations in the passion, death, and Resurrection of Jesus, and in the faith of the early disciples of Jesus subjectively. Through their faith, the disciples are transformed from death to new life, from hopelessness to hope, from sorrow to joy. The common vision and understanding of the early disciples of Jesus was that their community, their being together in the faith of the Lord's resurrection, was not simply the result of their human initiative but an action of God. They were "called out" (*ek-klesia*, Εκκλησία) by an act of God that was intrinsic to the Resurrection itself. As God had acted in the transformation of Jesus from death to life, so God had also acted in their own lives. This reflects the importance of the church as apostolic, one of the classical four "marks" of the Church. The church has to be intimately connected to the earliest apostles and disciples of Jesus, thus rendering all subsequent faith in Jesus as also faith in the community of his disciples, those who bore witness to his mission and God's work in Jesus' life, death, and transformation.[30] Finally, the resurrection is the manifestation and crystallization of what Dermot Lane calls the "seeds of indestructibility" in every human person; it is the revelation of the perfect child of God or the true Self of every person.[31]

3.9 The Paschal Mystery

The church is a community both rescued from the darkness of estrangement and sin and the living sacrament of this saving presence for all times and all peoples. The celebration of the church's foundation, nature, and destiny takes place in the Paschal mystery celebrated in the Eucharist and in all the sacraments. The Paschal mystery is the term that signifies the life, death,

[27] Acts 3:12–26, perhaps the earliest Christology in the New Testament.

[28] See Lane, *The Reality of Jesus*, 76–81.

[29] See Dwyer, *Son of Man, Son of God*, 193–96.

[30] See Küng, *The Church*, 80.

[31] Lane, *The Experience of God*, chap. 5.

Resurrection, Pentecost, and Ascension, of Jesus the Christ as one saving act of God. The Paschal mystery refers to two realities: *pasch* and mystery. Pascha was the Greek translation of the Hebrew *Pesach*, the Hebrew word for the feast of the Passover, the night of God's passing over the houses of the Israelites, sparing their families a visit from the angel of death. What God first accomplishes in the Passover of the Angel of Death in the time of Moses, God completes in God's full presence in Jesus. Jesus is not only God's promise of Passover, he is the Paschal Lamb who has been sacrificed in the unconditional expression of God's saving power (1 Cor 5:7). Hence, at its root, the mystery of Easter, the Christian Passover, is grounded in death and transformation. The Paschal mystery expresses that in Jesus, God has saved all persons and all creation from decay and death. God loved us so much that God shared in the most awe-full (or "awful," a word that has lost its power in contemporary use) experience of human conditions, death itself, even death on a cross. The Jewish experience of Passover was one of liberation from bondage to Egypt. The Christian experience is similar: bondage is now the enslavement to sin and self-isolation. At the heart of the Paschal mystery is God's liberating us from slavery—to a political power, to the power of sin, to the heart of our ego-selves trapped in darkness. In addition to the word "Paschal," the word mystery (mysterium in Latin, *mysterion* or μυστεριον in Greek) is also important to consider. For some centuries, the Greek word was translated as sacramentum in Latin. This fact, that mystery and sacrament were used interchangeably, was a vital insight in the early church, but lost after the high Middle Ages and with the coming of the Reformation. The mystery of God from all ages and the visible embodiment of this mystery in Jesus and the church are united in the two words signifying the same thing. The Catholic Church at the Second Vatican Council used the term Paschal mystery to describe the central Christian mystery: "[Christ] achieved this task principally by the Paschal mystery of the blessed passion, resurrection from the dead, and glorious ascension, where by dying, He destroyed our death, and rising He restored our life."[32]

3.10 The Paschal Mystery in Christian Life

According to Dermot Lane, Christians encounter the Paschal mystery at three levels. These levels are the ontological/moral, the sacramental, and the

[32] *Sacrasanctum Concilium*, Constitution on the Sacred Liturgy, December 4, 1963, 5.

eschatological.[33] Thus they meet the mystery of God's redeeming love in the invisible depths of their beings, in the visible rituals that celebrate the unity with God, and at their death.

3.10.1 The Ontological/Moral Level. The ontological/moral level is the level in which one lives and expresses Being. In friendship and love, one gives up one's self-assertive ego; one dies to one's self-centeredness for the sake of the other. Thus, love is a window into the Paschal mystery just as the mystery itself beckons us to love or to agape, love in its purest form. In this outward movement of our being, the call of Jesus to *metanoia* is answered. This change of heart or repentance is to move away from the self as the center of high seriousness, to reject oneself as the center of the universe. Positively, it is to turn to God as the center of life and meaning; it is to acknowledge that the divine Kingdom is near, nearer to oneself than the ego is. This is the same as Jesus' own life and mission: to make God, not himself, the center of life. Jesus remained in unity with his Father. In this way, Jesus was without sin—not that he was "unable to sin" but that he was "able not to sin."[34]

Sin is the opposite of God's love revealed in the Paschal mystery. Sin's power comes from self-absorption, a failure to trust anyone or anything but oneself. This is *hybris*, the Greek word for pride, which envelops persons and makes the individuals slaves to their ego-driven desires. If people deceive themselves into believing that they are the centers of the universe, then they can draw whatever one desires into this center. This desire is concupiscence, intense desire that flows from *hybris*. (Concupiscence should not be confused or reduced to sexual desire as it sometimes is.) The inevitable and absolute consequences of sin are manifested in the symbol of "hell," a state of being where the triumph of the ego-self and the state of isolation from and hatred towards oneself, the other, and God is finalized for eternity.

3.10.2 The Sacramental Level. Jesus' Paschal mystery is also visible in symbol and sacrament. Each sacrament, especially the Eucharist, celebrates the Paschal action of dying and rising, of passing over, of letting go of the ego-self and self-deception. A sacrament is not a magical ritual, but a symbolic action that points to a reality beyond itself while participating in the reality to which it points.[35] When Jesus says, "this is my body given for you," he utters in sacramental words the ontological and moral truth: God in Jesus has given divine life to us in creation, redemption, and sanctification. In Jesus,

[33] Lane, *Christ at the Centre*, chap. 5.

[34] Lane, *The Experience of God*, 23.

[35] This definition of a symbol is from Paul Tillich's *Dynamics of Faith*, 42–43.

the ideal of divine-human love, humanity returns this love to God. In love, death of the ego-self, and the triumph of our divine self, or the image of God within us, are made real, and the message becomes real: "Those who find their life will lose it, and those who lose their life for my sake will find it." This text is found six times and in all four Gospels, indicating its importance and centrality to Jesus' message: Mt 10:38–39; Mt 16:25; Mk 8:34–35; Lk 9:23–24; Lk 17:33; and Jn 12:24.

All of the church's actions are sacraments of the Paschal mystery, especially the breaking of the bread: what God has accomplished in Jesus' Passover in bringing life from death is made present to the church as food. The sacraments are not isolated actions but crystallized expressions of what is essentially possible at all times and in all places: darkness is vanquished by light, sadness by joy, sin by grace, and death by life. While the actual power of the Paschal mystery may be experienced in the emergency rooms of hospitals and on deathbeds, this same power of life over death is present symbolically in the church's rituals and sacraments.

The meaning of every liturgical action is always the same: the visible ritual embodies an inner and ontological reality. This is most powerfully expressed in the liturgy of the Blessed Night or the night of the Lord's passage from death to life. The Cross and Resurrection are archetypes of all personal and historical existence. The Paschal mystery does not mean the end of sorrow, suffering, and death, of course. Sorrow and sadness remain, but they are now part of the deeper mystery of joy and bliss; suffering and death remain but they are now part of the deeper mystery of life. God gives us new life through the ritual action of the church. The nature of the church is a communion of persons united in the human experience of faith in God's love and God's power over death.

3.9.3 The Eschatological Level: Dying in Christ. The fullness of the Paschal mystery is manifest in a person's own death and resurrection—that eschatological reality to which the movement of a person's life and the celebration of every sacrament points.[36] The central paradox of the Paschal mystery remains the same: finding life through death. *Metanoia* reaches it culmination in death itself. What had been represented in every sacramental action, embodied in every limited act of love and self-donation, now becomes actual and fulfilled in the encounter with God in death, humanity's only "last thing." Death signifies the completion of the Paschal mystery and the church as the Mystical Body of Christ, where, in Saint Augustine words, "there will be one Christ loving Himself."

[36] Lane, *Christ the Centre*, 112–14.

3.11 The Paschal Mystery in All the Sacraments

How is the Passover of the Lord made real in our lives today? The church has seven sacraments that embody the mystery of death and resurrection. Baptism is the entrance rite into the Christian mystery in which individuals, as Paul tells us, enter the tomb with Christ so that they may be raised up with Christ. Confirmation is a strengthening of baptism, the rite of passage into Christian adulthood. Eucharist is the central sacrament, celebrating God's triumph over death and the gift of new life. Reconciliation heals Catholics from sinfulness and invites them to accept forgiveness. Anointing of the sick is the visible ritual in which the Church pledges the presence and support of God and the church to the sick or dying person. The sacrament heals the person's spirit, and often has a limited effect on the physical well-being of the sick individual. Holy Orders celebrates dedicating one's life to service in the Church.

Finally, in marriage, the paschal mystery is made present in a human relationship. Husband and wife are the actual sacraments of god's hope and love in the face of sin and death; therefore, husband and wife are the ministers of the sacrament to one another. Through a whole-hearted commitment to another in the sharing of all of life and love, god touches the lives of the couple, invites them to die to their self-centeredness, and to grow in love for each other. In marriage, the central paradox of the Paschal mystery is realized: finding life through death. Marriage fulfills the central theme found at the heart of the Gospels mentioned above: to live one's life truly, one must give it up. This is the meaning of sacrifice and the finest expression of love.

The Paschal mystery is manifest throughout history in the church and its actions, in its creeds and moral precepts, in the whole reality of the things of the earth. Catholicism is primarily a religion of symbols: doctrines are the symbols of the faith as sacraments are the symbolic actions of God's saving power. No group of individuals understood this fact more clearly than the people of the medieval period; their lives were filled with symbols and sacraments, relics and pilgrimages. Many people have lost their understanding of the power of religious symbols; this is why Catholic sacraments make such little sense to the young in the church. In symbols and myths, the truth of our faith is located in the deepest mystery of life.

4.

ECCLESIOLOGY FROM THE APOSTOLIC TIMES TO THE THIRTEENTH CENTURY

4.1 The Church in the New Testament Era

The word for "church" comes from a community of people "called out," from *ek kaleo* (εκ καλεω, Greek), in Latin, *ecclesia.* The Latin and Greek roots of church define exactly what the church is, a people called out. "Church" in English is from the Old English word, *cirice,* Germanic, *kirika*, which in turn comes from *kuriakē* (Κυριακή, Greek) which means "of the Lord," the possessive form of *kurios* (κύριος, Greek), "ruler" or "lord."

The church was a living reality many years, indeed centuries, before any self-reflection by the community about itself or a "doctrine" of the church developed. The earliest members of the Christian community in the decades following the death and resurrection of Jesus could not imagine a systematic or formal interpretation of the church's inner life, nature, and mission. Indeed, they could not even imagine a church or community as a distinctly independent society within the broader culture. For the first few decades after the Resurrection, the earliest believers in Jesus were called "Nazarenes" or "People of the Way," not "Christians." The followers of Jesus in Jerusalem reveal a community that had faith in the Lord but without self-reflection on their significance as a community. Not unlike a newly born baby who possesses little or no sense of his/her identity or potential for growth, the early community had little self-awareness about its life and nature. After the death of Jesus, most likely in the year 30 CE, the "church" was born in the disciples' experience of the Paschal mystery, but without the self-awareness of the community as "church" at the time.

The earliest of Jesus' followers—the Twelve and the other disciples—with their hopes shattered in the events of the crucifixion, experienced the most extraordinary of realities. Like Cleopas and his companion on the road to Emmaus, their eyes were opened in faith. They came to see and understand that Jesus of Nazareth, the Crucified One, was raised from the dead and was now present in their midst. From a Catholic perspective, as soon as the disciples encountered the living Jesus and affirmed that he was alive in a new and startling way, the community that Paul would later call "church" came into historical existence. As Hans Küng says: "The church sprang not from imaginings, not out of a baseless credulity, but from real experiences of encounters with one who was truly alive....Jesus the preacher becomes Jesus the preached, the bearer of the message becomes the central substance of the message."[1] In other words, "some type of bond between Jesus and his followers was quite evident not only from his call to others to associate with him in his proclamation but also from the response of his followers after his resurrection *who saw themselves immediately as a community*."[2] Put differently, the experience of Resurrection was not given first to individuals who subsequently formed a community because of their own decision to do so. Rather the communal and shared nature of acknowledging that Jesus was alive was essential and intrinsic to the communal experience itself of the new life in Christ.

In the first few decades after Jesus' death, the focus of the early disciples was on the return of the risen Lord. The Nazarenes had expected Jesus to return soon, while some of them were still alive, in order to fulfill the Kingdom of God.[3] Jesus' preaching, his death, and Resurrection heralded the end times, and they expected the Lord's return soon, in their lifetimes. Saint Paul, in a famous text, says, "listen, I will tell you a mystery! We will not all die, but we will all be changed, in a moment, in the twinkling of an eye, at the last trumpet" (1 Cor 15:51–52). Likewise, Paul describes the end times, in probably the first book of the New Testament, this way: "For the Lord himself...will descend from heaven, and the dead in Christ will rise first. Then we who are alive, who are left, will be caught up in the clouds together with them to meet the Lord in the air; and so we will be with the Lord forever" (1 Thes 4:16–17).

---

[1] Küng, *The Church*, 80.

[2] Frederick J. Cwiekowski, *The Beginnings of the Church*, 60. (Italics mine.)

[3] For example, Paul's view in his early epistle, 1 Thes 4:13–17.

More than a generation passed before the disciples realized that Jesus would not return immediately; they understood that survival and life in the world was now necessary for some time. Much of the theology of Luke in his Gospel and in the Acts of the Apostles shifts the focus of Jesus from the end time to the midpoint of time, establishing a historical "time of the church."[4] The year 70 CE was a crucial date in the development of this realization; the temple in Jerusalem was destroyed by the Roman army under Titus, severing Jewish Christians from their religious roots and signaling the end of ancient Judaism.

As the *parousia* or the end time became less imminent, the community inevitably developed structures for its survival. Younger converts to Jesus had no contact with the Jesus of history. The original followers of Jesus had been all Jews, but Gentiles, with Paul's journeys, also heard the message of new life in Christ. From approximately 70 to 95 CE, the Gospels were written to teach converts the life and message of Jesus; persons were chosen to replace the earliest disciples. The first theologies also took shape in the writings of Paul and John. Not until the fourth decade after Jesus' death did the Christian community begin to develop its own organizational identity, its own tentative social and political structures, and an understanding of its mission and ministry. Preaching the Gospel and holding the communities together in a common faith was essential. Each community struggled with some significant problems: its relationship to Judaism and the Mosaic Law; the influx of Gentiles into the faith; and accommodation to a diverse and sometimes hostile social and political world beyond itself.[5] During the 50s and 60s of the first century CE, it is more proper to speak not of a single community or church, as subsequent generations would later come to understand it. Rather, the church of the first century was comprised of many local churches—the Jerusalem church, the church in Corinth, in Antioch, in Thessalonica, and the church of Rome.

These local communities, united by faith in the God who raised Jesus of Nazareth from the dead, were first described by the word "church" in the writings of Saint Paul. The Greek term *ekklesia*, was not a new word. In Athens, in the fifth century BCE, the *ekklesia* was the assembly of free citizens (all male and all landowners) called out by the herald to cast their ballots on an

---

[4] See John Dwyer, *The Word Was Made Flesh: An Introduction to the Theology of the New Testament* (Kansas City: Sheed and Ward, 1989), 77–80.

[5] See Cwiekowski's book for an excellent treatment of the church from 30 to 100 CE.

issue of the day. Likewise, *ekklesia* was the term employed in the Septuagint, the translation of the Hebrew Scriptures into Greek in the third century BCE, to signify the People of God or *qahal Yahweh*, the assembly of Israel.[6] The Hebrew word *qahal*, people or assembly, was translated into *ekklesia* in the Septuagint, occurring about one hundred times. By Jesus' time, the Greek influence of Alexander the Great had spread throughout the ancient world, necessitating the translation of the Hebrew Bible in the common language of the people. Greek became the *lingua franca* of the Mediterranean world. (All of the books of the New Testament were written in Greek.) Greek was spoken on the streets of Rome as well as Jerusalem at the time of Jesus. Pontius Pilate probably spoke Greek, not Latin, to the soldiers under his command.

Paul's original use of the term *ekklesia* during the 50s CE was a clear reference to this Jewish People of God. He needed a word to describe the followers of Jesus, so, as a Jew, he naturally turned to Scripture, to *qahal* or *ekklesia* to designate a community of Christians in a particular place—those "called out" to be the People of God in Corinth, in Galatia, and in other places where his preaching was effective. These churches, often very small communities, gathered in a home belonging to a newly converted Christian of some financial substance. We are familiar with the names of some of these people through Paul's letters.[7] In an individual city where the letters of Paul were circulated, there may have been a number of houses where early Christians met, thus creating more than one "church" in that area.[8] Sometimes the word *ekklesia* or "church" appears in the singular, sometimes plural, often with the phrase "of God" or "of God in Christ" after it.[9] God is the one who summons and gathers the community.

When the letters to the Colossians and Ephesians were written in the 70s and 80s CE—according to most scholars, not written by Paul himself—the focus of the term "church" shifted from designating houses and local communities to the universal and idealized community of believers. "Church" was now the term used to designate the center of God's plan of salvation, becoming "the fullness of him who fills all in all" (Eph 1:23). Likewise, Ephesians

---

[6] See Edward Hill, "Church," *New Dictionary of Theology*, ed. Dermot Lane, Mary Collins, and Joseph Komonchak (Wilmington: Michael Glazier Books, 1987), 195–97. See also Donald McKim, *Theological Turning Points: Major Issues in Christian Thought* (Atlanta: John Knox, 1988), 45.

[7] See, for example, Acts 18:2–3, Col 4:15, and Phlm 2.

[8] Cwiekowski, *The Beginnings of the Church*, 119.

[9] McKim, *Theological Turning Points*, 46.

3:9–10 says, "through the church, the principalities and ruling forces should learn how many-sided God's wisdom is, according to the plan which he had formed from all eternity in Christ Jesus our Lord."[10] Thus, in the half century after Jesus' death, the church evolved from small communities expecting the imminent return of the Lord to a more fully developed understanding of itself and its universal mission in the history.

4.2 Ecclesiology during the Period of the Fathers

With the settling of the Christian community, it continually found it necessary to clarify and expand its interpretation of Christ and the Gospel message. New social and political situations confronting the church inspired new theological and moral questions; these questions in turn required new, more sophisticated answers that had to consider the growing diversity of Christian experience. At the beginning of the second century, the church moved from a predominately Judaic to a Hellenistic community, passing through a complex and sometimes difficult transition from a sect within the Jewish tradition to a predominantly Gentile Christianity in the Greco-Roman world. The integration and assimilation of the Christian message with Greek philosophy, especially Neoplatonism and Stoicism, made necessary for the church to understand the mystery of God's action in Jesus in a philosophical and cultural framework other than its original Hebraic origins. For example, much of the theological debate in the third, fourth, and fifth centuries about three persons in one God and the two natures in Christ would have been unimaginable to a first century Jewish Christian.

This Greek philosophical framework also required the church to define the nature of God and Christ against those selecting questionable interpretations and creating a belief system that the later tradition would find false. The word for selecting or choosing, *hairesis* (αἱρεσις, Greek) means to choose. Heretics made choices that ultimately lay outside the Christian consensus. Members of the church who were leaders in answering these theological questions were later honored with the title "Fathers of the Church." We can date the period of the Fathers from the end of the New Testament period at the beginning of the second century to Gregory the Great (d. 604 CE) or Isadore of Seville (d. 636 CE) in the West and John Damascene (d. 749 CE) in the

[10] Cwiekowski, *The Beginnings of the Church*, 140.

East.[11] The Apostolic era, where the church was guided by the apostles and disciples of Jesus, takes up the middle third of the first century. The next generation, or the "sub-apostolic" era, comprising the last thirty years of the century (70–100 CE), witnessed much of the writing of the New Testament. The period of the Fathers thus begins with the post-apostolic generation of Christians in the second century.[12]

4.2.1 The Second, Third, and Fourth Centuries. During this time, the fundamental theological doctrines of God as Trinity, the Holy Spirit, and the Person of Christ were debated and defined for the church. These definitions took place at the great Councils of Nicea (325 CE), Constantinople (381 CE), and Chalcedon (451 CE). Yet, no treatise on the church emerged from these three great councils. Likewise, no comprehensive theological work on the church—such as Augustine's *On the Trinity* (*De Trinitate*)—was written in the patristic era. Of course, there were many references to the church in the writings of the Fathers, most notably in the sub-apostolic Fathers such as Clement of Rome, Justin Martyr, Ignatius of Antioch, and the Shepherd of Hermas. While their theological concerns were primarily not ecclesiological in the present-day meaning of the term, the church did play a significant role in their thought, providing a framework and a foundation for their overall theology. For example, Ignatius of Antioch, at the beginning of the second century, was the first to use the term katholikos (καθολικός, Greek), that is, catholic or universal, to describe the church. "Wherever Jesus Christ is, there is the Catholic church," he writes.[13]

Likewise, the Shepherd of Hermas, an anonymous author from the mid-second century and perhaps the first authentically lay theological voice speaking on the church, presents a mystical image of the church.[14] For him, the church was closer to God than human beings, and was the historical expression of God's grace. This preexistence of the church is a distinctive feature of Jewish Christianity. In two famous images, he compares the church, first, to a mystical tower inhabited with the elect and, second, to a venerable old woman. In Vision One, he reveals to a young man the identity of the old woman as the church, who was "created before all things; that is why she is

[11] Thomas Halton, *Message of the Fathers of the Church* (Wilmington: Michael Glazier Books, 1985), 9.

[12] Cwiekowski, *The Beginnings of the Church*, 160.

[13] Halton, *Message of the Fathers of the Church*, 17.

[14] Halton, 20.

elderly, and for her the world was made."[15] Thus, a rapid movement in ecclesiology took place in the century from St. Paul's historical communities to the transcendent church of the Shepherd of Hermas.

Even though Irenaeus, Tertullian, and Origen at the end of the second and beginning of the third century contributed theological insight into ecclesiology, the church did not define its theological mystery in a formal, systematic way because there was no reason to do so. All doctrinal reflection *on* the community *by* the community was too close, too immanent, too much of a lived experience as opposed to a system of formulations. In Origen, for example, the church is idealized as a transhistorical reality, "without spot or wrinkle, existing before the creation of the world and comprised of all those saints united with the Logos of God."[16] In his *Commentary on the Song of Songs*, Origen writes in the same spirit of Shepherd of Hermas: "Do not believe that the Bride, that is, the church, has existed only since the Savior's Incarnation. She exists since the beginning of the human race…even before the creation of the world."[17]

In the middle of the third century, St. Cyprian (d. 258 CE), the bishop of Carthage in North Africa, composed an important treatise on church unity, *De Unitate* (251 CE). Alone of all the writings during the period of the Fathers, this work examines the church in some detail.[18] Yet even for Cyprian, the real issue was not the theological nature of the church but the legal question of unity within the church under the bishop.[19] His treatise was in response to the priest and theologian, Novatian (200–258 CE), after the persecution of Christians by the Roman Emperor Decius. Novatian believed that those who denied the faith during the persecution—those who were "lapsed" Christians—were no longer "holy" and members of the church. The debate raged about the theological foundations, *besides* holiness, of the church's unity. Cyprian argued that the episcopate and apostolic succession alone were the

---

[15] Johannes Quasten, *Patrology* (Utrecht-Antwerp: Spectrum, 1966), 1:100; Halton, *Message of the Fathers of the Church*, 32.

[16] McKim, *Theological Turning Points*, 50.

[17] Halton, *Message of the Fathers of the Church*, 35.

[18] Tractates on the church were also written by two little-known early Fathers, Optatus and Pacian, though they did not try to give us an ecclesiological synthesis. See Gustave Weigel, *Catholic Theology in Dialogue* (New York: Harper and Brothers, 1961), 10.

[19] E. G. Hinson, ed., *Understandings of the Church* (Philadelphia: Fortress, 1986), 1. For Cyprian's work, *De Unitate*, see pages 69–86. Also see B. C. Butler, *The Idea of the Church* (Baltimore: Helicon, 1962), 87–104.

sources of the church's unity. Thus, with Cyprian, membership in the church shifted from an interior holiness and personal commitment to an exterior norm. It no longer depended, as it did for Irenaeus, on an individual's "acceptance of the teaching guaranteed by the episcopate as apostolic, but submission to the bishop himself."[20] The church's validity exists by unity of the faithful with the bishop in true apostolic succession. As Cyprian states, "you ought to know that the bishop is in the church and the church in the bishop; that if anyone not be with the bishop, then he is not in Christ's church."[21] Cyprian affirms that one "cannot have God for his Father who does not have the church for his mother." Thus, he concludes, there is no salvation outside the church, a phrase of contention for millennia, from Cyprian to Vatican II and the twenty-first century.[22]

The ecclesiology of Cyprian was one of the first theological efforts to create criteria for church unity and membership. His treatment of the visible faith and loyalty to the bishop saved the church from more division at a time of confusion, permitting it to survive with new vigor into the fourth century that witnessed the conversion of Constantine to the Christian faith. Cyprian, along with Ignatius of Antioch a century earlier, was one of the bedrocks of "Catholic Christianity," which was grounded in three elements: the canon of Scripture, the creed, and, perhaps most significantly, the person of the bishop himself.[23]

Cyprian's concern was with the practical life and unity of the church, not its objective nature. All the Fathers understood the church as the existential community in which faith in the Gospel is alive and active. Whenever they mentioned the church in their writings, they did so for pastoral and practical reasons, either to enhance the life of the community or to protect it from false leaders and ideas. More than a doctrine among others, *the church was viewed as the subjective presupposition of all doctrinal formulation*. In their minds, the church could not be separated from the entire mystery of God's revelation and salvific plan. It was an intrinsic part of the saving act of God made visible in Jesus and through history in the Holy Spirit.

The Fathers knew that, theologically, the incomprehensible mystery of

---

[20] J. N. D. Kelly, *Early Christian Doctrines*, 2nd ed. (New York: Harper and Row, 1960), 206.

[21] McKim, *Theological Turning Points*, 52–53.

[22] Kelly, *Early Christian Doctrines*, 206.

[23] Joseph Lynch, *The Medieval Church: A Brief History* (London: Longman, 1992), 6–8.

God precedes all other mysteries of faith. The church is a constitutive but a secondary dimension of this ineffable mystery, taking form as historical grace and community. In their experience, the church, comprised of living persons in faith, was the dwelling place where the mystery of God and the gift of salvation in Jesus first came to life as a transforming reality. The church was the existential milieu of all that God accomplishes in Jesus, the locus of reflection on the divine mystery. Only secondarily was it the locus of reflection about itself. Thus, the church is the living presupposition of the theology of God as Trinity, of Jesus Christ, and of the grace of the Spirit. In this light, ecclesiology, the objective study of the church, can be understood as a kind of synthesis of all theology, the subjective home where theology comes to life. In Henri de Lubac's phrase, the church is "the meeting place of all mysteries."[24] No one had a clearer understanding of this truth than the Fathers who saw the church not so much as an object of theological examination but a comprehensive home for the Christian mystery. Catholic Christians today, who wrestle with the problems of institution and authority, might do well to return to the implicit ecclesiology of the Fathers. They understood that the church, like all human families, defied simple objectification but was the Body of Christ and a community of love. The hierarchy today, defensive of their own authority in an age of sexual scandals and the rise of the 'Nones," should compare their institutional ecclesiology to the ecclesiology of the Fathers.

Both the Eastern and the Western Fathers understood the dynamic unity of Christ and the church. They were not concerned about conceptual terms but biblical imagery: the People of God, Body of Christ, temple, house, flock, vineyard, kingdom, field, net, and the like.[25] The ecclesiology of the Eastern Fathers was especially underdeveloped. Cyril of Alexandria (378–444 CE), for example, never considered the issue of the church's existence. Unlike some of the Western Fathers such as Cyprian and Augustine, they did not discuss the church's hierarchy or the ecclesiological relationship between the historical, visible society and the invisible community of grace. Cyril emphasized the unity of Christians with one another in the Body of Christ and in God's Holy Spirit. This Spirit "joins together the many distinct spirits in unity, making them as it were a single spirit in Himself."[26] For John Chrysostom, unity is

[24] Henri de Lubac, *The Splendour of the Church* (New York: Deus Books, 1962), 14.

[25] See Paul Minear's classic work, *The Images of the Church in the New Testament* (Philadelphia: Westminster, 1960).

[26] Kelly, *Early Christian Doctrines*, 405–6.

the outstanding characteristic of the church, a unity grounded in the mutual love of its members. In his view, the Catholic Church, spread throughout the world, is "indestructible and eternal, the pillar and ground of faith."[27] They had little to say about the church as a social and political reality. Here one can clearly see the predominance of twentieth-century Avery Dulles's model of the church as mystical communion.[28]

Although the ecclesiology of the Fathers rarely contained explicit content other than biblical images, one can discover some formal and implicit theological principles essential to an understanding of the church. According to M. -J. le Guillou, these principles include the following: (1) the Holy Spirit and the Eucharist were at the core of the church's being; (2) through faith, love, and prayer, the spiritual motherhood of the entire church was held together; (3) charity, peace, and concord must exist among all the local churches; (4) the whole church is fully present in all the local churches united in the collegial unity of the bishops who govern each church; and (5) the Bishop of Rome is the guardian of charity and the principle of unity of the universal church.[29] While institutional and jurisdictional elements of the church were often present and the subject of some dispute in their writings—at least in the Western Fathers—they were never considered independently of the church's mystery of persons united in Christ and the Holy Spirit.[30] Put simply, the Fathers "give us much material for ecclesiological investigation but they do not give us a formal ecclesiology."[31]

4.2.2 Augustine and the Fifth Century. In the writings of St. Augustine (d. 429 CE), the greatest of the Western Fathers, no formal theological treatise on the church exists. Nevertheless, Augustine's insight into the church, implicitly present in many of his works, became normative for many centuries in

---

[27] Kelly, 402.

[28] Avery Dulles, *Models of the Church*, chap. 3.

[29] M. -J. le Guillou, "History of Ecclesiology," 1:314. It is historically inaccurate to call the Bishop of Rome the "Pope" until the sixth century. The term *papa* (Latin) or *papas* (Greek), meaning "daddy," was originally used by many Christians in a filial relationship to their bishop. Not until the sixth century was the term "pope" exclusively applied to the Bishop of Rome. Likewise, the title "vicar of Christ" did not develop until Pope Innocent III at the beginning of the thirteenth century. See Robert A. Markus, "From Rome to the Barbarian Kingdoms," in *The Oxford Illustrated History of Christianity*, ed. John McManners (New York: Oxford University Press, 1990), 35–37.

[30] See le Guillou, "History of Ecclesiology," 313–15.

[31] Weigel, *Catholic Theology in Dialogue*, 10.

the West. Much of his ecclesiology, like that of Cyprian before him, resulted from his defense of church unity, in his struggle with the heretical group, the Donatists.[32] Akin to Novatian, Donatists possessed an unrealistic view of holiness and perfection in the church, believing that unless the clergy were without sin or fault, their mission would not be effective. Donatists divided the church in Carthage in much of the fourth and fifth centuries.

While Augustine's ecclesiology was more comprehensive than Cyprian's, because of the Donatist heresy, it was inevitably rooted in an apologetic approach. For Augustine, the church is the third mode of Christ's existence, after, first, the Logos, God's eternal Word, and second, Jesus of Nazareth, the Mediator between heaven and Earth.[33] He described this third mode of existence as "mystical," emphasizing the divine reality of Christ in the church. The church of invisible grace sharply contrasts to its visible and institutional form. Like the Shepherd of Hermas centuries earlier, Augustine intimately connects the church with the Body of Christ, creation, and the fellowship of the Holy Spirit.[34] This mystical identification between Christ and the church is described by Augustine in his *Commentary on the Psalms* in this way:

> There are many Christians but only one Christ. Christians together with their head who has ascended into heaven are one Christ. Not that he is many and we are many; but we who are many are one in him. Therefore, there is one man, Christ with his head and body. What is his body? It is his church.[35]

Augustine's spiritual and mystical understanding of the church made him an important theological source for the Protestant Reformers, Luther and Calvin, more than a millennium later. In particular, Calvin grounded his ecclesiology, as well as his theology of sin and grace, in Augustine's clear distinction between the visible and the invisible church, the outward society in

---

[32] Donatism was the error taught by Donatus, bishop of Casae Nigrae, that the effectiveness of the sacraments depends on the moral character of the minister. In other words, if a minister who was involved in a serious sin were to baptize a person, that baptism would be considered invalid.

[33] Augustine, Sermon 341, cited in Eric G. Jay, *The Church: Its Changing Image Through Twenty Centuries* (Atlanta: John Knox, 1980), 84.

[34] Augustine, Sermon 341, cited in Jay, *The Church*, 86.

[35] Augustine, *Commentary on the Psalms*, quoted in Edward J. Gratsch, *Where Peter Is: A Survey of Ecclesiology* (New York: Alba House, 1975), 35. For Augustine's idea of the church, see also Butler, *The Idea of the Church*, 105–22.

history and the communion of saints elected by God. For Augustine, public members of the church who do not love God and their neighbor are not truly part of the invisible communion of saints. Thus, Augustine said of the visible church that within its bosom, "many sheep are without, many wolves are within."[36] For this as well as other reasons, Augustine was to become, in Jaroslav Pelikan's words, "the principal ancestor for the distinctive doctrines of the Reformation."[37]

4.3 Political and Social Factors in the Early Centuries

4.3.1 From Counterculture to Power. In addition to the theological writings of the Fathers, other vital changes in the living experience of the Christian community were taking place during the patristic period. These changes profoundly changed the church's self-understanding for the next thousand years. The church of the first few centuries was closely bound together as a rejected minority within the Roman Empire, forming, in Avery Dulles's phrase, a "contrast society."[38] By the beginning of the fourth century, even before the final period of persecution under the Emperor Diocletian (244–311 CE), which began in 303 and lasted eight years, more people were entering the church, sometimes out of deep faith but often for political and social reasons. Regardless of the fury and the systematic effort behind Diocletian's persecution, the persecution failed because there were already too many Christians in the mainstream of Roman society. Roman officials were willing to seize property of Christians under their jurisdiction but they refused to comply with the emperor's command for their unbridled and ruthless slaughter.[39]

With the conversion of Constantine to Christianity in the year 312, the

---

[36] *Exposition on the Gospel of John*, 45.12, quoted by Calvin in his *Institutes*; Donald McKim suggests a number of texts that highlight Augustine's ecclesiology, including his *Exposition on the* Psalms, 32.21, *On the Trinity*, 15.33–37, and *On the Unity of the Church*, 74. See McKim, *Theological Turning Points*, 55–59 and notes 30–34 on page 184.

[37] Jaroslav Pelikan, *The Christian Tradition: A History of the Development of Doctrine*, vol. 4, *Reformation of the Church and Dogma* (Chicago: University of Chicago Press, 1984), 253.

[38] A term used to describe the church in the first few centuries by Avery Dulles in *Models of the Church*, chap. 13, in which he discusses the church as the community of disciples.

[39] Lynch, *The Medieval Church*, 9–10.

gates of the church were opened for good, and conversion to Christianity, now the religion of the emperor, became the socially and politically acceptable, even the correct, thing to do. The distinction between those Christians willing to live and die for the faith as martyrs (literally, witnesses) and others content to live by minimal Gospel precepts suddenly became clear. Where once conversion to Christ took courage and often the ultimate sacrifice of both status and life, now it was convenient and politically proper for some to enter the church as the emperor had done. This greatly increased the sheer number of Christians and, for the first time, necessitated the erection of large buildings or churches for prayer and the Eucharist. The community understood itself differently: the focus of church membership shifted from a living and demanding commitment to respectability and status within society. The bond of unity within the church ceased to be the eschatological hope of the Lord's return and the blood of martyrs, which was "the seed of the church,"[40] and instead became the visible sacraments administered by the clergy.[41]

Prior to the fourth century, the dividing line was clear between the community of faithful disciples on one side and the unredeemed pagan world on the other. Now, with the advent of the officially Christian world, the external distinction between church and world shifted to a distinction within the church itself, particularly between clergy and laity. The *Apostolic Constitutions* early in the fourth century, for example, defined the role of the laity with more precision, clearly distinguishing the unique power of bishops and separating the clergy and laity in worship. Laypersons were also gradually eased out of positions of financial authority within the church. Important issues were no longer decided upon, as St. Cyprian had suggested more than a century earlier, "with the consent of the whole people." Pope Leo in the fifth century banned laity from preaching, and Pope Gregory in the sixth century replaced all of his lay servants with clerics or monks.[42] Thus, the unfortunate tendency to understand the church primarily, even exclusively, in terms of the hierarchy and the clergy was initially rooted in the decline of Rome and the rise of the church as the normative institution of Western culture.

4.3.2 Monasticism. Another important development in the church in the fourth century, which would significantly influence future ecclesiology, was

---

[40] A well-known phrase of Tertullian in the early third century, cited in McKim, *Theological Turning Points*, 51.

[41] G. H. Williams, "The Ancient Church," in *The Layman in Christian History*, ed. Stephen Neill and Hans-Rudi Weber (Philadelphia: Westminster, 1963), 29.

[42] Frend, "The Church of the Roman Empire," 59–62.

the emergence of monasticism. Christians were no longer required to be witnesses or "martyrs" for the faith as they were during the earlier Roman persecutions. Dedicated Christians, or those true martyrs in the spirit of an earlier time, sought new ways to express the unconditional nature of their commitment to Christ and church that literal martyrdom had once provided. Thus, monastic life began as an expression of complete commitment; monks rejected both sexuality and their life in the world. As a seventh-century monk says, monasticism arose "from men's desires to become martyrs in will, that they might not miss the glory of them that were made perfect by blood."[43]

Monasticism began in the East in the fourth century with St. Anthony of the Desert and St. Pachomius. It began primarily as a lay movement within the church, attracting deeply committed people, often from the educated and the aristocratic classes, in search of new modes of spiritual expression. Initially, monks lived alone (*monos*, one in Latin), called eremitic (ἐρημος, desert) monasticism. Eventually, they gathered in community and lived and ate together in cenobitic (κοινόβιον, or a common life). Monasticism gradually became more and more a clerical practice as some monks received ordination while some priests embraced that monastic spirituality.

The most important person in the development of monastic life was Benedict of Nursia (ca. 480–543), a small town in northern Italy. Benedict authored his famous Rule and established a monastery at Monte Cassino, about eighty miles south of Rome, in 529. A member of his community was elected Pope Gregory I (Gregory the Great) in 590 and served as pontiff and leader of the besieged city of Rome until 604. The Rule of Benedict and the Benedictine Order was enormously influential in the life of the church during the Middle Ages, keeping the literacy of the West alive in monasteries and inspiring the foundation of other orders in the revival of Europe in the eleventh and twelfth centuries.

As monks became the "successors of the martyrs," the Indian summer of the Roman Empire in the fourth century faded, and the ancient world was slowly melting into centuries of tribal conflict and societal lawlessness.[44] With the end of the Empire in the West in the fifth century and the gradual conversion of the barbarian tribes, the church filled the political and social vacuum left with the fall of Rome. It became the dominant force within the whole of society and helped to create the medieval world as we have come to

---

[43] Cited in Frend, 82n15.

[44] Frend, 79.

know it.[45] By the beginning of the sixth century, the church, once a small contrast community, often an object of derision and persecution by the established order, had become not only the religious but also the social and political center of Western Civilization. The pattern that subsequently transformed ecclesiology from the biblical images of the Body of Christ and the People of God into the political metaphor of Christendom or Christ's earthly Kingdom was firmly established.

4.4 The Early Medieval World: Theology and Ecclesiology Static and Dormant

With the end of the Roman Empire (nominally in 476 CE) and the beginning of the medieval world, the field of theology would lie fallow for centuries in the West. Almost without exception, theology in the early Middle Ages was essentially and exclusively biblical, maintaining and faithfully observing the patristic principle of the sufficiency of Sacred Scripture.[46] The theological enterprise often consisted of a restatement of Augustinian thought and was usually no more than a commentary on the text of Augustine's writings. Only one Western theologian, John Scotus Erigena (ca. 808–870, the Irish Neoplatonist philosopher, poet, and theologian of the ninth century, is recognized as an original thinker, perhaps the only one of note from Augustine until the end of the eleventh century.[47] His theology is much akin to the mystical thought of Pseudo-Denys, or Pseudo-Dionysius (fifth and sixth centuries, more exact dates unknown), and Maximus the Confessor (580–662). Perhaps he is most known for his contribution to the interpretation of doctrine.

The fourth century marked the last period of a literate and educated laity in the Western church for a millennium. Some have erroneously called this the "Dark Ages," a term that most scholars prefer not to use today. The world had become static, and so too the church and its theology. Feudalism became the reigning social and political system for centuries, with the strict social hierarchy of emperors, nobles, knights, and serfs or peasants. The church, too, became enormously powerful, in part because of the vast lands that it owned. These lands were important in subsequent history, and the problem of church property was not resolved until the nineteenth and early twentieth centuries.

---

[45] See I. N. Wood, "The Conversion of the Barbarian Peoples," in *The Christian World: A Social and Cultural History*, ed. Geoffrey Barraclough (New York: Harry Abrams, 1981): 85–98.

[46] Congar, *A History of Theology*, 51.

[47] Congar, 63.

The church as a political and social power dramatically changed the church's self-understanding. Ecclesiology became the study of the church's institutional and political power. The mystery of the church was submerged into its institutional expression, into the milieu of kings and nobles, into what erroneously appeared to be a static and changeless world. Such a worldview changed dramatically at the beginning of the sixteenth century with the Protestant Reformation.

In the early medieval period, monasteries became the only places where serious academic learning occurred, almost all by the monks and other clergy. Since the culture appeared static and unchanging, with the average person in the feudal system illiterate and uneducated, the entire period was steeped in symbols and rituals that approached superstition. Theology from the sixth to the eleventh centuries tended to have little life and no creative spirit; ecclesiology likewise lay dormant.

The static nature of the culture made any objective development in ecclesiology unlikely. The problem of the church as a visible and political institution, so prevalent in the second millennium of Christianity, was neglected—or more properly, unimaginable in this feudal and sacramental world. In the spirit of Augustine, the church was understood as a mystical reality, closely identified with God, Christ, and the sacraments. Christians of this period had the simple but profound sense of participating in a church and a spiritual reality that engulfed every dimension of their lives. While the Eucharist lost some of its mystical sense during this period, the church, taken in its totality, did not. This loss in the theology of the Eucharist was the unfortunate result of the theology of Bérengar (Latin, Berengarius) of Tours (ca. 999–1088), who was accused of questioning the real presence of Christ in the Eucharistic bread, believing the elements of bread and wine became the body and blood of Christ only in a symbolic sense. Most notably, he rejected the then-current view of transubstantiation, made popular in the ninth century. His accusers responded by emphasizing the objective nature of Christ in the visible sign of the sacrament. Bérengar was forced to recant his spiritual and symbolic interpretation in 1059.[48] Bérengar has been described as one of the "inciters of modern heresy."

This objectification of the Eucharist was a foretaste of ecclesiology in the centuries to come. Unlike the Eucharist, however, the church was not yet

---

[48] Jaroslav Pelikan, *The Christian Tradition: A History of the Development of Doctrine*, vol. 3, *The Growth of Medieval Theology (600–1300)* (Chicago: University of Chicago Press, 1978), 186–87.

ready for objectification in a formal ecclesiology. Perhaps the church, as the family of God in the world, is not unlike a human family where growing children have little or no objective critical sense of the small community in which they live until they grow up. This simultaneous growth and loss of innocence are inevitable for everyone. So too the "childhood of the church" was coming to an end: adolescence and a loss of cultural and historical innocence were soon to shake the church to its foundations in the following centuries. In the High Middle Ages, the Christian community ceased to live simply, comprehending the mystery of the church from the inside out, so to speak. The time had come for the church to examine itself objectively, from the outside in.

4.5 The Twelfth Century

The twelfth century marks a crucial turning point and a dramatic shift in ecclesiology. Indeed, this was a special moment of transition in the entire intellectual, sociopolitical, and economic life of Europe.[49] For the first time, the church was threatened with domination by the lay aristocracy and the secular power of emerging European governments. One of the weapons used by the church's leaders to free itself from the threat of secular rule was the development of a legal system within the church called canon law. This law served to control human life and society more rigidly, to enhance the legal power of the papacy, and to affirm papal autonomy and independence, especially from the emperor. In this period, ecclesiology was to undergo an important change in its orientation: from an understanding of the church as the whole mystery of God present in human community to a perfect society modeled on a city or earthly kingdom. *Legal and sociological categories were applied to the church for the first time*; this was to have the most significant impact on ecclesiology in all of the centuries to follow.

Christians no longer saw the church as a way to the inner life of God. The church, no longer the mystical communion in the minds of the faithful, was now understood in the same interpretative categories as other human societies and institutions. Theology also became more than a commentary on a text. Peter Abelard (1079–1142), in his famous work, *Sic et Non*, attempted to reconcile conflicting texts in theology. For Peter Lombard (1096–1160, theologian and bishop of Paris), theology became more than a moral and allegorical interpretation of Scripture; theological data was now subject to the

[49] See Marie-Dominique Chenu, *Nature, Man, and God in the Twelfth Century* (Chicago: University of Chicago Press, 1968).

same categories of thought as any other object of scientific knowledge. The most famous theological work of the twelfth century, the *Sentences* of Peter of Lombard, described as a "textbook" and "companion" to the Bible itself, contained no special section devoted to a theological presentation of the church.[50] Likewise, no formal and systematic ecclesiology can be found in the hundreds of commentaries on the *Sentences* that were written in the late twelfth and thirteenth centuries.[51]

The twelfth century marked a turning point in the history of Western theology, and thus in the development of ecclesiology. Several theological movements were also factors in developing a new self-understanding of the church. These movements defined the world in radically dualistic terms: light versus darkness, matter versus spirit, body versus soul. The goal of life, much in the tradition of Plato, was the escape of the good spiritual self from its evil worldly reality. The Albigensians, sometimes known as the *Cathari* or the Pure Ones (Greek katharos, καθαρός, pure) exemplified the dualism of the time. Like all dualists before and after, matter was evil and spirit was good. Thus, they attacked the earthly church for its worldly power. Hence, the church's "matter," its visible and worldly institutional form was condemned. Likewise, the spiritualist Waldensians (from Peter Waldo, ca. 1140–1217) attacked the hierarchical priesthood and the spiritual mediation of the church, thus calling into question the entire sacramental nature of the church's life. The Waldensians, sometimes confused with the Cathari, considered themselves loyal members of the church. Preaching a doctrine of poverty, they renounced worldly goods and, consistent with their spirituality, they understood the church as an invisible community of the elect who are known only to God.[52] The first attack on the pope as the "anti-Christ" dates from this period, thus anticipating the demands for reform embodied in the Reformation.

Moneta of Cremona (unknown–1240) entered the fledgling Dominican order (founded in 1216 by St. Dominic) in 1220. He vigorously defended the visible church against those who reduced the church to an invisible community. In his treatise, *Against the Cathari and Waldensians*, he was the first theologian to demonstrate the impossibility of understanding the mystery of the church separated or abstracted from the concrete forms of its life on earth.[53] This had the unfortunate side effect of reducing the power of the mystical and

[50] Congar, *A History of Theology*, 84, 78.

[51] Pelikan, *The Christian Tradition*, 4:71.

[52] Jay, *The Church*, 124–25.

[53] Jay, 315.

spiritual understanding of the church and enhancing the image of the *ekklesia* in sociological and political categories. Furthermore, these spiritualistic and dualistic attacks on the church, as well as the church's defensive reaction, were to create a pattern of ecclesiology as situation and response, action and reaction. This pattern of ecclesiology as a defense against critics across the whole spectrum would continue to develop more abundantly in the following centuries and subsequently flourish from this period into the twentieth century.

4.6 The Thirteenth Century: From Plato to Aristotle

In the thirteenth century, the so-called golden age of theology in the West, a most significant shift in theological emphasis took place. Before this period of the High Middle Ages, Aristotle had little influence on the Fathers of the church, both in their theological method of doing theology and theological formulations; indeed, they suspected him of inspiring heresies. Boethius, who flourished in the early part of the sixth century, had translated Aristotle, but the Middle Ages studied only his logical works. Aristotle was admired as a master of grammar and of reasoning. In the thirteenth century, however, through the influence of Arabic philosophers in Moorish Spain, especially Al-Farabi (d. 950), Avicenna (d. 1037), Al-Gazelle (d. 1111), and Averroes (d. 1198), the metaphysics of Aristotle was reintroduced into Western thought, particularly at the University of Paris. With this reintroduction of Aristotelian philosophy into Western consciousness, the nature and method of theology shifted. Aristotle became more than a logician and grammarian; his metaphysics too were studied and applied, thus making him, in Congar's phrase, "a master of the knowledge of man and his world."[54] Theology was no longer an ascent to mystical truth as it had been for Augustine. With Thomas Aquinas, and especially those who followed him, Duns Scotus and William of Ockham, theology became the study of the data of revelation. To paraphrase the central methodology of Aristotle and Aquinas, "nothing exists in the mind unless it first exists in the senses." Theology, as Yves Congar says, became "a rational and scientific consideration of the revealed datum," or a "scientifically elaborated copy of faith."[55]

Behind this thirteenth century shift in theological method was a deeper change in the way human beings understood themselves, God, and the world. The Platonic-Augustinian worldview, which dominated the theology of

[54] Yves M. -J. Congar, *Lay People in the Church* (Baltimore: Helicon, 1965), 58–59.

[55] Congar, 102.

Western Christianity from its beginning, was slowly passing away. For Plato, knowledge and love were the same; to know something or someone meant to love it, that is, enter into communion with it and participate in its life. Knowledge of the divine did not mean to know God as an object of knowledge nor as the conclusion of an argument; rather an individual understood the divine as the *prius* of all thought, the infinite source of all being that preceded the finite and was inseparable from it. The whole of things, being-itself, was accepted and understood as primary, before individual being was an object of consideration. *Esse, verum, bonum*—universal being, the fullness of truth, absolute goodness—were the transcendent and real ground of all individual beings, the very presupposition of anything which was and could be known. These were "the principles of truth which were the divine light within us."[56] Hence, before Thomas, there were no proofs for the existence of God, only the reality of God as given, as ground of all that is. A person could not ask the question of God without first presuming God's being. This understanding of God was embodied in medieval Franciscan theology and spirituality, especially in the greatest theologian between St. Augustine and St. Thomas, St. Bonaventure. As Bonaventure says, "God is most truly present to the soul and immediately knowable."[57] At the beginning of chapter five of *The Soul's Journey Into God*, Bonaventure writes:

> We can contemplate God not only outside us and within us but also above us; outside through his vestiges, within through his image and above through the light that shines upon our minds, which is the light of eternal truth, since 'our mind itself is formed immediately by Truth itself.'[58]

In this passage, Bonaventure uses Augustine's words to describe the unmediated presence of divine truth as the source of the mind's truth. Thus, God is knowable without mediation and directly through the divine light in the mind and, like Augustine, in the soul's depth. One cannot know anything as true without also knowing Truth itself as its presupposition. The soul's journey into God is possible because all creatures "have their archetypes in the divine mind and flow out of the divine fecundity." As creatures, we are

---

56 Paul Tillich, *A History of Christian Thought*, ed. Carl Braaten (New York: Harper and Row, 1968), 184.

57 See Paul Tillich, "Two Types of Philosophy of Religion," in *Theology of Culture*, ed. Robert Kimball (New York: Oxford University Press, 1959): 10–30.

58 Bonaventure, *The Soul's Journey Into God*, trans. Ewert Cousins, Classics of Western Spirituality (New York: Paulist, 1978), 94.

"shadows, echoes, pictures, vestiges, representations, or footprints of the Trinity."[59] For Bonaventure, the path to God is both within the self and in all creation as sacrament.[60]

With Thomas Aquinas, Duns Scotus, and William of Ockham—all followers of Aristotle—theology took a 180-degree turn. Instead of standing in the divine center and looking at the world, one stood in the world and looked at God. Instead of beginning with God as first in the order of human knowledge, this approach placed God last. Instead of *sapientia* (wisdom), the goal was *scientia* or knowledge. Instead of understanding God from the inside out where the divine light was present to the soul and mind, God became knowable only from the outside in. Inevitably, God became an object of knowledge, one fact to be known among others. Even as a "Supreme Being," God was one being among others, and therefore an object of doubt and suspicion. If the starting place is the self, one can move from the finite mind to the infinite itself only by the logic of the finite order.

This is the flaw in Thomas Aquinas's five proofs for the existence of God; one presumes that St. Thomas knew that "conclusions reached in this way, though they are logically correct, do not produce a real conviction about god."[61] If the finite was no longer able to reach the infinite cognitively through the divine light immediately present in the soul, or if the finite understands God by proofs that move from the finite order to the infinite, then an impasse is reached. With Duns Scotus, an unbridgeable gap between the human and the divine opens up because God could never be reached through autonomous knowledge. Hence, this gap could only be overcome by the power of the church in which people had to subject themselves to biblical and ecclesiastical authorities for the certainty of faith they needed.[62] With William of Ockham, the father of nominalism, the real could be found only in the individual; hence, God was the *ens singularissimum*, the most single being. God is therefore separate from other individuals, removed from the center of life to a place beside other realities. In Paul Tillich's words,

In this way, the unity of all things in God has come to an end. The

[59] Harvey Egan, "Bonaventure," in *An Anthology of Christian Mysticism*, edited and introduced by Harvey Egan (Collegeville, MN: The Liturgical Press, 1991), 237.

[60] On Bonaventure, see John Dourley, *Tillich and Bonaventure: An Evaluation of Tillich's Claim to Stand in the Augustinian-Franciscan Tradition* (Leiden: E.J. Brill, 1975), 115–57.

[61] Tillich, *A History of Christian Thought,* 186.

[62] Tillich, 191.

> consequence of their individual separation is that they cannot participate in each other immediately in virtue of their common participation in a universal. Community...is replaced by social relations, by society. As a consequence of this nominalism, we live today in a society in which we relate to each other in terms of cooperation and competition, but neither of these has the meaning of participation. Community is a matter of participation; society is a matter of common interests, of being separated from each other and working with or against each other.[63]

Both the theological and ecclesiological implications of this shift in epistemologies are clear. Theologically, modern atheism and agnosticism is a result of this cognitive separation of the human and the divine. Instead of the "ground of being," God becomes an individual and the subject of debate about his existence. Ecclesiologically, the Body of Christ becomes a moral ideal instead of a metaphysical truth. Unfortunately, for a number of reasons, modern persons today have little or no access to the Augustinian-Franciscan worldview in which one begins with God or being itself—that which is the universal ground and source of all life—and not the individual self. At the same time, it remains the only authentic alternative in Western thought to the scientific vision of reality often naïvely accepted by the contemporary world as the best or the only understanding of the real. Without it, the sacramental and mystical are reduced to the positivistic and mechanistic. The result is that many people have little or no sense of liturgy, ritual, or the power of the sacraments today. The interest in Asian religions in America since the 1960s does not suggest that many people truly understand Buddhist epistemology but rather that they are searching for something which they sense they need and which has been lost in their own Western tradition. The modern Islamic scholar, Seyyed Nasr, laments the loss of *sapientia* or sacred knowledge and the triumph of *scientia* or secular knowledge. Both, of course, are essential and are the bulwarks of Western civilization. *Sapientia* is the source of religion and *scientia* the foundation of scientific knowledge and technology. In Nasr's words

> A further eclipse of the sapiential dimension and the secularization of knowledge was to come in the twelfth and thirteenth centuries with the spread of Aristotelianism and Averroism in the west and their wedding with various forms of Christian theology, especially those schools which followed upon the wake of Saint Thomas. Until this period, Augustinianism had still preserved the primacy of illumination in the act

[63] Tillich, 200.

> of knowledge, whereas Saint Thomas, trying to preserve the primacy of Scripture, denied the possibility of the illumination of the mind by the Intellect, and considered all knowledge as having a sensuous origin. Despite the imposing theology created by Saint Thomas, his adoption of Aristotelian categories for the expression of Christian doctrines and emphasis on the sensuous origin of knowledge played a further role in the desacralization of knowledge, although Saint Thomas himself did not accept the separation of faith and reason which he in fact had sought to harmonize....Had Thomas continued to be interpreted by Meister Eckhart, the intellectual destiny of the West would have been very different.[64]

If the church had been understood in a transcendental, mystical, and sacramental way up to this historical moment, it was because all of reality was also viewed in the same light. With Duns Scotus and William of Ockham, philosophy took a different orientation: the whole of things had no meaning prior to a knowledge of the parts. The starting point for understanding reality was no longer located in the infinite itself but in its finite manifestations. Likewise, the knowing subject began to have an autonomy and an independence grounded in its unique individuality. This subject could then examine and consider any object in question with some distance, some sense of separation. Before this change in epistemology (the part of philosophy which studies how human beings know and understand), it was unimaginable for human beings to separate God and Christ and church from one another and their own meaning and destiny. With the change in the thirteenth century, however, God and the human person could be conceptualized as separate realities. The church, therefore, inevitably shifted its own self-understanding from the mystical reality of grace that was *of* and *from* God, a community that, in some *a priori* sense, defined human destiny, to a society of persons subject to the categories and laws of historical interpretation.

Although Aquinas's epistemology marked an important turning point in the method and the direction of theology, his own writings continue to treat the church in the tradition of the Fathers and other medieval theologians before him. Like his predecessors, he centered the church in the mystery of salvation which takes place in God's action in Christ and which is embodied in the Eucharist. He understood the church as mystery, a transcendent reality unconfined by space and time. For him, the true church is the heavenly church

---

[64] Seyyed Hossein Nasr, *Knowledge and the Sacred* (Albany, NY: State University of New York Press, 1989), 37.

upon which the earthly church is modeled and to which all persons move. Thomas applied his theory of instrumental causality to the Body of Christ, thus continuing the Pauline tradition of a theology of the church with Christ as the head and the church as his body. He understood the church as a spiritual community of persons united in Christ and the Holy Spirit, a community grounded in the Paschal mystery or the saving act of God in Christ. This community exists from its historical origin in the Cross and Resurrection of Christ until its completion at the *eschaton* or the return of all things to Christ at the end of time.[65]

In the same tradition of the Fathers much earlier, one could make a case for the church as the implicit center of all of Thomas's theology, the milieu in which God's grace becomes present. Indeed, the substance of the church for Thomas is "the new life which men receive by the virtues of faith, hope and love and is a life driven Godwards, with God for its end....[It is] the whole economy of the return towards God, *motus rationalis creaturae in Deum* (the rational movement of the creature towards God)."[66] Yet, in spite of his extensive theological writings and an age that did not lack theological treatises, Thomas, like other medieval theologians such as Albertus Magnus and Bonaventure, wrote no distinct and formal treatise on the church itself, nor did he study its distinctive marks, its organization and authority. Surprisingly, no "questions" of the *Summa Theologica* deal with objective ecclesiological issues. The great theologian of the church in the twentieth century, Yves Congar, believes that Thomas acted deliberately when he wrote no treatise on the church. Congar vigorously affirms that, "it is also true to say the entire *Secunda Pars* of the *Summa Theologica* is ecclesiology," an ecclesiology that "had a different drift from that which developed subsequently."[67]

Unfortunately for the future of ecclesiology, a more objective and explicit theology of the church in the writings of the great medieval theologians did not exist among the canon lawyers of the period who were quick to define the nature of the church in their own juridical and canonical terms, reducing the ecclesial mystery to objective legal categories.[68] This again established a

---

[65] Avery Dulles, *A Church To Believe In: Discipleship and the Dynamics of Freedom* (New York: Crossroads, 1982), 151. See his entire chapter, "The Church According to Thomas Aquinas," 149–69.

[66] Yves Congar, *The Mystery of the Church*, 2nd rev. ed. (Baltimore: Helicon, 1960), 59. For the role of Congar in contemporary ecclesiology, see the section on the twentieth century below.

[67] Congar, 54–56.

[68] Pelikan, *The Christian Tradition*, 4:71.

regrettable pattern for the future ecclesiology. In the next two centuries, the church's self-understanding would be confined within social, political, and legal categories because the church itself would be entrapped in a world of political intrigue and struggles for temporal power.

5.

THE RENAISSANCE AND THE REFORMATION

5.1 The Fourteenth Century and Formal Ecclesiology

In the fourteenth century, the church was compelled to reflect on its identity in a formal and systematic manner. Unfortunately, a tragic irony in the church's self-understanding began to develop, creating a pattern of ecclesiological thought that survived into twentieth century. The church, the environment in which doctrines were formulated and that is only implicitly a doctrine itself, now took a different turn. The factors involved in this important shift included, first, the decline of the Augustinian-Franciscan approach to theology with Aristotle's return as the philosophical master of the West; second, the change in the political and economic conditions in Western Europe beginning in the twelfth century.

Ecclesiology, of necessity, became aware of its own importance as a distinct and explicit part of theological reflection. Once the church became self-conscious of its place of importance in creating theology at the beginning of the fourteenth century, it quickly became, as Jaroslav Pelikan says, "the primary issue" of all theology. From this time until the Reformation two centuries later, the church continually affirmed its position as "the first and most universal principle of doctrine and of the science of faith." At the Council of Basel, for example, in the early fifteenth century (which will be considered later), all of the participants, both the orthodox and the heretics, "found themselves compelled to discuss the concept of the church as the basis of all items on the program."[1] The church was no longer simply the place where orthodoxy and heresy could debate; now it was to become itself an object of fervent orthodoxy and heretical interpretations.

The change in theological focus introduced in the fourteenth century is clear and unequivocal. While one can read the Fathers and Doctors of the Church for their interpretation on *any* subject *except* the church, the fourteenth and the fifteenth centuries, by contrast, produced a vast number of texts that deal explicitly and *exclusively* with the doctrine of the church and all matters ecclesiastical.[2] Once the floodgates of formal ecclesiology were opened, the church became the center and primary concern of its own theological enterprise. To add to this irony, the first distinct theologies of the church were not written by theologians with the status of Church Fathers and Doctors but by men who are no more than footnotes in the history of theology. The oldest theological treatise on the church is thought to be James of Viterbo's *De regimine Christiano* (Christian Government), appearing in 1301. (Viterbo was a small town about sixty miles from Rome.) This treatise was followed in the next several years by two other writings of note: *De ecclesiastica potestate* (Ecclesiastical Power) by Giles of Rome and *De potestate regia et papali* (Royal and Papal Power) by the French Dominican, John of Paris.[3] John also penned the treatise *De potestate papae* (The Power of the Pope), which specifically defended the hierarchy against the claims of the lower clergy.[4] The titles of these earliest works suggest their theological orientation: treatises that examine and defend the church's right to power and authority rather than doctrinal expositions on the mystery of the church. John's thesis is that spiritual power and temporal power both have their origins in the divine itself, and, while temporal power has its own autonomous sphere, spiritual power is greater. Translated into the political framework of the day, the priest is greater than the prince; the pope has authority over the king or emperor.[5]

These early ecclesiological treatises were occasioned by the bitter dispute between Pope Boniface VIII and King Philip IV of France over the question of whose power was the greatest on earth, the *Imperium*, the earthly power of the king, or the *Sacerdotium*, the sacred power of the church. Of course, this

---

[1] Pelikan, *The Christian Tradition*, 4:71.

[2] Pelikan, 4:71.

[3] On Giles of Rome and John of Paris, see J. R. Eastman, *Papal Abdication in the Later Middle Ages* (Lewiston, NY: Mellen, 1990), 70–80.

[4] le Guillou, "History of Ecclesiology," 1:316.

[5] Jay, *The Church*, 127.

was not the first time such a battle took place. In the struggle between Henry IV of Germany and Pope Gregory VII at the end of the eleventh century, Gregory forbade the clergy from accepting investiture as bishop from a lay person. In 1076, he excommunicated Henry and deposed him from office. Ironically, many of the bishops in Germany sided with the king while many lay nobles stood with the pope. The King, barefoot and supplicant, appeared before the pope at Canossa; accordingly, Gregory rescinded the excommunication. When the dispute broke out again in 1080, Gregory ordered a second excommunication. Henry responded by attacking Rome and sending the pope into refuge in southern Italy. The dispute was not settled until 1122 with the Concordat of Worms, a compromise between Pope Calixtus II and Henry V. This agreement greatly enhanced the power of the papacy in the following centuries.[6]

Relations between the two seats of power, church and state, have always been a matter of conflict. After the Concordat of Worms, the papacy in the twelfth and early thirteenth century reached the pinnacle of its power during the Middle Ages, culminating with Pope Innocent III (1161–1216). His papacy held political control over all of Christendom. In John Dwyer's words, Innocent "was destined to bring the office to the summit of its political power and, perhaps in virtue of that fact, to prepare for its decline as a spiritual and moral force."[7] In less than a century, the papacy declined from the acme to the nadir of its power. The pope began the century as the undisputed ruler of the West. By the pontificate of Celestine V (Celestine resigned his office after only six months as pope in 1294) before the end of the thirteenth century, the papacy was virtually a subject of the state under King Philip IV of France. Known as "Philip the Fair," King Philip embodied the emerging philosophy of Statism that placed civil rule over ecclesiastical governance. By definition, Statism was antagonistic to the power of the Holy See. The king met his match in Celestine's successor, Pope Boniface, but the circumstances that had permitted the papacy to triumph almost two centuries earlier in the Investiture battle between Henry IV and Gregory VII had dramatically changed; now it was far more favorable to the civil rulers.[8]

Perhaps more than any other medieval pope, Boniface's pontificate

---

[6] See Lynch, *The Medieval Church,* 141–45.

[7] John Dwyer, *Church History: Twenty Centuries of Catholic Christianity,* rev. ed. (New York: Paulist Press, 1992), 173.

[8] Robert McNally, *The Reform of the Church: Crisis and Criticism in Historical Perspective* (New York: Herder and Herder, 1963), 20–21.

marks the end of an epoch and the beginning of a new age in papal-state relations, when, in Robert McNally's words, "the Popes and religion gradually cease to be taken into account as factors in the public life of Christian nations."[9] Boniface, in a bitter dispute with the French king over control of the clergy in France, issued the bull, *Unam Sanctam*, in 1302. This famous medieval document strongly supports the principle that in jurisdictional conflicts between Church and state, the papacy possesses supreme power and no civil ruler has authority in Church matters. Boniface writes:

> Both [*sacerdotium* and *imperium*] therefore, are in the power of the Church, that is to say, the spiritual and the material sword, but the former is to be administered for the church but the latter by the Church; the former in the hands of the priest; the latter by the hands of kings and soldiers, but at the will and sufferance of the priest....However, one sword ought to be subordinated to the other and temporal authority, subjected to spiritual power.[10]

The bull concludes with these often-cited lines: "We declare, say, define, and pronounce that it is absolutely necessary for the salvation of every creature to be subject to the Roman Pontiff."[11] Of course, the pope included Philip in this declaration. What poor Boniface did not know was that this document exemplified the last pronouncement of the triumphant medieval papacy.[12]

At the beginning of the fourteenth century, the first treatises on the church were not comprehensive treatments of the mystery of the church as it emerged from faith in the Resurrection but simply ad hoc responses to those who were challenging the church's political authority at the time. Nor were these treatises in any sense dogmatic, that is, systematic presentations of faith. Instead, they were apologetic, defending not only the principle of the Church's historical authority, but also, more specifically, the particular powers of the papal office and often an individual pope. In this same spirit, Augusto Trionfo wrote his *Summa de potestate ecclesiastica* (Summa on Ecclesiastical Power) during the early years of Pope John XXII (ca. 1316). He affirms the positions of both James and Giles of a few years earlier that proclaimed that the pope is supreme in both spiritual and temporal matters. His justification

---

[9] Philip Hughes, *A History of the Church,* vol. 3, (New York: Sheed and Ward, 1949), quoted in McNally, 21.

[10] Umam Sanctum, trans. Ronald L. Conte Jr., www.catholicplanet.com.

[11] Quoted in Edward. J. Gratsch, *Where Peter Is: A Survey of Ecclesiology* (New York: Alba House, 1975), 94.

[12] McNally, *The Reform of the Church*, 26.

is based upon this simple logic: the spiritual is more important than the temporal; all bishops derive their jurisdiction from the pope; the pope has the power of the keys directly from Christ; finally, since the emperor is a vassal of Christ, he is also the vassal of the pope or the Vicar of Christ. The pope can demand an account of the emperor's reign, impose penalties upon him, and depose him if he sees fit to do so. Even though the separation of spiritual and temporal power—which is our modern presumption—was unimaginable to the theologians of this time, this treatise of Augusto Trionfo is, nevertheless, a neat summary of every papo-centric ecclesiology found in different forms in later centuries.[13]

5.2 Avignon and the Great Schism

To understand the milieu that created the ecclesiology of the fourteenth and fifteenth centuries, one need only explore in depth a papacy characterized by political intrigue and jurisdictional struggles with secular powers. While to the papacy, the temporal and the spiritual orders were still inseparable, the pope was no longer the undisputed temporal and political leader of Europe; his spiritual authority and credibility was also weakened. This situation inevitably led to an ecclesiology that was unusually narrow, one-sided, and self-serving. Any discourse on the church was reduced to taking a theological position on the pope and his power vis-à-vis the political and/or spiritual forces attacking him. The decline and the fragility of the papacy as part of a church in transition from the medieval world to the modern is most obvious in the move of the papacy from Rome to Avignon. This resulted in the period of the Great Schism where two men claimed the throne of Peter at the same time. In the bitter debate over *Unam Sanctam*, Philip IV had Pope Boniface shamelessly arrested in 1303, but the pope died before his trial. His successor, however, and all the popes from 1304 until 1378, resided in the small southeastern French city of Avignon where the great fourteenth century palace of the popes still stands. These seven French popes, as John Dwyer says, "were Frenchmen first and Popes second," serving as "pliable and willing tools in the hands of the French monarchy."[14] This period in the life of the church has been aptly called the Babylonian captivity. For more than a century, confusion over papal authority and the authenticity of claims to the papal throne reigned, creating a time of great scandal to the average person with a piety often deep but

[13] Gratsch, *Where Peter Is*, 95.

[14] Dwyer, *Church History*, 195.

untutored and uncritical.[15]

Since the papacy was on French soil and under the protection of the French king for more than seventy years of its "captivity," the throne of Peter surrendered its universal character for the first time, which its autonomy in the city of Rome had given to it. The Avignon papacy, with its bureaucracy established to levy taxes on all of Christendom, "prepared the way for the rebellion of Northern Europe against the papacy and the papal church in the sixteenth century and it ranks high on the list of causes of the Reformation."[16] In 1377, when Gregory IX at last returned and reentered Rome, the restoration of the papacy to Rome seemed definitive. Unfortunately for the Church, however, Urban VI, an Italian, was elected pope the following year in 1378 as Gregory's successor. He revealed himself to be an unbalanced tyrant, unquestionably a man with a serious mental illness by today's standards. Thus, the cardinals were forced to meet again just six months after the first election to depose Urban and name a Frenchman, Clement VII, to the papal throne. Unfortunately, his first act was to remove the papacy from Rome and restore it to Avignon. This action forced the cardinals to gather again and elect a pope who would remain in Rome. As a result, an even greater crisis now beset the Church since two men, one at Rome, the other at Avignon, claimed the papacy at the same time. This created an "incurable cancer" at the heart of the church's life.[17] The Great Schism or period of two popes generated seven antipopes who remained at Avignon while others duly elected in Rome maintained the papacy there. Even the saints of the era were divided over which claimant to the throne of Peter was legitimate. St. Catherine of Siena and St. Vincent Ferrer, both Dominicans, supported different men, one in Rome, the other in Avignon. The tragic impact of the Great Schism on the consciousness of the whole Church is described by Robert McNally this way:

> The scandal was enormous....In the eyes of the common man, the vast moral prestige of the Holy See was brought down, for obedience to the Chair of St. Peter was determined for him according to national interest. The long wrangling and intricate litigations to terminate the schism fatigued men who began to consider an ecclesiastical system,

---

[15] For more information on this period, see the classic work by Guillaume Mollat, *The Popes at Avignon 1305–1378* (London: Thomas Nelson, 1963).

[16] Dwyer, *Church History*, 198.

[17] Cited in Jaroslav Pelikan, *The Christian Tradition: A History of the Development of Doctrine*, vol. 2, *The Spirit of Eastern Christendom (600–1700)* (Chicago: The University of Chicago Press, 1974). 72.

which was incapable of securing unity of obedience, to be effete and passé.[18]

The Babylonian captivity remained a scandal until the Council of Constance (1414–1418). As a result of this council, during which time three men claimed the papal throne, Martin V was at last declared the legitimate pope in 1417. The Council restored the papacy to Rome where it remained. This "monstrous and unimaginable scandal," as Joseph Lortz calls it, was more than just a theological and academic matter, but "permeated the entirety of public and private life."[19] The damage to the Church and its credibility was immense and irreversible. In a little more than a century, the sacramental/mystical mind of the Middle Ages, which could not imagine an alternative to the church as the center of the religious worldview, had become little more than a memory. The church in fact had become a temporal princedom, not catholic as universal, but Roman Catholic, politically, sociologically, and canonically.

If the papacy was losing its credibility, so too were its theological apologists and supporters. In reducing ecclesiology to a defense of institutional and papal power, theologians created a consistent historical pattern, discernible in different forms with changing antagonists, from the beginnings of formal ecclesiology at the time of Boniface VII to the Second Vatican Council. Virtually all ecclesiology put the emphasis on the church as a visible and hierarchical society; any theology of the church was an apologetic defense of church authority or a defense of ecclesiastical power in both the spiritual and temporal orders. The earliest and sometimes primitive expressions of this one-sided ecclesiology are visible in the theology of the fourteenth and fifteenth centuries, forecasting the tragic separation within the church that was to come a century later.

Formal ecclesiology was born, then, in a time of transition and strife. The entire period from Pope Boniface VIII to the reformer Martin Luther (1300 to 1517) was characterized by an increasing number of attacks on church authority. Some of these attacks were undeniably justified because of the abuse of ecclesiastical power, especially at the highest levels of the clergy. In addition, Church leadership was in severe institutional and moral decline, and endless cries for reform of both ecclesiastical structures and spiritual life were on the lips of many from every walk of life. Europe was changing, and the Church as a visible institution, instead of serving as a spiritual leader and

---

[18] McNally, *The Reform of the Church*, 42.

[19] Joseph Lortz, *How the Reformation Came* (New York: Herder and Herder, 1964), 43–44.

prophet in a time of change, was entrapped in endless political intrigue, both ecclesiastical and secular. Without question, these two centuries marked the nadir of church history. Since ecclesiology can be no better and more creative than the historical community out of which it develops, the ecclesiology of these pre-Reformation centuries reflects the profound confusion and corruption in the church's life and leadership. The "little flock," a phrase peculiar to Luke's Gospel, had lost its way, and its shepherds seemed too busy with mundane matters to care.

The church's demise in this period began with the weakening of church authority. Radical Reformers like John Wycliffe at the end of the fourteenth century and John Hus at the beginning of the fifteenth attacked or outright rejected the authority of the church. Wycliffe, an English reformer at Oxford and the person described as "the morning star of the Reformation," asserted that religious authority should be reserved for the righteous and moral alone.[20] His work, *De potestate papae* (Papal Power), was a strong condemnation of the papacy. In this work, Wycliffe proclaimed to the world the pope as the antichrist. Hus, a Bohemian, denounced the hierarchical organization of the Church and preached against an immoral clergy. His treatise *De ecclesia* (On the Church) clearly foreshadowed the ecclesiology of the Reformers of the following century. Hus was invited to the Council of Constance (1414–18) that settled the Great Schism and was promised his personal safety. In one of the saddest and most deceitful pages of church history, he came to the Council in good faith only to be burned at the stake as a heretic. Both Wycliffe and Hus were early expressions of rebellion against the absolutist power of the visible and institutional Church. Unfortunately, as church reformers, both of them worked out of a distorted interpretation of Augustine's concept of grace in which human effort counted for very little. This understanding forced them to take extreme positions on the spiritual nature of the church; because human free actions were of little or no value in the work of salvation, the church as a visible institution was likewise unimportant. Thus, in their view, the church was an invisible communion of the predestined or the elect.

[20] McNally, *The Reform of the Church*, 43.

5.3 Conciliarism

A second source of weakness and confusion for the universal church was in the theory of Conciliarism evident at the Council of Constance (1414–1418), the theory that an ecumenical council, not the papacy, held the final authority in the Church. This was a most serious threat to the credibility of Church authority especially when such authority was desperately needed after a century of a weak and divided papacy. The Council raised this fundamental ecclesiological question: who holds supreme authority in the Church, the pope or an ecumenical council? The Conciliarists responded that the Council was superior to the pope, establishing the principle that the Church was not a monarchy but an aristocratic oligarchy. In the minds of the Conciliarists, the pope possessed a primacy of honor, not authority; not the Roman Pontiff as an individual, but the ecumenical council of the world's bishops, including the Bishop of Rome, *alone* possessed absolute authority to govern the Church. In their view, while the pope is "the supreme administrator and custodian of the affairs of the Church," he is not "her chief judge and legislator endowed with the special authority of Christ."[21] Conciliarism emerged in part as a result of a century of frustration with the papacy, weakened first at Avignon, later devastated by the Great Schism. Perhaps, as the proponents of Conciliarism fervently believed, many in council could do what one with supreme authority had been unable to do for the reform of the structures of Church life and the elimination of the abuses in ecclesial governance. Yet was Conciliarism a viable theological alternative to a papo-centric ecclesiology? According to Robert McNally, the Conciliarist approach "colored the ecclesiastical atmosphere of the day with dark shadows by advancing an ecclesiology which, if left unchecked, would surely destroy the church in her essential constitution."[22]

In Conciliarist ecclesiology, the church was understood as a community of the faithful (*congregatio fidelium*) where what was normative in and about the church emerged from individualistic and representative opinions about the nature of the community. This was a classic expression of nominalism, the reigning philosophy of the day, applied to the theology of the church. In reducing the church to the community of the faithful or the sum of its members, the mystical awareness of the church as the mystery of God's grace, created before the world, was utterly submerged in the individual, social, and political reality of the institution. Conciliarism, of course, was but another effort to

[21] McNally, 52.

[22] McNally, 51.

change the abusive situation within Church governance of the time. Yet as a theology, it went beyond the limits of valid reform by unduly limiting the power of the Holy See and subordinating the power of the papacy to the ecumenical council. The theory was rejected by Pope Martin V, the first pope of a unified Church in Rome in over a century. Unfortunately, since the necessary reform of Church abuses had now become so closely associated with Conciliarist ecclesiology, the repudiation of one was viewed as a repudiation of the other. Thus, the much-needed Church reform became an innocent victim in the victory of the papacy over Conciliarism. In McNally's words: "This was a tragedy whose full significance would only be grasped in the following century, when reform would be sought without benefit of either church or council."[23]

In spite of Pope Martin V's rejection of Conciliarism, after the Council of Constance, an even more radical, anti-papal, pro-Conciliarist council was held at Basel beginning in 1431. Pope Eugene IV (1431–1447), successor of Martin V, moved this council to Ferrara in 1437, and its work continued until 1449 in Lausanne. This Council (rejected as schismatic by Bellarmine but accepted as authentic by subsequent Gallican sympathizers) was in constant battle with Eugene IV. At first, he disbanded it, then later capitulated to the most outrageous of its anti-papal decrees. While one could argue that within Conciliarist ecclesiology, some form of worthwhile democracy had manifested itself within Church structures for the first time, the Councils of Constance and Basel had also proven once and for all that if the papacy could not reform the church then neither could any council in rebellion against its excessive papal power.[24]

The year 1440, after the Council of Basel had ended and Conciliarism had been defeated, has been described by M. -J. le Guillou as a sort of "solstice" or turning point in the whole history of the church's ecclesiological thought.[25] Conciliarist ecclesiology was nurtured and defended by outstanding thinkers such as William of Ockham, Marsilius of Padua, and Jean of Jandun. While their theology and philosophy was sometimes controversial, it was surely not irresponsible nor without solid foundation. William of Ockham (d. 1349) defined the church as "the whole congregation of the faithful living in this mortal life at the same time."[26] The major weakness with

[23] McNally, 55–56.
[24] McNally, 63–69.
[25] le Guillou, "The History of Ecclesiology," 316.
[26] Quoted in Jay, *The Church*, 131.

Ockham's ecclesiology was that he placed little emphasis on the mystical body and, instead, greatly stressed faith and personal liberty as the constitutive elements of the church. Ockham, as has been pointed out, was the father of nominalism, a school of philosophy which insisted that the essence of what is real was in its particular and objective historical expression. Nominalism, in Joseph Lortz's words, "individualized and atomized the thinking process" inhibiting knowledge of the sacred or *sapientia*. In a strongly anti-mystical way, it had the effect of blocking the mind's access to the realm of mystery and its sacramental embodiment. In such thinking, the church becomes "only the sum of the individual faithful; they 'constitute' the church but are not born of the church who is indeed more than the sum of her members."[27] Conciliarism was steeped in this nominalist view of the church. In nominalism, we see the final end to the Platonic worldview which inspired the spiritual vision of the West from the time of the Fathers until the re-emergence of Aristotle; we also uncover an important strand of thought in the development of the Reformation, secular consciousness, as well as the science and technology of the modern world. It is no wonder that Martin Luther frequently spoke of William of Ockham in a most favorable light.

Perhaps more influential theologically in the creation of an anti-papal, pro-Conciliarist theology was Marsilius of Padua's (d. 1342) radical treatise on the church and the political order, *Defensor Pacis* (Defender of Peace) of 1324. This treatise proposed to redefine church-state relations by seriously reducing the role of the church in public life, making the church a dimension of the civil life of the state, and transforming her ministry into a public service. The work was revolutionary and filled with scorn and contempt for the church; it was a treatise, as McNally says, "the extent of whose evil influence is too vast to be measured."[28] At the same time, *Defensor Pacis*, by suggesting that church and state were ultimately separable realities, was also so much ahead of its time that it could have had no immediate effect on the life of the church in the fourteenth and fifteenth centuries. Its appearance, however, two full centuries before the Reformation, suggests that such a work "would not have been possible at all had it not been for the broad subsoil of discontent from which it sprang."[29] In *Defensor Pacis*, one has a very early taste of the ecclesiological questions of jurisdiction and secular control facing the church in the seventeenth and eighteenth centuries when movements such as

[27] Lortz, *How the Reformation Came*, 57.

[28] McNally, *The Reform of the Church*, 32–33.

[29] Lortz, *How the Reformation Came,* 49.

Gallicanism, Febronianism, and Josephinism (see chapter six) sought to control the church and place it under the authority of civil rulers and the secular state.

From the opposite perspective, defenders of papal authority against the Conciliarists included John of Turrecremata (or Torquemada), John of Ragusa, and Thomas Netter. The battle between these two different ecclesiological schools produced the first systematic or comprehensive treatises on the church: one by John of Ragusa, the other by Turrecremata, his *Summa de Ecclesia* of 1436.[30] These treatises were systematic because, for the first time, they dealt with the reality of the church in a more integral and complete way. Both works placed strong emphasis on kingdom and power as the foundation of church. The *Summa* of Turrecremata (not to be confused with his infamous nephew, Thomas, the Inquisitor) was, for example, divided into four parts: the church in its nature or its mystery, the primacy of the pope in Rome, ecumenical councils, and schism and heresies.[31] While its content was very much a product of its own century's theological disputes, the form of this treatise prefigured some of the schemata on the church which did not appear until Vatican I and Vatican II over four centuries later.

5.4 The Decline of the Institution

In addition to the weakening of the Church's power because of the Avignon papacy, the Babylonian captivity, and the Conciliarist crisis, the fourteenth and fifteenth centuries also witnessed a sharp decline in the quality of worship and the spiritual life of the faithful. Liturgy became increasingly removed from the life of the average Christian; rather than a rite shared fully and actively by its participants, it was more a mysterious rite performed in the apse of the Gothic cathedral that was observed by the faithful from some distance. Reception of the Eucharist as spiritual food and nourishment declined sharply while greater emphasis was placed on the sacred presence and pious adoration of the host itself. In the nominalist spirit of the times, the Eucharist, like the church, was more a distinct object of awe than a mystery requiring personal participation. Spirituality, too, became simple, direct, and almost nonsectarian, expressed to a great extent in what was called the *devotio moderna* (modern devotion), the uncomplicated, faddist spirituality of the time. Accessories to the spiritual life such as devotions to the saints, relics, and processions

---

[30] le Guillou, "The History of Ecclesiology," 316.

[31] Yves M. -J. Congar, *L'Eglise de Saint Augustin a l'époque moderne* (Paris: Les éditions du Cerf, 1970), 340.

multiplied, often obscuring Christ as the one mediator embodied in the mystery of Word and sacrament. It was an age of a new idolatry. As John Dwyer writes of the period, "There was an appalling lack of depth in the piety of the common people. Superstition was widespread, and the sacraments were often treated as a particularly effective form of magic." After the bubonic plague, or the Black Death (1348–1350), of the fourteenth century, people became obsessed with death and the tortures of purgatory. The goal of religious practice was merit, and achieving merit usually involved stipends—it was expensive to get out of purgatory. Masses for the dead, as well as priests to offer such Masses, multiplied in a grand effort to "guarantee a blissful existence in the future life."[32]

At the center of the church's life, tragic divisions existed: between piety and theology, between faith and reason, and between laity and clergy. Indeed, the separation between lay people and the ordained, as well as between lower and higher clergy, was acute. In terms of the church itself, its external aspect, especially the hierarchy, became more prominent as representing the whole church; hence, implicitly or explicitly, the church was understood and defined in this way. At the same time, the internal mystery of the church as Christ's body, prominent in the thought of the Fathers and Doctors of the Church, faded into the shadows.[33] The church in both its governance and its spiritual life was in desperate need of reform during these struggling years of the fifteenth century. A cataclysm awaited the institution in the radical reform of the Protestants in the next century.

An endless series of efforts at the reform of abuses in the Church took place in the second half of the fifteenth century, with each new pontificate showing promising signs that change would occur at last. The great cardinal and philosopher, Nicholas of Cusa (1401–1464) advanced one such courageous program of reform, prepared at the request of Pius II himself (1458–1464). Cusa identified the Roman Curia, the centralized bureaucracy that governed the Church, as the root cause of the Church's universal moral decay and recommended systematic reform from pope to peasant.[34] Unfortunately, his suggestions were not implemented and all other such efforts at reform during this time accomplished very little. In McNally's opinion, this period of true ecclesial *deformatio* (deformity, corruption) as a long and painful chapter in Church history remains a scandal that plagues Christians down to this

[32] Dwyer, *Church History*, 208–9.

[33] McNally, *Reform of the Church*, 34–36.

[34] McNally, 8

day.[35] The Church at the brink of the Reformation was adrift, consumed with unimportant questions, cut off from the faith of the apostles and martyrs, the Fathers and mystics. The energies of the popes of the period were likewise spent on peripheral matters at a time when both a strong visionary papacy and a spiritual renewal of the whole Church were desperately needed.[36] The litany of distractions from true reform from the thirteenth to the fifteenth centuries is long and complex: crusades against the incursions of Islam into Eastern Europe; a fixation with Renaissance life and art as well as a humanism as pagan as it was Christian; the politics and the political machinations of France, Spain, Germany, and all the Italian city-states; lavish enrichment of nephews, sons, and families of popes and cardinals; intrigues of major Roman families—the Orsinis, the Colonnas, the della Roveres, and the Borgias—who virtually controlled the papacy at this time. Abuses were also widespread: corruption in levying tithes and annates;[37] rampant nepotism where nephews of the pope were commonly named cardinals; the neglect of clerical celibacy and religious life in general; simony or the selling of church offices to the highest bidder; a lack of pastoral concern by the higher clergy due to flagrant episcopal absenteeism. At the time of the Council of Trent, for example, seventeen of the twenty-two bishops who held dioceses in France were permanently on leave in Rome enjoying high living of the Renaissance Eternal City; finally, the holding of the office of bishop in more than one diocese at the same time in order to collect more revenues. For example, the incompetent Bishop of Mainz, Germany during Luther's life held two other sees simultaneously.[38] The Church was on a path for disaster, but few people in power could see it, and if they could, they lacked the power or the will to do anything about it.

In addition, the Sacred Liturgy had been supplanted by questionable private devotional practices and placed at the core of Christian life. Likewise, heavy taxation to support the Church and the Roman Curia burdened the average Christian. This was especially true in Germany where Christians at every level of society were disgruntled at the burden of taxes just before the beginning of the Reformation. Sadly, the throne of Saint Peter had been

---

[35] See Yves M. -J. Congar, *Vraie et fausse réforme dans l'Eglise* (Paris: Les Éditions du Cerf, 1950), 356–57; defined by McNally, *Reform of the Church*, 103.

[36] For more information on the popes of the fifteenth century, see John A. Thomson, *Popes and Princes, 1417–1517: Politics and Polity in the Late Medieval church* (London: Allen and Unwin, 1980).

[37] Annates were payments of the first year's revenues made by a cleric to the papacy for a patronage appointment reserved to the Holy See; see Thomson, 216.

[38] Lortz, *How the Reformation Came*, 81.

transformed into another Renaissance princedom, and the pope's credibility as a universal spiritual leader was greatly diminished. The tragedy of the period was not merely in the abuses themselves but in the callous unconcern and indifference with which they were accepted on all sides.[39] For nearly three centuries, the cry for reform was heard on everyone's lips, yet the situation continued to deteriorate, reaching its nadir in the second half of the fifteenth century. The decay of the church, like a formal medieval procession, advanced under the logic of its own law.[40] In McNally's words, this decay was "a form of moral degradation that invaded the highest places in the Church in the last days of that century and prepared the way for the almost universal disaster of the sixteenth century."[41] It was the late autumn of the medieval world, only the popes and the cardinals of the time did not know it. Soon this world, awaiting the right catalyst, would collapse on top of them in a winter of discontent. The rulers of the *ecclesia* had lost themselves and their mission to preach the Gospels, feed the hungry, and heal the sick. Ecclesiology, by the standards of almost any other time, was embarrassingly narrow-minded, defensive, self-serving, and petty. As McNally says

> The writing was on the wall but it was not read; if it were read, it would not have been fully understood; and had it been fully understood, one wonders what measures would or could have been taken to turn back the overpowering tide which corruption, carelessness, irresponsibility, and abuse had created.[42]

Using the metaphor of windows, the Protestant historian Jaroslav Pelikan described the institutions of the Church at the Reformation this way:

> The institutions of the medieval papacy were in trouble, and everyone knew it. Intended as windows through which men might catch a glimpse of the eternal, they had become opaque, so that the faithful looked at them rather than through them. The structures of the Church were supposed to act as vehicles for the spirit—both for the spirit of God and the spirit of man....Instead what [an individual] found was a distortion of faith.[43]

---

[39] McNally, *Reform of the Church*, 90.

[40] Lortz, *How the Reformation Came*, 48.

[41] McNally, *Reform of the Church*, 100.

[42] McNally, 96.

[43] Jaroslav Pelikan, *Spirit versus Structure: Luther and the Institutions of the Church* (New York: Harper and Row, 1968), 5.

5.5 The Protestant Reformation

On October 31, 1517, Martin Luther, an Augustinian friar, posted his Ninety-five Theses to the door of the Wittenberg Cathedral. With this simple yet dramatic gesture, the separation and the splintering of the Christian world in the West had begun. Luther served as a catalyst to unleash the spirit of dissatisfaction and rebellion long festering within the consciousness of many Christians, especially Northern Europeans. This spirit, virulent in Germany, Switzerland, and England, brought the unity of the church to an abrupt end. From this time on, it is no longer strictly proper to speak of the church in the West but of churches in the plural. The idea of one Catholic Church, one expression of the Body of Christ, was no longer a historical reality; now it became a theological and eschatological ideal, that is, something no longer actual but an object of hope and desire. (The first tragic historical split to affect the church was the separation of the Orthodox church of the East from the Catholic Church in the West in 1054. Unfortunately, this story of theological debates, cultural differences, and political intrigues lies outside the scope of this volume.)

After 1517, the word "church" meant different things to different people, making the history of ecclesiology several histories as individual communities developed different identities and diverse self-understandings. The Catholic community, which once understood itself as "universal" as its name signifies, was now fragmented. For centuries, it failed to make the necessary reforms from within and inevitably suffered the consequences. Not until the sundering of Christendom did the Catholic tradition work to reform its spiritual and ecclesial life, rediscovering and renewing the meaning of church given to it from the beginning.

Thus, properly speaking, there was not one reformation but two—first, the Protestant and then the Catholic—sometimes inaccurately called the Counter-Reformation. Within Protestantism itself, the reform was not a single and united event but a number of nonsynchronous movements, each antagonistic to the others and sharing only the common thread of the rejection of Roman authority. One can study four clearly discernible strands within the Protestant Reformation, each with its own unique identity and different understanding of church polity: first, the Lutheran, grounded in the work of Martin Luther (1483–1546) and Philipp Melancthon (1497–1560); second, the Reformed, associated with Jean Calvin (1509–1564), Huldrych Zwingli (1484–1531), and William Farel (1489–1565), based in the city of Geneva; third, the Tudor or Anglican, instigated by King Henry VIII (1491–1547) and his dispute with Rome and Pope Clement VII over his marriage; finally, the Radical, which found expression in the Anabaptists, the Mennonites, the Hutterites, and other groups. The Radicals so completely redefined church polity and the practice of Christianity that they themselves were condemned and severely persecuted not only by Catholics but also by the mainstream reformers, Luther, Calvin, and Zwingli. They rejected both the hierarchical structure of the Catholic Church and presbyterian or synodal polity of the Reformers' church, accepting instead a spiritual and congregational view of the community in the form of a Free Church or a Believers' Church. As early as the first part of the sixteenth century, Sebastian Franck (1499–1543), a religious individualist and spiritualist, "coolly classified his contemporaries into four main groupings—Catholic, Lutheran, Zwinglian, and Anabaptist."[44] Thus, as a result of the Reformation, three kinds of church polity had emerged: the Catholic Church of Rome, the classical Protestant Church of Luther, Calvin, and Zwingli, and finally, the Church as the "Fellowship of the Spirit," represented by the radical reformers. This tripartite division, as we shall see, failed to delineate the primary difference between Luther and Calvin, a distinction that remains an important part of twenty-first-century Protestant America.

In an ideal history of the development of ecclesiology, each movement within Protestantism should be considered separately and, of course, always one in light of the other. The Reformation was not a seamless garment, but a most complex quilt of forces—theological, socioeconomic, and political—all set into motion by Luther's Ninety-five Theses. These forces—the breakdown of the medieval world, the profound discontent within the Church, the desperate need for both spiritual and institutional reform, the decline of papal authority and credibility, the emergence of the modern political state, and the desire of many for a different and more personal spirituality—had been present in the church and culture for some time and ready to be set free. As Lortz reminds us, "Revolutions are not simply created, they are released."[45] Wilhelm Neuss best describes this situation:

> If, without the slightest notion of the Reformation, we were suddenly transplanted into the religious-ecclesiastical situation of the year 1500, what would we see? A Catholic world with a rich, very rich Church life, numerous clergy, numerous monastic establishments; the Church,

[44] Donald F. Durnbaugh, *The Believers' Church: The History and Character of Radical Protestantism* (Scottsdale, PA: Herald, 1985), 22.

[45] Lortz, *How the Reformation Came*, 106.

> and no one else, the uncontested leader of all sectors of public and private life. And in a sudden, incomprehensible catastrophe, this world collapses. Until yesterday, the mothers of Nuremberg brought their daughters to the Poor Clares so that they might lead a nun's life of perfection. And "today"—the same mothers show up with horses and wagons, screaming and howling abuses to rescue their daughters by force of arms from a place of idolatry. Overnight, thousands of monks forget their vows and join Luther in reviling the monastic life in terms that cannot be outdone. What had happened? Life had undergone a profound change that had been long in coming—only nobody knew it. In its appearance, life had been Catholic, but it was an illusory picture.[46]

5.6 The Debate over Grace

Since our primary concern here is the history of what can now be called Roman Catholic ecclesiology, the significant questions from a Catholic theological perspective are these: What was the impact of the Protestant Reformation on the Roman Catholic Church's self-understanding? How effectively did the Catholic Church reform itself and change its ecclesiological abuses in response to the historical emergence of non-Catholic Christian traditions? Did the uniquely Catholic element in the church survive and flourish as a result of the tragedy of ecclesial estrangement? How has the ecclesiology of the Catholic Reformation affected Catholicism's self-understanding from the Council of Trent to this post-Vatican II era? Finally, what has Catholic ecclesiology learned from the Protestant Reformation? Put differently—and in a question that would shock the sixteenth century Catholic theologian—how has Catholic ecclesiology accepted a Protestant element within itself for a more comprehensive and complete vision of the church?

At the core of the Reformation and of the profound changes in the subsequent social life of Europe was the theological debate about grace: is it by grace alone that salvation or justification comes? What role do good works play in salvation? Luther's answer to this last question was the resounding *sola fide*, that is, God's saving grace transforms the person by *faith alone*. Only faith justifies the person, making the sinner just and righteous before God. Paul Tillich, the twentieth-century Lutheran theologian, corrects the popular misunderstanding about justification by faith by suggesting that the Lutheran doctrine of justification, strictly speaking, does not mean justification *by faith*

[46] Quoted in Lortz, 105.

but justification *by* grace *through faith*.[47] The grace of salvation is a gift of God alone through the revelation and mediation of Christ; faith is the human reception and response to divine grace. Nothing a human person does merits God's grace because it is God's pure gift. No church or sacrament is necessary for this grace to be effective; nothing need facilitate a person's response in faith.

For Luther and the other Reformers, the good news of the Gospels and Paul's message of righteousness had been swallowed up by a pharisaical and sometimes magical system of merit in Catholicism. Salvation was turned upside down: from God's utterly free gift to a human achievement through ritual, devotion, and a commitment to the Church as an institution, financially and politically. Of course, with the long-standing abuses in the Church and the inability or unwillingness of the institution to reform itself, the Reformers' position was not without cause and justification. In addition to their purely theological objections to Church authority, sociocultural, political, and economic factors, which helped create the acrimony between Protestants and Catholics that lasted for centuries, were also at work in the division not only within the Church but also throughout Europe itself. One must also add to this the confusion, misunderstanding, and ill will which reigned on both sides at the time. In this light, the Reformation appears as a tragic yet inevitable moment in the history of Western Christianity, as much of a debate about power, politics, and economics as it was about theology.

Still, in a narrower perspective, it is ironic that the debate over grace was unfortunately misplaced and misunderstood. The dilemma that the Reformation posed was not between grace and human effort or between faith and good works but a protest against the historically corrupt and distorted way in which human effort and good works appeared as a substitute for grace. Today we can acknowledge that what *appeared* to divide Christianity centuries earlier is no longer the issue. No Christian today, Protestant or Catholic, would disagree with Luther that it is God's grace alone that justifies and saves. Salvation is God's gracious and loving act, given freely to persons out of the infinity of divine love, not something merited by religious ritual or moral living. Ecclesiologically, the issue of the Reformation, then and now, is the manner in which God's saving grace becomes present, the form grace puts on to become effective in concrete life. Does grace take human and communal form? Is it inseparably bound to an institution with hierarchical authority—an

[47] Paul Tillich, *Systematic Theology*, vol. 2 (Chicago: University of Chicago Press, 1957), 79.

institution capable of corruption and the abuse of power? Put differently, the question of the Reformation is the question of the role the visible and historical church plays in divine salvation. Given the state of *deformatio* in the Church at the beginning of the sixteenth century, the visible church's role in Christian life was a stumbling block that many intelligent and committed Christians had to confront. It is of little wonder that Calvin returned to Augustine's idea of an invisible church of the elect and Luther rejected the visible, hierarchical priesthood, replacing it with the priestly ministry of every Christian.

This seminal debate about church and grace can be explored from a different point of view by asking this fundamental theological question: *finitum capax infiniti?* Is the *finite capable of the infinite*? Does God's grace come directly to the soul of the Christian in faith, justifying the person? Or can grace be embodied in the finite and fragile things of life, in the signs and rituals of the community, regardless of the worthiness of its ministers and members? Can justifying grace be made visible and celebrated in good works? Is grace incarnate in the finite order or not? The entire Catholic sacramental system depends on the answer to this particular question. If grace is present in the finite order, then it must exist as an intrinsic part of the human person, not foreign to human freedom and human action.

The Catholic understanding has always been that, in scholastic terms (it can be found in Aquinas), *gratia perficit naturam*, grace perfects or completes nature. Grace can and must be found within nature, within the visible and earthy realities of life, including human activity in which a person is engaged. Historically, neither the Lutheran nor Anglican reformations denied the capacity of the finite to embrace the infinite nor did these traditions reject the importance of sacramental mediation in the bestowal of salvific grace. The significant break with the traditional understanding of grace—and thus in the whole interpretation of Christianity—took place, first, with the ideas of Jean Calvin and others in the Reformed tradition and, second, with the so-called Radical Reformers. Calvin and the Reformers held that all things human and finite were corrupt, unable to serve as vessels of grace. In Protestant theology, this is called the "*extra Calvinisticum.*"[48]

Hence, for the Reformers, God justifies the soul directly, without the essential mediation of finite ritual and sacrament, priestly office, or ecclesial authority. The human person's freedom cannot be limited by sacramental

[48] See E. David Willis, *Calvin's Catholic Theology: The Function of the So-Called Extra Calvinisticum in Calvin's Theology* (Leiden: E. J. Brill, 1966).

mediation since salvation is the work of divine grace alone. The Radicals affirmed that there are no sacred words, no sacred things, no holy places, no sacred time, no special sacred person—sacredness and holiness can be found everywhere in the human heart.[49] On the other hand, in the Catholic view, human freedom and divine grace, present in sacramental form, cooperate in the work of salvation. This cooperation does not take place between partners as if God and the human person were equals who, in simplistic categories, divide up the saving operation. Rather their relationship is paradoxical: grace, by its embodiment in the things of the earth, allows personal freedom to act by itself for its own salvation. The Lutheran view is in complete agreement with the Catholic view, what is known in Lutheran theology as the "*infra Lutheranum*."[50] In reflecting the central paradox of grace in St. Paul, Karl Rahner writes that "the situation of this freedom to say Yes or No to God is not that of autonomous emancipated choice. When a person says No, it is his/her own work; when s/he freely says Yes, s/he must attribute this to God as God's gift."[51]

Ecclesiologically, if God's grace comes directly to the soul of the person through God's saving Word, the church for the Reformers must be understood as the fellowship of the justified or those persons predestined for grace. As a historical community, the church is the *congregatio fidelium* (the congregation of the faithful), the fellowship of the saved. For Calvin, membership in the Body of Christ is coextensive with the invisible church; not everyone in the visible church is necessarily predestined for salvation.[52] The church would not be, in the Catholic sense, a community that essentially mediates divine salvation and makes it present. The Catholic understanding of the church is intrinsically sacramental; the church itself is the sacrament of justifying grace, the unique finite, historical vessel of God's infinite saving power. This church possesses two interdependent elements: first, the congregation of the faithful mystically united in Christ; second, the visible means that brings such

---

[49] Walter Klaassen, *Anabaptism: Neither Catholic nor Protestant* (Waterloo, ON: Conrad Press, 1973), 11–13.

[50] See Carl Braten, *Principles of Lutheran Theology* (Minneapolis: Fortress Press, 1983).

[51] Karl Rahner, "Grace," in *Sacramentum Mundi: An Encyclopedia of Theology*, vol. 2 (New York: Herder and Herder, 1968), 420.

[52] See Jay, *The Church,* 169–76. Calvin himself is quite sacramental in his emphasis on divine concession to human weakness. Calvin*ism,* on the other hand, followed Zwingli's sacramental theology that placed much less emphasis on the external sacrament.

community about. God's saving grace exists and is accessible to persons in the structures, doctrines, priestly office, ecclesial authority, and sacramental rituals of the visible and historical church—albeit in finite and imperfect form. While grace is God's alone, God meets us where God finds us. For the Catholic, God's gift of salvation is mediated through the historical community, which is the earthly sacrament of Christ's heavenly body.

Although Catholic theology is in accord with the Protestant position of salvation by the grace of God alone, it also affirms that this saving or justifying grace is present *in* and *through* the historical and structural forms of the church. The church as a visible community, therefore, plays an essential role in making the grace of God actual and effective in human history. To paraphrase the Catholic theologian Karl Rahner, Christians are not so much persons in possession of grace; rather, they are vessels in and through which grace wishes to reveal itself visibly and historically.[53] Paul Tillich likewise acknowledges that grace cannot be present without a Gestalt, without some visible expression. Ecclesiologically, for Tillich this means that the visible church is "essentially a form of grace." In other words, the church as the Gestalt of grace means more than "merely pointing to the transcendent"; it must also be the "Glory of God made visible."[54] Thus, in the Catholic view, there is one church, visible and invisible, in which the visible embodies the invisible and brings it to form and historical life. In Yves Congar's terms, the one church, visible and invisible, is "a historically constituted society and a mystery of heavenly life."[55] With this fundamental truth in mind, the Second Vatican Council (1962–1965) has called the church the "sacrament of the world's salvation."[56] In this definition, the term church does not represent an invisible community of the saved but the historical, sociological, and hierarchical body in which divine grace takes on human, though imperfect, form.

---

[53] Karl Rahner, *Nature and Grace*: *Dilemmas in the Modern Church* (New York: Sheed and Ward, 1964), 92.

[54] Tillich, *The Protestant Era*, 25, 26, 212.

[55] Congar, *Lay People in the Church,* 33.

[56] *Lumen Gentium*, The Dogmatic Constitution on the Church, in *The Documents of Vatican II*, ed. Walter Abbott (New York: America-Guild Press, 1966), para. 9. The actual text of this most significant document reads "visible sacrament of this saving unity." The term "sacrament" is found four times in the conciliar documents: articles 1, 9, and 48 of *Lumen Gentium*, and article 5 of *Sacrosanctum Concilium*, The Constitution on the Sacred Liturgy.

5.7 The Catholic Response or Catholic Reformation

The Catholic Church, for more than a millennium unified and truly "catholic," had surrendered its homogeneous ecclesiology not for a simple, uniform alternative but rather a set of complex and different theologies of both grace and church polity that survive into our own time, especially on pluralistic American soil. After this breakdown of unity within Western Christianity and the emergence of diverse Christian churches, the Roman Catholic Church—given its history of *deformatio* in the two centuries prior to the Reformation—finally reestablished and purified its self-understanding in the reforms of the Council of Trent (1545–1563).[57] Post-Reformation Catholic ecclesiology has its foundation in this great council of the Catholic Reformation, during which most, but not all, of the abuses of the late Medieval and Renaissance Church were corrected. The reform of the clergy and the bishops was successfully accomplished at Trent. Less successful, however, was reform of the papacy and the papal bureaucracy, the curia, even though the cries for more than a century called for reform of the Church "in head and members." The final decrees of Trent were passed on December 4, 1563, under the pontificate of Pope Pius IV.

Ironically, the Council did not formally consider the Church or the papacy in a systematic way, perhaps out of its concern about reawakening the issue of Conciliarism and weakening the power of the papacy. However, as a response to the Protestant interpretation, it did examine the teaching of the Church on the sacrament of Holy Orders and the role of the bishops. In its theology, the Council addressed Luther's doctrine of the priesthood of all the faithful, denying Luther's belief that all Christians are priests of the New Testament endowed with equal spiritual power and authority. The classical Protestant tradition grounded the power of any individual to preach the Word and administer the sacraments by incorporation into the priesthood of Christ by baptism and the consent of the community. The Radical or Free Churches based their fellowship on personal and Spirit-moved experience and were suspicious of any formulae of faith, worship, ministry, and organization.[58] Trent, on the other hand, emphasized that the authority for ministry came from Christ himself and that this authority was passed down exclusively through

---

[57] For all of the documents of the Council of Trent, the best text can be found in Norman P. Tanner, ed., *Decrees of the Ecumenical Councils* (Washington, DC: Georgetown University Press, 1990).

[58] Angus Dun, *Prospecting for a United Church* (New York: Harper, 1948), 46–58.

the apostles and their successors; this authority could only be granted through priestly ordination.[59]

Before its end in 1563, the Council ordered the composition of a catechism that was to be written in the vernacular for the entire Catholic world. Drafted by Charles Borromeo, revised by a papal commission, and completed in 1566, it was published under Pope Pius V (who was later canonized, as was Charles Borromeo). Its structure of four sections—a theological exposition of the Apostles Creed, the seven sacraments, the Ten Commandments, and prayer—became normative for Catholic catechisms for centuries. Part one, chapter ten examines the creedal article "I believe in the Holy Catholic Church." In the first section, which discusses the word "church," the catechism cites Augustine's definition that the church "consists of the faithful dispersed throughout the world" and is comprised of all those persons "called by faith into the light of truth and the knowledge of God."[60] If this were all, many of the Reformers would have endorsed this definition just as it was, since they themselves were heavily indebted to Augustine's theology. But the catechism proceeds to identify the church with the "prelates and pastors," making it clear that the ultimate authority in the church is exercised by the Roman Pontiff and the curia. The church is thus identified exclusively with the Roman Catholic Church. All infidels, heretics, schismatics, and those excommunicated are excluded from this one, true church "until they repent." No reference is made in the catechism to the idea of an invisible church, though the distinction between a church militant on earth and a church triumphant in heaven, as constituent parts of one church, is present in the document as part of the discussion of the communion of saints. However, unlike Calvin's invisible church of the saved, the church militant on earth is composed of good and bad persons, like the chaff mixed with the wheat until the end of time. In the theological logic of the catechism, then, only baptized members of the visible Roman Catholic Church were considered members of the Body of Christ, be they worthy or not. By these criteria, all Orthodox Christians of the East and Protestants in the West, as either schismatics or heretics, were outside Christ's body. Furthermore, the Roman Catholic Church, marked by unity, holiness, catholicity, and apostolicity, was created not by human power but by the power of God. Not by human reason but only by faith is one able to understand and accept the Roman Catholic Church as the sole possessor of the keys to the Kingdom of heaven and the power to

---

[59] Gratsch, *Where Peter Is*, 126–27.

[60] Quoted in Jay, *The Church,* 197.

remit sin. While the church has one ruler, the invisible one, Christ himself, the visible ruler of the whole church on earth is the legitimate successor of Peter, the one who holds the See of Rome.[61]

The most prominent of the theologians of the Catholic Reformation was Robert Bellarmine (1542–1621), a Jesuit, a cardinal of the Church, and a saint. In his lectures called *Disputationes de controversiis christianae fidei* (Debates over the Controversies of the Christian Faith), Bellarmine presented a pointed response to the ecclesiological questions raised by the Protestant Reformers, especially their rejection of the visible structure of the church. He affirmed that Christ is the head of the universal church that includes the church militant on earth, the church suffering in purgatory, and the church triumphant in heaven. He insisted on the church as an ecclesiastical monarchy, and he emphasized the primacy of the Roman Pontiff, which dated from Peter himself as the first bishop of Rome. Bellarmine went so far as to believe that, while the apostles received their jurisdiction from Christ, their successors, the bishops, receive it only from the pope, the bishop of Rome. Likewise, in an opinion that anticipated the principal decree of the First Council of the Vatican in the nineteenth century, the pope had the authority to rule the entire church and all its members to the extent that his laws could oblige an individual's fidelity in conscience.[62]

Bellarmine, of course, is perhaps most remembered by Catholics of later times for his famous definition of the church that became the standard theological description of the Roman Catholic community until the changes of the Second Vatican Council. This definition was transcribed word for word in the *Baltimore Catechism* of the late nineteenth century and memorized by every American Catholic for generations. In Bellarmine's words, the church "is the congregation of persons bound together by profession of the same Christian faith and participation in the same sacraments under the government of legitimate pastors and especially of the one Vicar of Christ on earth, the Roman Pontiff."[63] While this definition maintains a rigorous Catholic orthodoxy, most notable is the criteria for church membership as well as what it neglects to say about the mystery of the church. First, people are not members of the church by predestination, grace, or charity; membership requires only visible participation in the hierarchical community by accepting the doctrines of the church, visibly receiving the sacraments, and submitting to the

[61] Jay, *The Church*, 199–201.

[62] Gratsch, *Where Peter Is*, 129–30.

[63] Quoted in Gratsch, 130.

rule of pope and legitimate pastors. Thus, people who publicly profess the faith but do not believe in their hearts are church members; those who believe in their hearts but do not publicly profess the faith, are not members of the church.[64] Second, neglected in the definition is Jesus himself and his preaching on the Kingdom of God, his death and Resurrection as central to the inner mystery of the church, and the Holy Spirit as the soul of the church and the source of its spiritual life. By answering the Protestant Reformers, Bellarmine created a one-sided apologetic for ecclesial visibility and hierarchical structure. His influence on the understanding of the church since Trent has been enormous, and his conception of the papal power became the foundation of the First Vatican Council's definition of papal infallibility (1869–1870). Pope Pius XII repeated his limited and confining norms for membership in the church in the twentieth century in his encyclical *Mystici Corporis* (The Mystical Body of Christ) in 1943.[65]

In the second half of the sixteenth century, the Church of the Catholic Reformation succeeded in saving its institutional identity. Through Bellarmine and others, such as Thomas Stapleton (1535–1598), who examined the relationship of the papacy to temporal power, Ignatius Loyola (1491–1556), the founder of the Society of Jesus, and Francisco Suárez (1548–1617), who established the beginnings of a modern understanding of church and state, the Roman Catholic Church survived the loss of almost half of Europe to the Protestant Reformers. In its own reformation, or as some prefer, the counter-reformation, Catholicism was successful in eliminating those glaring abuses which plagued the church in the fourteenth and fifteenth century.[66] Seminaries were established to train future priests properly, new regulations for bishops promulgated, and more authority was centralized in the Roman government of the Church. In the area of liturgy, more uniformity was established in response to abuses and superstitions that were prevalent in the late medieval period. With the publication of the Roman breviary in 1568, the Roman missal in 1570, and the Roman ritual for administration of the sacraments in 1614, the entire Western Church adopted a common mode of worship. Ecclesiologically, this was to have significant implications: while removing many of the abuses which plagued the Church in an earlier era, it also, as one

---

[64] Dulles, *Models of the Church*, 16.

[65] Dulles, 132.

[66] For a discussion of the terms "Catholic Reformation" and "Counter-Reformation," see John O'Malley, *Trent and All That: Renaming Catholicism in the Early Modern Era* (Cambridge, MA: Harvard University Press, 2000).

commentator suggests, "encouraged the idea that Rome was the norm of ecclesiastical life in all areas, and that one must go to Rome for the solution of all problems."[67] The Roman Catholic Church was forced by the political and theological circumstances after the Reformation to become ever more centered in the supremacy of Roman authority and less and less "catholic" in the ancient meaning of the term. The spirit of this Tridentine (that is, the Council of Trent) ecclesiology survived with very few changes until the Second Vatican Council in the mid-twentieth century.

Before leaving the Council of Trent, an important distinction must be made between the Council itself and the system of thought that emerged in its implementation called "Tridentinism." Many progressive Catholics in the post-Vatican II era mistakenly see Trent as the source of ecclesial intransigence in recent times. Trent itself was a pastoral council with its primary goal to restore the visible church to its spiritual roots in the mission of the Gospel. It was concerned primarily with the *cura animarum*, the care of souls. The danger facing the Catholic Church in the second half of the sixteenth century was the implementation of the conciliar decrees. There were significant pockets of opposition by some bishops and priests to the demands that the council would inevitably make on the lives. Pope Sixtus IV took implementation of Trent very seriously. Giuseppe Alberigo, the distinguished historian of the church from Trent to Vatican II, writes:

> In the five short years of his reign (1585–1590), Sixtus V launched an array of institutional changes that would have ramifications for centuries to come. Not all of these initiatives directly concerned the implementation of the council, but each one strongly influenced the way the council was received, sometimes far more than many official decisions about interpretation.[68]

Some of these changes related directly to the council, such as the obligation of all bishops to make a visit *ad limina apostolorum* (i.e., to the threshold of the apostles) every five years. Another was the centralization, again in Rome, of the process for nominating bishops. The reports of nuncios, rather than those of cities or provincial councils, came to govern these nominations.

---

[67] O'Malley, 137.

[68] Giuseppe Alberigo, "From the Council of Trent to 'Tridentinism,'" trans. Emily Michelson, in *From Trent to Vatican II: Historical and Theological Perspectives*, ed. Raymond F. Bulman and Frederick J. Parrella (New York: Oxford University Press, 2006), 35.

A third was the production of an official edition of the "Sistine" Vulgate (1590) as an instrument for controlling the use of the Bible. Other changes concerned the *reformatio in capite* (reform of the head), which the popes had vigorously opposed at the council. These included the bull *Immensa Aeterni Dei* (1587) The Immensity of the Eternal God, which instituted Roman congregations as regular and standard tools of government; these congregations were committees of cardinals, each assigned to a particular sphere of competence. Such innovations signaled the inexorable decline of the Consistory as an entity for governing the universal church, and at the same time, paved the way for Rome to intervene much more frequently and thoroughly in individual dioceses. Even the decisions of diocesan and provincial synods came under centralized, lengthy, and sometimes financial scrutiny.[69]

In short, the system called Tridentinism, described by Yves Congar as "an all-embracing system of theology, ethics, Christian behavior, religious practices, liturgy, organization and Roman centralization brought about by the reforms of the Council of Trent," had begun.[70] Giuseppe Alberigo's distinction between the reforms of Trent and post-Tridentine legislation and implementation is crucial for understanding the pastoral nature of Trent itself, subsequent ecclesiological developments in the centuries to follow, and the context and text of Vatican II as well as post-conciliar ecclesiology into the new millennium.

[69] Alberigo, chap. 2.

[70] Congar, *Fifty Years of Catholic Theology*, 3–4.

6.

THE TRIDENTINE CHURCH: THE SIXTEENTH TO THE NINETEENTH CENTURIES

6.1 In the Aftermath of the Protestant Reformation

The hemorrhage of the faithful during the Protestant Reformation forced the Catholic Church to take the necessary steps toward significant reform. The cry for reform had gone unheeded for centuries and tragically only the cleavage within Western Christianity compelled Catholicism to respond. The Catholic Church took steps to correct many of the ecclesiastical abuses in its household and restored a much healthier spiritual and institutional life. Yet, as a result of this Catholic reformation in the sixteenth century, there persisted an ecclesiology marked by the historical pattern of one-sidedness that had characterized formal ecclesiology since the fourteenth century. This emphasis on the visible, hierarchical church had unfortunate consequences in light of the many ecclesiastical and political questions facing the church in the centuries to come. While the Fathers and the medieval theologians understood the church in its spiritual and sacramental nature as an organic reality intimately linked to Christ and the Spirit, the first written ecclesiologies were narrowly focused defenses of institutional and papal power. With its decline in the fourteenth and fifteenth centuries, the Church was reduced to a temporal princedom, which was constantly under siege from both within and without. In response to the tragic split of Christian Europe during the time of the Protestant Reformers, the Church (henceforth signifying the Roman

Catholic Church, although some recent developments in Protestant ecclesiology will be considered later) was successful in reforming itself in light of many of the social and political abuses that had plagued it in earlier centuries. Doctrinal questions were clarified, and liturgical practices were made uniform.

Unfortunately, however, in response to the Protestant Reformers who denied the essential nature of the visible church, the Catholic tradition was forced to defend its visible and institutional identity, including the authority of the Roman Pontiff, *even more forcefully* in the centuries following the Reformation itself. Put differently, the traditional pattern in ecclesiology that underscored the visible and institutional elements within the church continued; the church was mired in an apologetic and defensive ecclesiology in response to all the forces that threatened its existence. This inevitably tended to reduce the church as the historical mystery of God's grace to its visible and societal manifestations. More than Trent itself, the legislation and implementation of the Council under Sixtus V was the major factor in creating this ecclesiological one-sidedness and the emphasis on centrality and authority that defended and supported it.

The historical roots of this ecclesiological pattern lie, as we have noted, in the late medieval and early Renaissance application of political and sociological categories to the church's self-understanding. From the twelfth century onward, by modeling itself on the emerging state, the church was transformed from a divine mystery of historical grace to a "perfect society" open to examination and interpretation by the same categories applied to society as a whole. Ecclesial hermeneutics—the levels of the church's interpretation and understanding of itself—had shifted. The church as mystery, the dominant theme in the ecclesiology of the patristic and medieval periods, had been submerged while the model of the church as perfect society became the ecclesiological norm. Add to this picture a second factor: the tendency towards civil government by absolute monarchy within the broader society, visible from the end of the thirteenth century onward, was transferred to the "perfect society" of the church. Thus, more and more power was centered in the Roman Pontiff and the Roman Curia. (The Curia comprised the congregations or departments of government of the Roman ecclesiastical establishment). The ideal in which the church was the goal and model of secular society had been reversed; ecclesial self-understanding no longer began in eternity, as with the Pastor Hermas, but on earth in the monarchies and oligarchies of civil governments.

Not unlike the kings and royal courts of the seventeenth century, in the aftermath of the Council of Trent, the Church understood itself, implicitly and explicitly, as a pyramid society with the pope at the summit of authority surrounded by his own papal court. The pope and the Curia ruled the church with supreme power. Perhaps Francis I (1515–1547), the flamboyant French monarch of the sixteenth century, served as a more accurate model of absolutist papal government than did the Bishops of Rome of the first few centuries; they held the church together while the church was a "contrast society" and often subject to persecution.[1] In Yves Congar's words, the post-Reformation Church understood itself "not as an organism animated by the Holy Spirit but as a society or rather even an organization where Christ intervened at its origin as its founder and the Holy Spirit as the guarantor of its authority."[2] One could justifiably argue, of course, that the times required a Church of absolute authority and uniformity, given the doctrinal confusion, spiritual and moral decay, and the loss of papal credibility in the fourteenth and fifteenth centuries. Such authority seemed even more necessary for the survival of the Roman Church after the emergence of the churches of the Reformation in the sixteenth century. The fact remains, however, that this ecclesial model, perhaps necessary during the Catholic Reformation to correct the pervasive abuses of the pre-Reformation Church, unfortunately assumed an eternal character of its own, becoming the norm of ecclesiological understanding for the five centuries to follow. Thus, not until the Second Council of the Vatican did Catholic ecclesiology attempt to move beyond the apologetic and triumphalist Tridentine ecclesiology of the sixteenth to the nineteenth centuries.

After Trent, the Roman Catholic Church, once master of medieval Europe at the beginning of the thirteenth century, was forced to withdraw into its own safe harbor, besieged on all sides by civil and religious powers. Nevertheless, the Church in the fractious sixteenth century triumphed in its own way, uniform in its faith and secure to its own supreme authority. By the beginning of the seventeenth century, Catholic theology quite naturally concerned itself with the consolidation of the doctrinal achievements of Trent. In response to the Protestant emphasis on Scripture alone as the source of faith, the Roman Catholic Church also reaffirmed tradition in addition to Scripture as a locus of ecclesial authority. Unfortunately, the focus of Catholic theology was not its commitment to a balanced exposition of the Christian mysteries but a polemical stand on the inadequacies and errors in the

---

[1] The term "contrast society," as mentioned above, is from Dulles, *Models of the Church*, 204.

[2] Congar, *L'Eglise de Saint Augustin a l'époque moderne*, 382–83.

Protestant teachings on grace, the nature and authority of the church, and the meaning of the sacraments.[3] The seventeenth and eighteenth centuries provide ample evidence of a Church in Rome that remained defensive against various challengers to its authority. Much of the Church's post-Reformation theology, and particularly the ecclesiology implicitly present in all of it, was protective of its supreme authority and defensive about its claims to possess the absolute truth of Revelation. Surprisingly, even in the midst of this Catholic-Protestant debate, the Church had not given its formal ecclesiology a fundamental reconsideration; though many theological issues implied the question of the meaning of church, systematic ecclesiology surprisingly remained "relatively peripheral" to the overall theology in the Church.[4]

6.2 Jansenism

In the middle of the seventeenth century, the authority of the Catholic Church was threatened again by a movement called Jansenism, named after Cornelius Jansen, the Bishop of Ypres, France, who died in 1638. While the ecumenical councils of the Church during its early centuries had struggled with the formal theological definitions of the Trinity and the person of Christ, they had little to say about sin and grace. This essential dimension of Christian life and faith, which was at the core of much of the argument between the Reformers and the Catholic Church, now became a major problem within the Catholic tradition itself. The central question was the relationship of human freedom and God's saving grace. The Louvain professor, Michael Baius (de Bay) (died 1589), believed that because of original sin, human nature is intrinsically corrupt and all human actions are necessarily sinful. This was much closer to Calvin than to the Scholastic understanding of nature and grace. Although Pope Pius V condemned the substance of Baius's teaching in 1567, the theological battle over the power of human freedom and the irresistibility of God's grace raged during the last third of the sixteenth century. The principal protagonists were the Portuguese Jesuit Luis Molina, a strong defender of free will and human activity, and the Spanish Dominican Dominic Banez, an ardent proponent of the irresistibility of God's grace and will in the process of salvation. The debate between Jesuits and Dominicans on grace versus free will, first begun during this time, continues to this day and remains

[3] Pelikan, *The Christian Tradition*, 4:374–75.

[4] Jaroslav Pelikan, *The Christian Tradition: A History of the Development of Doctrine*, vol. 5, *Christian Doctrine and Modern Culture (since 1700)* (Chicago: The University of Chicago Press, 1989), 288–89.

unresolved.[5]

While this debate between Molina and Banez took place within orthodox confines, Jansen once again took up the more radical opinions of the condemned theologian Baius. Jansen's three-volume work, *Augustinus*, which appeared two years after his death in 1640, affirmed, in the spirit of Baius, that human nature was so radically corrupted by original sin that free human action was virtually impossible. Salvation could come only through the love of God which creates faith and which was predestined for the individual. To many Catholics, this was Calvinism in Catholic clothes, for one could argue the theory of Jansenism was the Catholic counterpart to the most rigid and puritanical strand within the theology of the Protestant Reformers. After a decade of careful examination, the ideas of Jansen, like those of Baius before him, were condemned by Pope Innocent X in 1653. Jansenism, as a system of thought, however, remained a powerful force within the Church and, as one commentator states, tragically "died a slow death."[6] It was continually brought to life again, taking different forms in a number of subsequent theological works, most notably Pacquier Quesnel's *Reflexions morales* (Moral Reflections) in 1693. This work, attacked by the renowned churchman Francois Fénelon, Archbishop of Cambrai, was finally condemned by Pope Clement XI in his bull *Unigenitus* (Only Begotten) of 1713.[7]

Centered at the celebrated abbey of Cistercian nuns, Port-Royal in northern France, Jansenism attracted many intellectual and spiritual elites as converts, including the famous mathematician and philosopher, Blaise Pascal (1623–1662).[8] After a profound religious conversion in 1654, Pascal entered the Jansenist community there. His *Pensées*, published posthumously in 1669, contains a summary of ecclesiology emphasizing the importance of tradition and the church of the past for the church of the present. In his discussion of the papacy, his strongly negative reaction to the papal condemnation of Jansenism is clear. Thus, in spite of its official condemnation, with powerful intellectuals such as Pascal sympathetic to its principles, Jansenism survived and remained an influential system of thought in the Church in a number of ways. The Irish, persecuted by the English in the eighteenth century, sent many

---

[5] Gratsch, *Where Peter Is*, 142.

[6] Gratsch, 142.

[7] Gratsch, 142. See also L. Cognet, "The Jansenist Conflict to 1713," in *The History of the Church*, ed. Hubert Jedin and John Dolan, vol. 6, *The Church in the Seventeenth Century* (New York: Crossroad, 1981), 41–57.

[8] Pelikan, *The Christian Tradition*, 4:374–85.

seminarians for study to northern France where they inevitably came under Jansenist influence. Since human nature was corrupted by the fall of our first parents, matter and everything human was highly suspect. In the nineteenth century these same Irish, trained by French Sulpicians, brought the Catholic faith to America, leaving an indelible confusion toward the material world in general, and sexuality in particular, in the American Catholic psyche. Many American Catholics, nurtured in this type of faith, continued to identify sin with the individual's sexuality well into middle of the twentieth century. Only with the Second Vatican Council has a healthier attitude toward sexuality emerged along with a broader and more comprehensive understanding of Christian morality that includes social and economic justice. It is also from Jansenism that the idea of infrequent Holy Communion or Communion only after confession had its origin. Religious people, concerned about their worthiness, often refrained from communion for months, even years. In regions affected by Jansenism, its influence survived well into the twentieth century.[9] Thus, within both Roman Catholic theology and popular Church culture, the Jansenist spirit indeed died a very slow death.

Jansenism's impact on ecclesiology was two-fold: first, as a threat to Christian life, it required papal intervention, an action that once again weakened papal authority. It forced the Holy See to continue its defensive position and prevented it from assuming a more positive role as the leader of Christian spiritual life. Second, Jansenism also affected Catholic ecclesiology at a much deeper level. In its condemnation of the intrinsic, created goodness of human nature, it implicitly denied the human mediation of the church, its sacraments, and its human structures of authority. In creating a type of pessimism toward the created world, it muted what was truly and invaluably Catholic in this post-Reformation time: God's presence within the things of the earth, within the human community called church, within the church's visible signs and sacraments, and, finally, within the visible authority of the pope and the bishops as successors of the apostles. While claiming to be rigorously Catholic, the Jansenists ironically weakened the foundation of the most necessary part of Catholicism in this post-Reformation era, a strong church authority.

6.3 Gallicanism

The Catholic Church, especially Church authority and the institution of the

---

[9] Louis Dupre, "Jansenism and Quietism," in *Christian Spirituality: Post Reformation and Modern*, ed. L. Dupre and D. Saliers (New York: Crossroad, 1989), 124–25.

papacy, was further threatened by Gallicanism and its parallel movements of Febronianism and Josephinism. Gallicanism (from *Gallia*, the Latin word for France), a product of the French Church, was a theory that attempted to restrict the central authority of the papacy by subordinating it to either the civil power of the king or the ecclesiastical power of local bishops. The political roots of Gallicanism can be discovered as far back as the controversy between King Philip IV and Boniface VIII at the end of the thirteenth century when Philip claimed ecclesiastical power over Church offices. Its theological foundation is grounded in the theory of Conciliarism of the Council of Constance in the fifteenth century, which asserted the superiority of the bishops in ecumenical council over the pope. Gallicanism must be understood as not simply a battle between a united Church and civil rulers but a conflict within the Church itself. In the French Church, both the king and the bishops demanded a dimension of autonomy from the Roman Pontiff in civil as well as ecclesiastical governance. The classic Four Articles of Gallicanism, drawn up by Bishop Bossuet of Meaux and passed in 1682 at a general assembly of the French clergy called by Louis XIV, limited the authority of the Holy See in matters of faith and jurisdiction. These articles state that in matters of faith, the judgment of the pope is not final until the whole Church also adds its own assent. They also require the pope to conform to the customs and the law of the French Church and affirm, in accord with the conciliar theory, that the authority of general councils is superior to the pope as an individual.[10]

Condemned by two popes, the articles of Gallicanism were ultimately withdrawn by King Louis XIV in 1693, eleven years after he had sanctioned them with his own authority. Sometime after, a compromise between the Holy See and the French king and the French bishops was negotiated. The spirit of Gallicanism, the spirit of independence from Rome and local ecclesial autonomy, survived, however, and continued to challenge the central authority of the papacy until the First Vatican Council in 1870. With the loss of the papal states, Church authority was no longer grounded in civil politics as it had been since the time of Constantine in the fourth century; consequently, it was much less of a threat to secular governments. With the declaration of papal infallibility, the Vatican was free for the first time since the early Middle Ages to exercise its autonomous jurisdiction over the entire Church.

Ecclesiologically, the theories of Conciliarism and Gallicanism represent one historical pole in understanding the human mystery of the church and the source of its historical authority. These two theories stand in sharp contrast

---

[10] Gratsch, *Where Peter Is*, 144–46; see also Jay, *The Church*, 225–26.

to the opposite pole, the theory of "ultramontanism," which required all matters of faith and ecclesiastical governance to be referred to Rome and to papal authority. In contrast, Gallicanism demanded jurisdictional power for civil rulers in ecclesiastical matters as well as autonomy of local bishops to teach and govern the Church. Both schools in the history of ecclesiology have appeared under different forms and with different names throughout the centuries. Ideally, both of these elements should exist in a living and creative tension with each other. Practically, the history of the church tells a very different story. Theologically, universal agreement exists that the power of governance and authority in matters of faith come ultimately from the Holy Spirit, who is the soul of the church. The classical Gallican debate focused attention on where and how this authority should find its concrete historical expression: does it reside solely in the papacy or do bishops and civil rulers have a role to play in governing the Church?

With the advent of democracy and the *de facto* if not *de jure* separation of church and state in the nineteenth century, political Gallicanism ceased to be the same burning ecclesiological issue it was in the seventeenth. Rarely are Catholic ecclesiologists concerned with the infringement on the Church's spiritual power by kings and secular rulers. In most places, the Church has apparently won its final victory for political independence in the triumph of complete ecclesiastical jurisdiction in every local church as well as its freedom, at least in theory, from all political interference in internal Church affairs. This necessary victory has also carried a price, of course, the price of centralization and the creation of a Church that is theologically and structurally monolithic. In today's post-Vatican II Church, while most ecclesiologists affirm that the power and authority to govern the church must be fully present in the Roman Pontiff and the Roman congregations, they also believe that this authority must come to life in local, regional, and national communities of Christians under the leadership of the bishop. As cultural and theological diversity becomes a reality within what Karl Rahner calls a truly "world church," not simply a European church, the question of a central monarchical papacy and curia with supreme juridical power over the universal church needs constant theological reexamination in light of our changing social and cultural situation.[11] "Gallicanism" and "Conciliarism" thus reemerge in new forms without the serious threat to Roman authority at the political level they once

[11] Karl Rahner, "The Abiding Significance of the Second Vatican Council," in *Concern for the Church: Theological Investigations,* vol. 20 (New York: Crossroads, 1981), 90–102.

were. Now they suggest, in accord with a jurisdictional diversity to correspond to the Church's growing philosophical and cultural diversity, that the supreme authority of the Roman Pontiff must exist side by side with the collegial spirit of all the bishops and their unique sacramental charism to govern their local churches.

In the eighteenth century, Gallicanism once again took historical form in a German context through the ideas of the bishop of Trier, who, under the pseudonym of Justinus Febronius, wrote *On the Present State of the Church and the Legitimate Power of the Roman Pontiff*. Inspired by the Church in France, complaints by German Catholics against the Holy See, and a Germany split between Protestants and Catholics, Febronius, as Edward Gratsch says, "questioned the role of the papacy as it actually functioned at that time."[12] Febronius asserted that since the ninth century, the administration of the Church had been too centered in the papacy. He believed the power of the keys was given to the whole Church, not just the Holy See, and recommended such radical changes for the times as popular education, general councils, and national synods as ways of restoring proper balance between the centralized authority of the Roman Pontiff and the universal Catholic community. The discussion in today's Church on the teaching authority of national and regional bishops' conferences recasts for our own time some of the same questions raised by Febronius two centuries ago.[13]

Likewise, Josephinism, named after Joseph II (1741–1790), the Hapsburg Emperor of Austria, was another political form of Gallicanism that strongly resembled Febronianism. Emperor Joseph espoused the view that the church was an agency of the state and that the clergy were primarily responsible for the social welfare of citizens. He took over seminary education, permitted local bishops in place of Rome to grant certain matrimonial dispensations, and redrew the boundaries of both parishes and dioceses. This situation compelled Pope Pius VI to travel to Vienna in 1782 to negotiate concessions from the emperor, although many of Joseph's reforms remained in place until the end of the monarchy and the beginning of World War I. Once again, Josephinism, like Febronianism and Gallicanism, forced Church authority into defensive positions and weakened the bond between the Bishop of Rome and the universal church. In these movements, unlike the reforms of the sixteenth century, the attack came not from those poised to leave the Church

[12] Gratsch, *Where Peter Is*, 147.

[13] See Avery Dulles, "Episcopal Conferences: Their Teaching Authority," *America* 162 (1990): 7–9.

but loyal children of the household who were adjusting to the Church's role in an emerging political, social, and intellectual milieu. Gallican and Febronian ideas were not limited to particular schools of thought but were indications of a deep and hostile attitude towards Rome widely held throughout Catholic Europe.[14] Whatever remained of the medieval view of the church was now dead; the modern world, with a new understanding of the church, the state, and their interrelationship, was taking form.

6.4 The Enlightenment or the Age of Reason

The eighteenth century has often been called in retrospect the Age of Reason or the Enlightenment (in German, the *Aufklärung*), a period in which reason triumphed over supernaturalism, individualism over community, empirical data over given philosophical absolutes, and human resourcefulness over divine revelation. Philosophical rationalism and classicism in art and literature flourished throughout the period. In religion, the rationalist worldview was tempered by pietism, a spirituality in which feelings triumphed over ideas and heart over mind. By the end of the century, the romantic reaction took place in which emotion had vanquished reason. If one listens to a Mozart or Haydn symphony and then listens to a symphony of the late Beethoven, Mendelssohn, or Schubert, one will clearly understand the world of difference between classicism and romanticism. Descartes (d. 1650), Leibniz (d. 1677), and Spinoza (d. 1716), all rationalists, had prepared the way for the Enlightenment a century earlier. Isaac Newton (d. 1727) discovered the inner secrets of the universe. Likewise, Locke (d. 1704), Berkeley (d. 1753), and David Hume (d. 1776) established human experience, empiricism, and experimentation as the norm of what is real. With the notable exception of Hume, most of the significant thinkers of the age were not unbelievers. In the rationalist spirit of the day, they accepted a God who, as Locke says, is "the most obvious truth that reason discovers" and a truth "equal to mathematical certainty."[15] Yet, in the popular mode of religious thought known as deism, God exists but is aloof and transcendent; God creates the order of the universe and places upon humanity the task of discovering through human reason the rational structure of the created world and the laws established in creation. "Natural religion," what humanity could determine from the laws of nature based upon reason,

[14] Roger Aubert et al., *The Church Between Revolution and Restoration*, vol. 7, History of the Church Series, ed. Hubert Jedin and John Dolan (New York: Crossroad, 1981), 3.

[15] Quoted in Jay, *The Church*, 220.

was the cry of the day. In eighteenth-century thought, with God cut off from human affairs, social life was reordered on an expanding secular basis with the influence of religious truth on the practical life of people waning or disappearing. People no longer defined their identity solely by participation in a religious community; individuals gradually became more autonomous and free from all clerical and political authorities.[16]

Few treatises on the church of any significance were written during this period, and the initial impact of rationalism on formal ecclesiology, found in the catechisms and other documents of faith of the eighteenth century, was minimal or invisible. The Church categorically rejected rationalism, deism, or the triumph of reason in any form over faith. The Church, however, in spite of its efforts, could not change the world that was being born. Classical doctrines along with clerical authority came under attack. In a deist world, in which God is the ground of the reasonable, the starting point of Christian theology, the mystery of God's revelation, was obviously called into question. For the rationalists, the power of human reason made divine revelation unnecessary. Especially for the empiricists, who developed the understanding that knowledge is derived from sense experience, revelation was the remnant of an older superstition. Perhaps only John Locke, in his work, *The Reasonableness of Christianity*, affirmed that, in addition to the existence of God that was provable by reason, God also revealed Godself through the Sacred Scriptures.[17]

In the light of the rationalist thinking of the times, the ecclesiology in some Protestant communities transformed the church into a reasonable and ethical society in which toleration and denominationalism was accepted. While this period was a difficult time for all the churches, this was especially true of the Roman Catholic Church. The impact of rationalism on Catholic ecclesiology took a different and more threatening form. In a reasonable world with the transcendent God as the source of the natural order, the traditional supernaturalism of Catholicism became suspect. Why would it be necessary for humanity to attain the supernatural state of grace when God's law for the universe could be rationally discovered within the natural order of creation? Hence, the Catholic Church and its claims to divine authority for itself were viewed as unnecessary. Likewise, sacraments were called into question; the special mediation between the natural order and the supernatural order of grace was hardly important in a world that could discover divinity and divine

---

[16] Aubert et al., *The Church Between Revolution and Restoration*, 7:4.

[17] Jay, *The Church*, 221.

law with the power of reason alone. Thus, rationalism posed another threat and a challenge to the theology and the authority of Catholicism, requiring the Church to be ever more defensive against forces both outside and within. In short, Catholic ecclesiology of the period was defined not only by its anti-Protestant and anti-Gallican point of view but also its war over supernatural revelation with the rationalist thinkers from the eighteenth century onward. For Catholic theologians, the full mystery of the church remained submerged in an effort to defend the nature of divine revelation and to assert the validity and the authority of the institutional and hierarchical structure of the Church that for centuries had been under attack.

In this defensive posture that was often reduced, in Roger Aubert's phrase, to "stereotype and sterile protest," the Catholic Church grew weaker from within. Rome, with its antiquated modes of expression, unfortunately rejected any dialogue with the changing currents of thought that the Church encountered in the birth of the modern world. While the Holy See itself was immeasurably rich with countless privileges, including the support of the state, the Church's real authority in the personal and social affairs of Christian life was seriously weakened. Furthermore, the spiritual supremacy of the papacy was greatly reduced by the pope's role as a small Italian territorial ruler, made worse by the papal reputation of being backward and absolutist in governance.[18] The distinction between the universal spiritual authority of the papacy and the pope's political power over his territories was not yet clear; hence, to call one into question was to question the other at the same time. Furthermore, the man who filled the papacy for the last quarter of the eighteenth century, Pius VI (1775–1800), unfortunately revived the nepotism and other highly questionable policies of the late medieval papacy. At the crucial time of the breakdown of the *ancien régime* and the outbreak of the French Revolution, the Pontiff "lacked energy and acuity" and tended to be "absorbed by secondary problems of prestige."[19] Thus, the Church during this time interpreted any change in the social, political, and intellectual world as a threat to the status quo to which it was inseparably wed. Instead, the Church championed an understanding of both the theoretical and practical world that was immutable and closed to any progress. In Roger Aubert's words:

The disparity between a world which was in the process of full

[18] Aubert et al., *The Church Between Revolution and Restoration*, 7:3.

[19] Aubert et al., 9. Aubert and his coauthors suggest that while Pius IV was later idealized as a martyr because of his sufferings in the last years of his pontificate, there is a significant difference between the myth and the reality.

> economic, social, and cultural development and that of a clerical hierarchy which was simply incapable of differentiating between the real requirements of faith and the nonessential accessories with which the church and religion had surrounded themselves in the course of centuries became evident. The church clung tenaciously to completely obsolete positions.[20]

6.5 Ecclesiology in the Nineteenth Century

In order to comprehend fully the texture of Roman Catholic ecclesiology today, a careful study of the forces both outside and inside of the Church in the nineteenth century is essential. Twenty-first-century ecclesiology was shaped by the theological, philosophical, social, and political patterns of thought of the nineteenth century, so much so that the reforms of the Church at the Second Vatican Council (1962–1965) can be interpreted as both a reaction to, and development and completion of, the same ecclesiological forces a century earlier. These forces found their fullest expression at the First Council of the Vatican (1869–1870), which proposed a comprehensive treatise on the Church for the first time, yet all it accomplished was a definition of papal infallibility and Roman authority. The tension between the forces of liberalism and reaction, present within the Church during much of the nineteenth century, especially at Vatican I, approximates the shape and configuration of our own post-Vatican II Church and serves as an important lens into present day ecclesiological conflicts.

This "intra-ecclesia" (inside the church) view is only one part of the picture. Theologians do not create ecclesiology in a vacuum: the Church lives in a particular cultural milieu with philosophical, political, and socioeconomic forces, all influencing the way the church understands itself. The changing world context—demographic, governmental, social, economic, political—affect changes in points of view that in turn change both the way theologians perform their task and their particular conclusions. From the late medieval period, solidified at the Council of Trent, the church's ecclesiology was self-contained, that is, it developed out of certain *a priori* presuppositions that came from within the Church's tradition itself. Since its formal inception at the beginning of the fourteenth century, Catholic ecclesiology was primarily concerned with institutional protection and the mundane modification of ecclesiastical structures. Of course, political and social contexts were always a factor in ecclesiology, but they possessed the power to bring about change in

[20] Aubert et al., 3.

any theologically normative position *only* in a negative and defensive way. In most cases such external factors, such as changes in the political and social fabric of the society in which the Church lived, were not consciously considered essential to the world of theology and were dismissed as purely extraneous. Unfortunately, ecclesiology did not react to them; they were not the explicit context out of which the discipline worked.

The nineteenth century marked a significant turn in ecclesiology. A genuine reconsideration of the nature of the Church occurred as a result of two factors. First, the world itself became more complex and diverse, changing and developing in a radically new way. An industrial revolution took place, social sciences were born, empires rose and fell, populations migrated across oceans, democracy became the dominant form of government in the West, the forces that created the scientific and technological revolution in the twentieth century were created, and perhaps most importantly, vast numbers of people were educated and became literate for the first time. Second, theologians became conscious of this milieu, not simply as a given, not as something they themselves had created, but as a source of information that required reflection and integration. This information both provided the raw material for their work and patterned the conclusions they reached. Theologians began to acknowledge that what philosophy and theology had done for other doctrinal issues such as the Trinity and Christology centuries earlier, the emerging social sciences, especially history, could do for the theology of the church.[21]

When John XXIII opened the windows of the Catholic Church to the world in 1958, it was an indication that, unlike some of his post-Tridentine predecessors, he took the world seriously as autonomous and not an appendage of the Church. This change in attitude also revealed a significant change in theological method: from the elaboration of *a priori* truths to an awareness of the historical nature of truth and the relevance of historical experience. Although the Catholic Church in its official posture was never so isolated from the world and its changing thought patterns as it was at the time of the *Syllabus of Errors* in 1864 or the First Council of the Vatican six years later, one could already discern the undercurrents—such as in the theology of Johann Adam Möhler, the writings of John Henry Newman, and the spirit of the Church in America—that were to change the patterns of ecclesiology in the twentieth century. These nineteenth-century thinkers, and a church in the United States that took roots on democratic soil, served as harbingers of Vatican II and some post-Vatican II theology and ecclesiology. After a long

[21] Pelikan, *The Christian Tradition*, 5:290.

period of gestation, Möhler's ecclesiology, Newman's thought, and a more democratic worldview that came to life in the 1960s helped to foster a new ecumenical understanding among Christian churches. They became aware of their interdependence and developed a more positive appreciation of non-Christian religions and the secular order.

Beginning in the nineteenth century, ecclesiology could no longer be done in a cultural and historical vacuum; it could no longer be understood as the simple modification of institutional forms within Roman Catholic visible political confines. It could no longer be reduced to simple shifts in the theory or the tactics for defending ecclesiastical structures and governance; this had been the case for more than five hundred years. Yet the nineteenth century, which witnessed the advent of the modern world, also witnessed the pattern in which the Church of Rome, and all its accoutrements for that matter, continued to fall behind in recognizing the deeper changes affecting both Christian life and life in the world.

Historians date the nineteenth century, understood as a pattern of political movements and intellectual ideas, from the restoration of Europe at the Council of Vienna in 1815 to the outbreak of the First World War in 1914. Its roots lie further back, within the revolutionary spirit that overtook Europe and the Americas in the last two decades of the eighteenth century. Ecclesiologically, the century tells the story of the church in an age of political, social, intellectual, and scientific revolution. Just as it had been in the two previous centuries after Trent, the Church in the first part of the nineteenth century was once again placed on the defensive, guarding and protecting its political and ecclesiastical autonomy. This time, however, it was against different adversaries. In the period from 1800 to 1850, a study of catechisms and works on the Church suggests the same defect that could be found in the immediate post-Reformation ecclesiologies: a one-sided emphasis on the Church as an organized society, the "perfect society," governed and protected by its hierarchical and papal power. The century's crowning ecclesiological moment, the First Vatican Council, was not without its irony. During the Council, papal infallibility was defined as a dogma of faith, and the pope reached his highest pinnacle of power. In the very same year, the papacy lost all its political control over land in Italy, forcing the Church to understand its relationship to the world in radically different categories for the first time in more than a millennium. At Vatican I, ecclesiology had become, in Congar's phrase, "hierarchology"—in which the study of the church is reduced to the study of the power of the hierarchy, especially the Bishop of Rome.[22] This hierarchology distracted the Church for decades from the authentic challenge facing Catholicism: shedding its medieval mantle and confronting honestly and critically the modern age.

The nineteenth century witnessed several significant and contrasting currents in the development of the ecclesiology. The first was ultramontanism, which defined the Church as an institution or perfect society and greatly emphasized the centrality of Roman and papal power. The second was the movement to a more Spirit-centered, less institutional ecclesiology, which understood the church in terms of communion of persons united in the divine Spirit. This latter approach, closely related to the romantic movement, is associated with the thought of Johann Adam Möhler, a German theologian who taught at Tübingen in the first part of the century. As mentioned above, Möhler, along with Cardinal Newman, are by most standards the greatest Catholic theological minds of the nineteenth century.[23] Both of these ecclesiological currents triumphed within the Church at different times: Ultramontanism at Vatican I, and the Church as a mystical communion or Mystical Body in the middle of the twentieth century. Both currents are still powerful poles in the creative formation of the Church's self-understanding today. But perhaps the most important current in the creation of ecclesiology in the nineteenth century did not lie inside of the Church itself but was the horizon against which the Church struggled to understand itself: the growth and the triumph of secular thought. Ultramontanism emerged as a powerful force in the early nineteenth century and reached its zenith at the First Vatican Council. It grew in response to the emergence of the modern political and democratic state and developing secular worldview. The term "ultramontanism" (from *ultra* and *montes*, beyond the mountains) means across the mountains, a description given to the movement by the German and Northern European bishops on the other side of the Alps who regularly looked south to the popes of Rome for guidance. The path to Vatican I in 1870 from the beginning of the French Revolution in 1789 was not an easy one for the Catholic Church. It was marked by contrasting patterns of ecclesiastical and papal humiliation and triumph; likewise, it was the final period of the transformation of the medieval Church with its parochial political power over lands and people to an institution equipped to be a spiritual leader of all persons in

[22] Congar, *Lay People in the Church*, 58–59.

[23] See Philip Porter and Michael Hollerich, "Newman and Theological Conflict: An Exchange," *Commonweal* 145, no. 16 (2018): 25–28.

the modern world.

Ultramontanism has its origins in the French Revolution, which had abruptly destroyed most of the ecclesiastical world of France that had flourished during the *ancien régime*. At the time of the Revolution, church property was confiscated, some religious orders were disbanded, and clergy were required to take an oath of obedience to the French Civil Constitution that reduced them to civil servants. Perhaps one-third of the French clergy initially cooperated with the Revolution and became so-called Constitutionalist clergy; those Romanist clergy who refused were often executed or deported. In 1792–1793, in France, the mother country of the church, an amazing anti-Christian campaign of violence broke out against anyone Christian. This bloody campaign was actually a product of a small number of radicals consumed by a distorted rationalist understanding of the world along with an immense hatred for the power of the Church and the remnants of superstition they believed the Church to uphold. In spite of this fact, this was a shocking time for the Church and her loyal sons and daughters. Some relief and a lessening of the terror and oppression against Catholics took place when Robespierre took over the Committee for Public Safety in 1794, but the trials for the Church were hardly over. The pope, Pius VI, an invalid of eighty, was taken prisoner by the French General Berthier in 1798 and was shamelessly dragged across the Alps into France before his death.

Even Napoleon Bonaparte was moved by the treatment of the aged Pontiff.[24] But Napoleon, after ascending to the throne of France, also abused his power and grossly mistreated the next pope, Pius VII. After arresting Pius in 1809 and seizing all of the Papal States, he kept the pope a prisoner for five years in a bitter dispute over ecclesiastical jurisdiction. This humiliation of the Roman Pontiff took place at the same time as Napoleon's extraordinary military conquests. When Napoleon was finally defeated and compelled to abdicate in 1813, he was to find Pius a most gracious victor.[25] But in spite of this blatant misuse of military power over the pope and the Papal States, Napoleon, unlike the earlier revolutionaries, was, above all else, pragmatic about relations with the church. While his ultimate goal was to subject the Church to the state, he was also aware of the importance of compromise. In signing

---

[24] Gratsch, *Where Peter Is*, 157–58; for the best brief history of the church during this time, see E. E. Y. Hales, *The Catholic Church in the Modern World: A Survey from the French Revolution to the Present* (Garden City, NY: Doubleday Image Books, 1960).

[25] Hales, *The Catholic Church in the Modern World*, 64–71.

the famous Concordat of 1801 with the Holy See, Napoleon restored the Christian religion in France. This agreement, negotiated by the great Roman diplomat, Cardinal Consalvi, was to have the most important implications for the freedom of the Church from all civil control and marked the death of Gallicanism or the control of the state over the Church in any form. The Concordat stated that Rome could refuse to approve or invest any bishop chosen by civil rule. This principle prepared the way for the complete separation of Church and state in the twentieth century.

The circumstances that led to the Concordat along with the subsequent humiliation of Pope Pius VII created the reactionary and protective worldview in Catholicism that made ultramontanism flourish during the rest of the nineteenth century.[26] After Napoleon's attempt to subject the Church to the State, his demise resulted in the resurgence of the Church's power and independence. The Church was a significant player in the restoration of the *ancien régime*, or the old-world order, negotiated at the Council of Vienna in 1815 under the guiding genius of the Austrian Chancellor, Prince Metternich. Many sees, bishops appointed by Napoleon, had been left unoccupied according to the principle of the Concordat of 1801 which permitted the pope to refuse to accept any bishop chosen by civil rule. To consolidate his control over the Church, Napoleon had even ordered the Vatican records and archives to be removed to Paris. With the settlement in 1815, however, the Church entered a period of independence, reorganization, and revitalization.[27] Rome was free once more, signing concordats with many of the newly restored monarchies similar to the agreement made with Napoleon. The Papal States, thanks primarily to the efforts of British and French diplomacy, were returned to ecclesiastical control. The Church as a political institution, with control over its own lands, was firmly aligned with the aristocracy and the monarchies of Europe. In the minds of the European working class, this association with the aristocracy caused disillusionment and alienation from the Church, leading a significant portion of the population to see the Church as an archaic remnant of the past. At the same time, it would be a mistake, in conservative historian, E. E. Y. Hales's opinion, to claim that these concordats were indications that the church gave her special sanction to monarchy as the best or

[26] Hales, 77.

[27] See R. Aubert and R. Lill, "The Awakening of Catholic Vitality," in *The Church Between Revolution and Restoration*, Roger Aubert et al., vol. 7, History of the Church Series, ed. Hubert Jedin and John Dolan (New York: Crossroad, 1981), 206–26.

only form of governance.[28] The traditional Catholic position in this matter was that "the church is 'indifferent' to forms of government, being concerned only to defend the liberties of the Faith."[29] This principle would become more significant when evaluating the Church's later condemnation of some constitutional or democratic governments. Naturally, this distinction was lost on many in the working army of the industrial revolution who looked for alternate political and personal philosophies to structure and order their lives. The European Christian populace was slipping away from the political and spiritual power of the Church and the Church's response was caution and reaction.

6.6 The Pontificate of Pius IX and the First Vatican Council

Europe remained relatively calm during the period of the restoration until the Liberal Revolution of 1848. In 1846, Pius IX, "Pio Nono," was elected pope. As the longest reigning pope in history, occupying the throne of Peter from 1846 to 1878, Pius IX was unique in his impact on ecclesiology from the mid-nineteenth to the mid-twentieth century. During the first two years in the papacy, Pio Nono, unlike his predecessor, Gregory XVI, was a liberal; for example, he established a consultative assembly with lay representation to help him administer the Papal States and granted amnesty to those exiled or imprisoned by previous popes. Yet, he failed to see that his sympathy with liberalism and nationalism would bring the revolution of the liberals, under Mazzini and Garibaldi, to his own front door in Italy. Forced to flee Rome and into exile from Rome in 1848 in the guise of a peasant priest, he did not return until the spring of 1850, a profoundly changed man. The pope's exile at the hands of Italian nationalists and their attempted conquest of the Papal States in the name of a unified Italy were most important turning points in the church's ecclesiological direction. These events moved both pope and Church away from a liberal perspective to an authoritarian and reactionary position.[30] It is impossible to suggest what might have happened to ecclesiology in the nineteenth century had Pius *not* had to flee to Gaeta in 1848, but after his forced exile, the pope, and much of Catholic Europe along with him, underwent a profound transformation from the spirit of optimism and

[28] Aubert and Lill, 72–81.

[29] Aubert and Lill, 106.

[30] Aubert and Lill, 108.

openness to a cautious and a reactionary mood.[31] The triumph of papal power in the declaration of infallibility twenty-two years later was the result, in no small measure, from Pio Nono's experience of the dangers of liberalism, secularism, and nationalism to the institutional and political Church.

Thus, in the 1850s and 1860s, Pius IX became a strong supporter of ultramontanism. The father of the movement was Joseph de Maistre (1753–1821), a French layman and pupil of the Jesuits, whose book, *Du Pape* (The Pope) of 1819, had achieved enormous popular success. De Maistre believed that the social order would not survive without a strong and independent Church, governed by a sovereign and infallible pope who no longer possessed any civil or secular authority. Given the disastrous experience of the French Revolution, the shameless treatment of Pius VI and Pius VII, and the acknowledged evils of Gallicanism and any civil form of control over Church governance by the state, ultramontanism struck a sympathetic chord with many European Catholics. Supporters of ultramontanism were looking for security in the face of a liberalism which, in their minds, led inevitably to political and social anarchy. It is a mistake to judge the ultramontane spirit in the middle of the nineteenth century by placing it in our categories today in the twenty-first century and to fail to understand ultramontanism in its historical and ecclesial context. While it was reactionary, ultramontanism was not only against liberalism but also against liberalism's excesses. It was a movement that strongly defended the central role of the papacy not only against the tendency within the Church towards democratization but also against a Gallican and Febronian state which often usurped ecclesiastical jurisdiction in the appointment of bishops and day-to-day ecclesiastical governance. To be an ultramontane in the nineteenth century did not necessarily mean that the individual necessarily was a reactionary or anti-liberal. For example, Jean-Marie de Lamennais, a French priest (1782–1854), was a strong supporter of ultramontanism while at the same time a proponent of such democratic ideals as freedom of speech, freedom of assembly, and freedom of the press. He believed that the clergy, independent of state control and led by an infallible papacy, was the only defense against secular political tyranny and chaos in society. Unfortunately, another powerful ultramontane was Mauro Cappellari, whose book, *The Triumph of the Holy See and the Church,* published in 1799, mistakenly reduced the church to only its visible and juridical structure. Cappellari was elected Pope Gregory XVI in 1831, governing the

[31] T. M. Schoof, *A Survey of Catholic Theology 1800–1970* (New York: Paulist Newman, 1970), 31.

Church for the fifteen years before Pio Nono. As pope, he condemned his fellow ultramontane, Lamennais, for his liberal views in the papal encyclical *Mirari Vos* of 1832.[32]

The ultramontane movement was thus well established and growing in popular support when Pio Nono returned from exile in 1850. The next two decades witnessed four significant events in the development of ecclesiology: the declaration of the doctrine of the Immaculate Conception in 1854, the Syllabus of Errors of 1864, the fall of all the Papal States to the newly formed Italian government by 1870, and, perhaps most important, the First Council of the Vatican in 1869–1870. Each of these events solidified the Catholic church as the Roman Catholic Church, completing the transformation of the term *Roman* from a historical and cultural adjective to an intrinsic, absolute, and theologically normative part of the Church's definition.

6.6.1 The Immaculate Conception. The first significant moment for ecclesiology in the period from 1850 to 1870 was the papal declaration of the Immaculate Conception. While in exile, Pio Nono issued an encyclical asking the bishops for their advice and prayers concerning a definition of the doctrine of Mary's conception without original sin. After a draft of the definition was drawn up and amended by the bishops, on December 8, 1854, Pio Nono officially defined the doctrine that Mary was free from all stain of original sin at her conception. Apart from Mariological considerations—and virtually no bishop had any objection to the declaration—this definition established the precedent that it was sufficient for the papacy to act on its own in declaring a commonly accepted truth to be a formal dogma of faith with only such consultation with the bishops as the Holy See thought necessary.[33] While the Immaculate Conception was defined for worthy theological reasons, perhaps the timing of the definition had as much to do with political expediency as it did with theology. Threatened with the loss of temporal power over the lands the church still governed in what was to soon become the nation of Italy, Pius might have believed that the only way to reassert his temporal power was to demonstrate his spiritual authority. Since the early medieval period, the temporal and the spiritual power of the Church had been inseparable. Pio Nono's pontificate was the last in which these two powers were united in the mind of the papacy. Indeed, very few nineteenth-century Catholics, including the great thinker, Cardinal Newman, believed that the pope could fulfill his position as pope and spiritual leader of the Church *without* his secular power

---

[32] Gratsch, *Where Peter Is*, 161–63.

[33] Hales, *The Catholic Church in the Modern World*, 113.

over the Papal States to support him.[34] The Immaculate Conception, defined by the pope alone, prepared the way for the doctrine of papal infallibility sixteen years later, emphasizing that the Church was very much in the hands of one person, the Bishop of Rome.

6.6.2 The Syllabus of Errors. The second important ecclesiological event, the famous (or perhaps, better, infamous) *Syllabus of Errors*, was issued by Pio Nono in 1864. Eighty propositions were condemned as false, including many strains of modern thought, such as atheism, communism, and denial of Christ's divinity, upon which all Christians were in agreement. The last and perhaps the most famous propositions rejected the belief that "the Roman Pontiff can and should reconcile himself to progress, liberalism, and modern civilization."[35]

In condemning other ideas that were popular, especially in England and America, such as modern civilization, freedom of the press, and freedom of religion, the appearance of the *Syllabus* created a storm of controversy both inside and outside the Church. Separated from its immediate context of the Italian political situation, many non-Italians were shocked and horrified at the *Syllabus*. (On the one hundredth anniversary of the *Syllabus* in 1964, the *New York Times* thought the *Syllabus* still relevant enough to publish an editorial on its dangers). These condemnations were directed primarily, if not exclusively, at specific political and ecclesiastical conditions existing in Italy at the time. The tragedy of the *Syllabus* was the universal application of many of its condemnations for all times and places—as if this were the eternal teaching of the Church. A number of bishops, especially those from Northern Europe, were confused and concerned about some of the propositions and questioned the lack of wisdom and foresight embodied in the *Syllabus*. The *Syllabus* also had the unfortunate effect of curbing an emerging Catholic intellectual movement, embodied in historians such as John (later Lord) Acton in England and Ignaz von Döllinger at Munich.[36] In our categories today, the promulgation of the *Syllabus of Errors* was an enormous public relations blunder. Even in its time, it suggested an image of the Church as intransigent, immovable, and utterly closed to the new political, social, and intellectual world growing around it. Ecclesiologically, it perpetuated the image of the Church as negative, defensive, and fiercely protective of ecclesiastical power and jurisdiction. It further enhanced the absolute power of the papacy within the Church and

[34] Schoof, *A Survey of Catholic Theology*, 31.

[35] Quoted in Schoof, 123.

[36] Schoof, 124–26.

created the distorted impression that the *ecclesia* of Christ resided exclusively in the papal office and person.

6.6.3 Loss of the Papal States. The third key event in the ecclesiology of this time was the loss of the Papal States to the forces of nationalism in Italy in the 1860s. From early medieval times, the Church owned and governed a significant portion of the land that now comprises modern Italy. In May of 1860, Giuseppe Garibaldi led his army into Sicily and captured much of the territory of Italy up to Naples. When France and Austria were no longer able to protect the States as provided in the settlement of 1815, it was clear, especially to Cardinal Antonelli, the Papal Secretary of State and the last cardinal-deacon in the Church, that the States were doomed. Pius IX fought on with an international army of volunteers, but most of the States fell before the end of the year. A decade later, when the last of the French troops, who were protecting the city of Rome from attack by Italian forces, pulled out of Italy to join the Franco-Prussian War of 1870, Rome itself fell to King Victor Emmanuel of Piedmont in September of that year. In July of the following year, he quickly established Rome as the capitol of Italy and himself as ruler of a free and united Italy, taking residence in the former papal palace of the Quirinal.

In response to this action, Pio Nono decided to make no response at all, remaining silent throughout the entire time. For political, and perhaps for personal reasons, too, he refused to acknowledge that the events had taken place. He likewise rejected the Law of Guarantees that regulated with considerable fairness the position of the Church in Italy and the sovereignty of the pope in the Vatican. He also refused to accept any financial compensation for his losses. For the last seven years of his pontificate, Pio Nono, now an old man with his power over Rome and the adjacent lands vanished, "shut himself up in the Vatican and moved no more in the city."[37] This situation was resolved in 1929 with the Concordat established between the Vatican under Pope Pius XI and the Italian government under Mussolini.

6.6.4 The First Council of the Vatican. Finally, the crowning achievement of Pio Nono's pontificate and the most noteworthy ecclesiological event of the nineteenth century was the First Council of the Vatican, which opened on December 8, 1869. Although the last of the Papal States were under constant threat at the time and his Secretary of State, Cardinal Antonelli, was opposed to the idea, Pio Nono invited more than eight hundred church dignitaries to Rome for the beginning of the Council. Unlike the Council of

[37] Schoof, 121–22; 143–47.

Trent that considered the nature of the true Catholic doctrine in response to the Reformers, the purpose of Vatican I was to define the Church itself, its authority, and its relationship to secular states. Before turning its attention to ecclesiology, the Council Fathers unanimously passed the constitution *Dei Filius* in early 1870. This document was made necessary by the non-Christian philosophies that had emerged since Trent. In it, the church rejected the rationalism of the eighteenth century that denied revelation, the pantheism of the nineteenth century that reduced God to that which was immanent in nature, and the movement of naturalism that denied the supernatural in all its forms.[38]

The first drafts of the document on the church were prepared by two theologians at the Gregorian University in Rome, Giovanni Perrone and Klemens Schräder, both ultramontanes and supporters of papal infallibility. Along with Carlo Passaglia and their student, John Franzelin, Pio Nono's own personal theologian, these Roman theologians were the primary creators of ecclesiology before and at the time of the Council. Although Schräder was something of a "theocratic extremist," he was primarily responsible for the document presented to the Fathers in early 1870.[39] In the first chapter of this draft, Schräder proposed to define the church as the Mystical Body of Christ. The Council fathers, who were accustomed to describing the church as the "perfect society" and speaking about it in juridical terms, rejected this bold statement for the time. Schräder's original draft, nevertheless, reflected a most important shift in ecclesiology. In his *De ecclesia Christi* (On the church of Christ) of the 1850s, Passaglia proposed a new method and point of departure for a theology of the church in which theology was grounded not in the laws of human society and natural law, but instead in biblical images and spiritual ideas from the Fathers.[40] Thus, for the first time in centuries, the idea of the church as the "perfect society" was being called into question. This ecclesiological shift, as we shall see, was to resurface in the writings of French and German theologians after World War I, culminating in the encyclical *Mystici Corporis* (The Mystical Body) of Pius XII in 1943.

Although not formally part of the first draft of the document on the

---

[38] Schoof, 134–35.

[39] Roger Aubert, "La composition des commissions preparatoires du premier Concile du Vatican," in *Reformata Reformanda*, Festschrift for Hubert Jedin, ed. E. Iserloch and K. Repgen (Münster: Aschendorf, 1965), 465n80; Gratsch, *Where Peter Is*, 164.

[40] Gratsch, *Where Peter Is*, 164.

church, a tentative chapter on the infallibility of the pope was in circulation in March of 1870. After his initial attempts at neutrality during the sessions of the Council, Pius IX finally agreed that not only should this chapter be debated, it should also be taken out of sequence and be placed first on the agenda. This chapter, chapter eleven of the original schema or document on the church, was subsequently recast into a separate document of four chapters, *De Summo Pontifice* (On the Supreme Pontiff).[41] The Council was divided into two clear groups: the conservative majority, who were ultramontanes, led by Cardinal Manning of Westminster, England, and the minority liberals, led by Bishop Dupanloup, bishop of Orleans, France.[42] The pressure of the debate mounted not only inside the Vatican but also in both the Catholic press and the world press. Most of the bishops opposed to the document came from countries where Catholics were in the minority or were open to strong criticism from Protestants and nonbelievers. Within the French hierarchy, twenty-two bishops were anti-infallibilists, including the Bishop of Evreux, Jean Devoucoux. On his deathbed in the spring of 1870, while the debate over infallibility was raging, he was reported to have said, "I bless God for calling me to himself before this definition."[43] Likewise, Catholic intellectuals such as Acton and Döllinger were strongly opposed to infallibility. Some bishops who rejected the document were not necessarily against the concept of papal infallibility in principle but against its formal definition at the Council. John Henry Newman, perhaps the greatest Catholic mind of the day, accepted the theological concept of infallibility, but was opposed to its definition at this particular time.[44]

As important as the declaration on infallibility itself was, the first part of *Summo Pontifice* proposed that the Pope had the "full plenitude of supreme power," that is, universal jurisdiction over every bishop and diocese within the Church. This concept of the juridical authority of the pope over the universal church would have a much more significant impact on the life of the church than papal infallibility. Up until this time, many bishops, as successors of the apostles, believed that their ordinary jurisdiction in their own dioceses came

---

[41] Thomas Bokenkotter, *A Concise History of the Catholic church*, rev. ed. (Garden City, NY: Doubleday Image, 1979), 334.

[42] Hales, *The Church in the Modern World*, 135–37.

[43] Quoted in Margaret O'Gara, *Triumph in Defeat: Infallibility, Vatican I, and the French Minority Bishops* (Washington, DC: The Catholic University of America Press, 1988), 75.

[44] Hales, *The Church in the Modern World*, 137.

directly from God, not through the pope. The debate over the document continued throughout May and June until the vote was finally taken on July 18, 1870. Five hundred thirty-three bishops voted for the document, and only two voted against.[45] One of the two negative votes was that of the American Edward Fitzgerald, the Bishop of Little Rock, Arkansas, whose "no" vote was never satisfactorily explained.[46]

Two important reasons led to the fact of only two negative votes against *Summo Pontifice*: first, with the outbreak of the Franco-Prussian War and the immanent seizure of Rome by the Italians—recall that French troops were protecting the Vatican from the Italians at the time—the bishops left Rome in a hurry, especially the French and German bishops who gratefully excused themselves in order to return home and to tend to their flock. Second, Pio Nono had become enormously popular in the Catholic world, and his generosity and good humor endeared him to his opponents as well as supporters. Some of the minority, including many American bishops, who for the most part opposed papal infallibility, left Rome in order to avoid casting a negative vote against this unusually popular and universally admired man. When Pio Nono proclaimed the new constitution, *Pastor Aeternus*, in St. Peter's, the two bishops who voted against it fell at the feet of the pope and gave their full assent to the new doctrine. Likewise, in the months to follow, almost all the bishops who left Rome before the final vote wrote to the pope to express their loyalty to the new verdict.[47]

With the definition of papal primacy and papal infallibility proclaimed by Pio Nono in the document *Pastor Aeternus* in July 1870, the pinnacle of papal power over the Church was reached and the dream of every ultramontane fulfilled. Because of the military pressure on the Papal States and the outbreak of war, the agenda of the Council, which should have included a definition of the entire church, was reduced to only chapter eleven and then this single chapter expanded to the new document, *Summo Pontifice*. So, the First Council of the Vatican ended by investing the pope with supreme power and elevating his prestige to its highest level throughout the Catholic world.[48]

---

[45] Hales, 138–39.

[46] James J. Hennesey, *The First Vatican Council: The American Experience* (New York: Herder and Herder, 1963), 281. One popular story has it that the bishop of Little Rock said, in a press interview after the Council, that it was a question of the "little rock" against the "big rock."

[47] Hales, *The Church in the Modern World*, 140.

[48] Hales, 147.

At the same time, Pio Nono, now a self-proclaimed prisoner of the Vatican with no more temporal jurisdiction, saw his prestige and influence with the secular governments of the world fall precipitously after the loss of the Papal States. As one Catholic historian describes Pius IX: "At his death in 1878, the church was left in a virtual state of war with the rest of society—a *Kulturkampf* (cultural struggle) by no means limited to Bismark's Germany."[49] From this point on, the pope would have to find the source of his universal spiritual power elsewhere; the temporal power he had possessed since the decline of the Roman Empire in the fourth century could no longer serve as the foundation of his papal authority and jurisdiction. The agenda of the First Vatican Council would be completed at the Second Council of the Vatican (1962–1965). Once again, the Church would attempt to define itself and its role in the world. Except for the issues of papal jurisdiction and infallibility, Vatican I had failed to accomplish its mission. A comprehensive ecclesiology would not come until the twentieth century, the so-called "century of the church."

The contemporary understanding of the Catholic Church in popular Catholic culture is very much a product of the reign of Pius IX. Always a warm and hospitable man, Pius initiated the custom of papal audiences, receiving virtually any visitor to Rome who wanted to see the pope. This greatly enhanced the prestige of the papacy and increased its popularity. It was with Pio Nono that the devotion of Catholics included personal devotion to the papacy.[50] The worldwide respect and adulation that Pope John Paul II received during his journeys were made possible in part by both the style and the substance of Pius IX's pontificate a century earlier. With the emergence of improved transportation and communication, Pius IX also encouraged frequent *ad limina* visits to Rome by the bishops of the world, an expression of the primacy of papal jurisdiction that continues today. Pius conferred the Roman title "Monsignor" (literally, "my lord") upon the clergy as a sign of their special dedication to the Church, that is, of course, to the pope himself. In short, the centralization of authority within the Catholic Church, widely presumed in the popular Catholic mind as essential to its ecclesial identity today, took definitive historical form during the pontificate of Pio Nono in the last century. Ecclesiology under Pio Nono became even more narrowly focused than hierarchology; the study of the Church was a study of the pope and his supreme authority. With the pontificate of Pius IX, the centrifugal forces of Gallicanism in the political order and ecclesiastical jurisdiction of the Church

---

[49] Bokenkotter, *A Concise History of the Catholic Church*, 338.
[50] Hales, *The Church in the Modern World*, 142–43.

at a local and diocesan level were definitively conquered by the centripetal power of the papacy and the Curia in Rome.

6.7 Johann Adam Möhler: Pioneer in Ecclesiology

Just before the reign of Pius IX, a second important movement in the development of the ecclesiology of the nineteenth century was also taking place at Tübingen with the ecumenical theology of Johann Adam Möhler. Perhaps the greatest Catholic theologian of the century, Möhler was born in 1796 and died at the height of his career in 1838. Möhler's achievement was the refocusing of ecclesiology from its post-Tridentine concern with the defense of the institutional Church and its objective doctrinal tradition to an understanding of the church as a mystical union of persons united in the Spirit. His vision of the church was not a *Gesselschaft* or society. Möhler saw the church at its deepest level as a *Gemeinschaft,* a community with the common bond of spirit. Influenced by his two teachers, J. M. Sailer and J. S. Drey, as well as Protestant thinkers such as Friedrich Schleiermacher and August Neander, Möhler's work was characterized by its romantic, ecumenical, and mystical spirit. The content of his two major works, *The Unity of the Church* (1825)[51] and *Symbolism* (1836)[52] profoundly influenced the ecclesiology of the twentieth century, establishing the starting point and focus of much work in theology from the end of the First World War up until the Second Vatican Council. Had Catholic theologians in the second half of the nineteenth century not been so absorbed with the emergence of neoscholastic theology and the debate over papal infallibility, Möhler's influence would have been more clearly visible at an earlier time.

The ecclesiology of his first work, *Die Einheit in der Kirche* (The Unity of the Church), is marked by a complete pneumatocentricity, that is, a centering of the church in the Holy Spirit. The church is a community whose life comes from the Holy Spirit and is realized by the action of the Spirit. For Möhler, the essential fact of Christianity is not the communication of truth but the transmission of life in the Spirit. The interior element of the church, the Spirit, always takes precedence over the church's visibility; the external

[51] *The Unity of the church or the Principle of Catholicism Revealed in the Spirit of the Fathers of the Church of the First Three Centuries,* ed. and trans. Peter C. Erb (Washington, DC: The Catholic University of America Press, 1996).

[52] *Symbolism or the exposition of the doctrinal differences between Catholics and Protestants as evidenced by their symbolic Writings,* trans. J. B. Robertson, 5th ed. (New York: published privately, 1909).

ecclesiastical church is a visible manifestation of the interior ecclesial life. By focusing on the inner life of the church, he deemphasized the political and historical side of the church as well as the church's visible structure and the authority that flows from it. In this way, Möhler presents a more comprehensive vision of the church and restores to ecclesiology a proper sense of ecclesial mystery. Perhaps this restoration, coming as it did in reaction to years of ecclesiology that defended the visible institution of the church, is dangerously close, as one commentator has put it, to an "ecclesiological monophysitism."[53] Monophysitism means "of one nature." Like the Christological heresy in which the human in Jesus was swallowed up into his divinity, Möhler may have excessively divinized the church, where the community and the Spirit were too closely linked and the historical and sinful church relegated to the less important. Since he lived in the romantic age, his strong sense of the church as a single divine-human organism may have had "a touch of the tragic halo about it."[54] At the same time, *The Unity of the Church* was a groundbreaking work in the post-Tridentine Church.

In his second work, *Symbolik* (Symbolism), Möhler, aware of the criticism of his first volume, shifts the focal point of his ecclesiology from the Holy Spirit to the person of Christ. The church becomes the Incarnation in time of the Son of God made man. Christ is the archetype of the church: as Christ was divine and human, so is the church. The Spirit is not neglected, however, since the Spirit is now visible and perceptible through the visibility of Christ. Since the Word of God became flesh, the form in which his work was to be continued was likewise visible and human; Christ's mission had to be entrusted to human envoys.[55] In *The Unity of the Church*, the church is "a Pentecost, renewed without ceasing...above all, invisible, the church of the Spirit." In *Symbolism*, the church is "an uninterrupted Nativity...essentially human, or better, divine-human."[56] With these different but complementary interpretations of the church, Möhler presented the relationship of the divine and the human, the interior and exterior element in the church, in a way that was profoundly Catholic but often forgotten in the post-Tridentine tradition. As he writes in *Symbolism*:

---

[53] J. R. Geiselmann, "Les variations de la definition de l'Eglise chez Johann Adam Möhler," *Revue des sciences religieuses* 40 (1960), 159.

[54] Gieselmann, 158.

[55] Möhler, *Symbolism*, 258.

[56] Geiselmann, "Les variations de la definition de l'Eglise chez Johann Adam Möhler," 162.

> We are not living members of the external church until we belong to the interior one. What has been imparted to us from without must be reproduced by and within us; the objective must become subjective before we are entitled to consider ourselves members of the Christian church. Thus far, certainly, the invisible is to be ranked before the visible church. And the latter is eternally renovated out of the former. But this Kingdom of God begins, grows, and ripens within us after it has first externally encountered us, and made the first steps to receive us into its bosom....The act of exterior excitement, instruction, and education is internally excited, taught and educated; but as soon as the exterior has passed into the interior, then the inward in its turn becomes the outward; and the image which from without was impressed upon the interior is reflected from the interior on the exterior.[57]

Since Möhler grounded the divine and human elements of the church in the archetype of the Incarnation, one contemporary theologian suggests that perhaps "no other modern Catholic theologian seems to have treated this problem of the two aspects of the church and their relationship to each other as lucidly as Johann Adam Möhler."[58] His importance in ecclesiology was two-fold: first, he shifted the work of ecclesiology from an exclusively apologetic and defensive mode to one that was systematic and objective; second, he was the first serious Catholic theologian to dialogue with Protestants on objective theological grounds. In fact, Möhler prided himself on his effort to be objective, exemplified by his call in the preface to *Symbolism* for an intellectual honesty in considering the nature of the Protestant Reformation and the estrangement of the churches for three centuries. His hope in the entire work is, as he says, "that I might do something to bring about a religious peace, by revealing a true knowledge of the great dispute in so far as by this knowledge men must come to perceive that the contest sprang out of the most earnest endeavors of both parties to uphold the truth—the pure and genuine Christianity in all its integrity."[59] In the context of his dialogue with the great Protestant theologians at the University of Tübingen, Möhler was a century ahead of his time in ecumenical work and ecumenical spirit.

Möhler's ecumenical ecclesiology differed sharply from the ecclesiology of one of Möhler contemporaries, Jaime Balmes, one of the great minds of

---

[57] Möhler, *Symbolism*, 335–36.

[58] Thomas Sartory, *The Ecumenical Movement and the Unity of the Church* (Westminster, MD: The Newman Press, 1963), 116.

[59] Möhler, *Symbolism*, xv–xvi.

nineteenth-century Spanish Catholicism; his four-volume work, *Protestantism Compared with Catholicism*, appeared in 1841 through 1844, less than a decade after Möhler's death. Balmes's thesis is that Protestantism corrupts, while Catholicism alone develops all the social virtues; he even denied the very possibility of studying Protestant doctrines. This work, in contrast with Möhler's, is a polemic of the highest order, in which, in Catholic theologian George Tavard's words, "the only thing lacking is an effort towards interior understanding."[60] In the historical situation of the Church in which he lived, Möhler, unlike Balmes, was a breath of fresh air and the first flowering of change in the musty, static room of post-Tridentine ecclesiology. More than a century before Pope John XXIII, Möhler opened the windows of ecclesiology. As Dom Rousseau has said of his work, "Möhler has made us understand that the church is much more than an institution, that she is a living organism in which the institutional spirit ought only to be the spontaneous manifestation of her inner being."[61]

6.8 Fin de Siècle: The End of the Nineteenth Century

Although he did his theological work in the first half of the nineteenth century, Johann Adam Möhler was one of the harbingers of the theology of the church that was to emerge slowly after the First World War, reaching its culmination at the Second Vatican Council.[62] The idea of the church in Möhler's theology could not come to the center of the community's self-understanding until the right time—and the pontificate of Pius IX was certainly *not* the proper historical moment. In the minds of most people, the Church remained the "perfect society," a visible institution controlled by its hierarchy and papacy. At the end of the pontificate of Pius IX in 1878, one can clearly discern two radically different approaches to theology present and emerging: *first*, the institutional perspective, grounded in neoscholastic theology and philosophy, which understood faith as a set of unchangeable truths expressed in clear

---

[60] See George Tavard, *Two Centuries of Ecumenism* (Notre Dame: Fides, 1960), 75–76.

[61] Olivier Rousseau, "Les attitudes de pensée concernant l'unité chrétienne au xixe siecle," *Revue des sciences religieuses* 40 (1960), 360–61.

[62] Möhler's works became prominent in the 1930s, influencing the important writers of ecclesiology in French, especially Yves Congar who was himself interested in Möhler's theology. See Pierre Chaillet, ed., *L'Eglise est une: Homage a Möhler* (Paris: Éditions du Cerf, 1938); Yves M. -J. Congar, "La signification oecumenique de l'oevre de Möhler," *Irenikon* 15 (1938): 113–30.

propositions about God and the world. The significant names in this group include the theologians who created and later supported the theology of Vatican I: Carlo Passaglia, S.J., (d. 1887), Joseph William Kleutgen (d. 1883), Cardinal Giovanni Perrone (d. 1876), Cardinal Clemens Schräder, S.J. (d. 1875), Austrian Jesuit theologian, Cardinal Johann Baptiste Franzelin (d. 1883), and Louis Veuillot (d.1883), author and leader within France of extreme ultramontanism. The *second* perspective emphasized the historical and experiential nature of truth, interpreting history and human experience as playing an essential role in the creation of doctrine. Holding this perspective were some of the great Catholic minds of the century, including Möhler himself, Cardinal John Henry Newman, Ignaz von Döllinger (d. 1890), the German theologian who rejected the doctrine of the Immaculate Conception, broke with the church, and founded the Old Catholic Church. Later, Maurice Blondel (d. 1949) created the so-called "new theology," or *nouvelle théologie*, which played a great role in the deliberations and arguments of the Second Vatican Council. In a wider context, the conflict between these two distinct ecclesiological and theological approaches formed the backdrop for the tensions in the history of the Church's self-understanding from the beginning of the nineteenth century to this post-Vatican II conciliar era. Not until the Second Vatican Council did human experience and historical consciousness definitively triumph over the world of static neoscholastic truth.

In France, the origin of the distinction between neoscholastic/institutional theology and the newer historical/experiential method can be located in the separation of church and state in the nineteenth century. Since the seminaries tended to be self-contained and traditional, the conservative theology of the neoscholastic "timeless" manuals went unchallenged. Catholic theologians in the universities, on the other hand, were free to speculate about the current scientific, social, and philosophical problems that intellectuals in Europe were discussing and evaluating. Modern thought was readily available to them, and such an opportunity required an intelligent response. It is from this latter group, those open to a theology-in-the-world, that Modernism would emerge at the beginning of the twentieth century.[63] Because traditional seminary theology, backed by Rome's authority, was far more influential than the more creative and historical university theology for the half century after Vatican I (1870–1920), it is little wonder that virtually no new ecclesiology more comprehensive than a repetition and clarification of *Summo Pontifice*,

[63] James M. Connolly, *Voices of France: A Survey of Contemporary Theology in France* (New York: Macmillan, 1961), 19.

which defined the papal infallibility in 1870, appeared during the period from the last years of Pius IX until after the First World War.

The first of these two approaches to theology, neoscholasticism, developed through a significant shift in Catholic thought that took place during the pontificate of Pius IX. The development of scientific history and the social sciences in the nineteenth century fostered a new optimism in intellectual circles about human progress and the human capacity to grow in knowledge. By beginning with and emphasizing calculable phenomena and empirical data, the new scientific intellect tended to regard everything not easily accessible by scientific method, especially religion and the truth of revelation, as an illusion. Given the isolation of the church from the secular world at the time, intensified by the loss of the Papal States and the *Syllabus of Errors* of 1864, it is hardly surprising that Catholic theology was the product of reaction to this emerging scientific and technological worldview. Neoscholastic theology was based on the system of rational discourse that was prevalent in the late medieval schools of theology, such as at the University of Paris and at Oxford University, from the time of Thomas Aquinas and the creation of his system in the late thirteenth century. Catholic theologians who embraced neoscholastic philosophy and theology after Vatican I were ironically not unlike their secular counterparts in other disciplines since both emphasized the new objective and analytical ways of research. Probably these theologians, such as those from the so-called "Roman School" at the Gregorian University, sincerely believed they were entering into the spirit of the thought of the times by reviving the theological method of the medieval universities. This resulted from the fact that both neoscholasticism and the emerging scientific worldview "often contained a goodly measure of rationalism."[64] Unfortunately, whatever similarities of method existed, neoscholasticism and a scientific worldview also reflected radically different cultural and intellectual spirits. The neoscholastics thus created a theology closed to the world, one that was "even more apologetic and polemical than before" Vatican I and its precursor in the first half of the nineteenth century.[65] Neoscholastic ecclesiology was exclusively a defense against Protestantism and secularism.

In the neoscholastic pattern of thought, truth existed as an *a priori*, free from the perceived whims of history or experience. Thus, Catholic

---

[64] Oskar Köhler, "Neo-Thomism, Neoscholasticism, and the New Philosophers," in *The History of the Church*, ed. H. Jedin and J. Dolan, vol. 9, *The Church in an Industrial Age* (New York: Crossroad, 1981), 316.

[65] Schoof, *A Survey of Catholic Theology*, 34–35.

theologians of the time were no longer searching for new and imaginative categories to explain the Christian message, but instead, clear and reasonable concepts that had the unfortunate effects of hindering intellectual creativity, silencing real theological questions, and imprisoning faith in a series of objective propositions. Unlike the Tübingen theologians such as Sailer, Drey, and Möhler earlier in the century, neoscholastic thinkers regarded faith as timeless and unchanging, protected from the vagaries of different philosophical presuppositions. Perhaps the only important neoscholastic theologian in the period from Vatican I to the end of World War I was Matthias J. Scheeben, a German Catholic theologian and mystic who studied at Gregorian University in Rome under Carlo Passaglia and Giovanni Perrone from 1852 to 1859.

Although he explored the richness of the Greek Fathers, even Scheeben gives the impression that theology lives outside of time and the dynamics of history. The neoscholastic method lacked a sensitivity to historical movement and was unable to adapt and reform itself to any new cognitive challenges "except within the logical relationships of formalized scholastic concepts."[66] This type of mind might be best embodied in this statement of Abbé Maignen, one of the leading French "integralists"—which we will consider in the following chapter:

> Unlike a science which is constantly changing, the church is fully justified in not attempting to find a useless reconciliation between her dogmas and the provisional results of the sciences. She has only to be concerned with her own teaching, which is dependent on faith alone and to alleviate the distress of souls by protecting them from all that may give rise to doubt and against dangerous and rash views. Science may constantly change, but faith is unchangeable.[67]

The philosophy of neoscholasticism received its official approval and sanction (and St. Thomas Aquinas declared *the* theologian of the church) in the encyclical of Pope Leo XIII, *Aeterni Patris*, issued August 4, 1879. According to the encyclical, the philosophy of Thomas Aquinas contains an "invincible power" to overcome all those principles of modern liberal thought that threaten public order. Thomism, found in the form of neoscholasticism, became the definitive *modus docendi* (form of teaching) for the Church and all of its theology, rendering suspect anyone who rejected this unique Christian

[66] Schoof, 36–37.

[67] Schoof, 149; 36.

philosophy.[68] Cardinal Mercier (1851–1926) of Belgium became the first significant figure in the Thomistic revival, establishing a Philosophical Institute at the University of Louvain that was dedicated to the implementation of the pope's desires in *Aeterni Patris*.[69] Unfortunately, since Thomas himself was separated from his own historical context, neoscholastic ecclesiology remained abstract and unhistorical, grounded in *a priori* principles of the Roman Catholic Church's unique claim to truth and authority that were themselves never called into question.

Before examining the emerging conflict between the neoscholastic/integralist mode of thought with the emerging liberal/modernist perspective, the pontificate of Pope Leo XIII is noteworthy for a number of ecclesiological reasons. While little or no creative work was done to advance formal ecclesiology, Leo made significant changes in the relationship between the Church and the world near the end of the nineteenth century. Although he was not a liberal himself, he was a widely traveled diplomat and accomplished scholar who was aware that the Church had to break with the isolationism and the siege mentality that had plagued it in the concluding years of Pio Nono's pontificate. For example, in a movement of rapprochement between the Church and the world outside the Vatican, he relieved the tensions in Germany brought about by the *Kulturkampf* (war over culture), the cultural struggle between Otto von Bismarck and the Church. He also instructed French Catholics to reconcile themselves to the Republic.[70] In his 1888 encyclical, *Libertas*, the open-minded Leo rejected the accusation that the church looked unfavorably on almost all forms of modern political systems and rejected the new discoveries in science and technology. In this spirit, Leo began the slow reconciliation of the Roman Catholic Church with the modern world and "led the church in taking a firm grip on the problems of mass society."[71] Leo was well aware of the rise of Marxist Socialism as the growing popular alternative solution to the terrible problems afflicting the workers in the Industrial Age. He also knew that by 1880, with the general reactionary character of Church leadership and its reluctance to adapt to new democratic procedures, much of the working class was already lost to the Church. Some churchmen were already on the front lines, like Cardinal Manning of England, a strong

---

[68] Oskar Köhler, "The Encyclical *Aeterni Patris*," in *The History of the Church*, 9:307–9.

[69] Connolly, *Voices of France*, 20.

[70] Schoof, *A Survey of Catholic Theology*, 58.

[71] Bokenkotter, *A Concise History of the Catholic Church*, 343.

ultramontane at Vatican I but a progressive in social affairs who lectured on the rights and dignity of labor during the 1870s and supported the London dock strike in 1889. The American Cardinal Gibbons of Baltimore was a strong supporter of the Knights of Labor and, with Cardinal Manning's help, prevented the union's condemnation by the Vatican in 1886. Finally, the Fribourg Union, comprised of leaders of social Catholicism, was formed in the 1880s.[72]

While neoscholastic thought kept the theology of the church static and unmoved by historical and scientific method, the Church under Leo XIII began to move on the social and political front. The crowning achievement of Leo's pontificate was the encyclical *Rerum Novarum* (literally, Of New Things) of 1891, the so-called magna carta of social Catholicism. The encyclical presented the best and most progressive Catholic social thought of the day and established the main lines of Catholic social philosophy for much of the twentieth century.[73] Forty year later, the encyclical was developed in *Quadragesimo Anno* (Forty Years After) by Pius XI on its anniversary in 1931. *Mater et Magistra* (Mother and Teacher) of John XXIII (on its seventieth anniversary in 1961) and *Rerum Novarum* became the guiding spirit for a more developed social Catholic philosophy. The pursuit of social justice continued in Paul VI's *Populorum Progressio* (The Progress of the Peoples) of 1967 and John Paul II's *Solicitudo Rei Socialis* (Concern for the Social Fabric) of 1987. Four years later in 1991, John Paul II issued *Centesimus Annus*, on the one hundredth anniversary of Pope Leo XIII's *Rerum Novarum.*

As a realist, Leo knew the church of Pius IX would not survive in the modern world without adaptation and some compromise with the reigning social movements of the time. The terrible exploitation of workers, which was part of the Industrial Revolution in the early nineteenth century, called for a response from the Church to the injustices of a newly formed mass society. This society was created by great numbers of people brought from the land into the dingy confines of urban areas. Their work situation, consisting of long hours for little pay in smoky factories, could only propel them out of a Church unconcerned with their plight, into opposing ideologies of secularism and Marxism. Leo's groundbreaking encyclical was rejected by many Catholics, nor did it stop the spread of socialist and secular thought among the workers. Nevertheless, his stand was a powerful force in the creation of both Christian trade unions and Christian

---

[72] See Normand J. Paulhus, "Social Catholicism and the Fribourg Union," in *Selected Papers from the 21st Annual Meeting of the Society of Christian Ethics* (1980): 63–88.

[73] Bokenkotter, *A Concise History of the Catholic Church*, 345–48.

democratic parties that were to carry the battle for social Catholicism well into the next century. Ecclesiologically, the encyclical created a crack in the institutional fortress of the Roman Church, constructed after the Reformation and fortified during the pontificate of Pius IX and Vatican I. *Rerum Novarum* was the first important indication that *the church could no longer define itself only in opposition to the broader society in which it lived.* In retrospect, one might suggest that the servant model of the church, developed by Avery Dulles almost a century later, had its first formal historical manifestation in the social Catholicism inspired by Leo XIII.[74]

The Church as an institutional fortress, of course, continued to thrive for many decades after *Rerum Novarum*, nourished by neoscholasticism and its reaction to the Modernist crisis that will be considered shortly. The last decade of the nineteenth century is also notable for one other challenge to the authority of the Church called "Americanism." The term refers to a movement within the Church in the United States, inspired by leaders such as John Ireland, Bishop of St. Paul, John Lancaster Spalding, Bishop of Peoria, and Cardinal Gibbons of Baltimore to assimilate the Roman Catholic Church more completely into American culture. Its hallmarks were enthusiasm for freedom of conscience and American political life where church and state were completely separate. Mildly rebuffed in Pope Leo's letter of 1895 letter, *Longinqua Oceani* (literally, across the long ocean, that is, the Atlantic),[75] the matter might have been put aside completely if the life of Isaac Hecker, founder of the Paulist community of priests, was not translated into French in 1897 by Abbé Klein, a French priest and strong admirer of John Ireland. This work encouraged the adaptation of the Church to the American mentality. The book infuriated ultra-conservatives among the bishops and clergy in France since the American Church and religious liberty was suggested as a model for the future of the French Church, and Isaac Hecker was called the "priest of the future." After an inquiry into the so-called Americanist way of thinking, "Americanism" as a pattern and style of thought was condemned by Pope Leo in his letter in 1899 to Bishop John Ireland, *Testem Benevolentiae Nostrae* (literally, Witness to Our Good Will.) No American bishops were invited to visit Rome personally during the inquiry to reply to the charges. In the encyclical, Leo rejected the tendencies, first, to extol natural and active virtues over the supernatural and passive ones and, second, to adapt the Church to modern ideas of

[74] Dulles, *Models of the Church*, 95–108.

[75] Oskar Köhler, "The American Way," in *The History of the Church*, 9:165. At the same time, the letter of Leo XIII was full of praise for American Catholics and their zeal for the faith.

freedom and authority.[76] For some people of the time, Americanism suggested more of a crisis in the French Church than the American Church at the end of the nineteenth century. At the same time, conservative historian E. E. Y. Hales cautiously notes that Americanism "advocated a way of life that was liable to lead to secularism and indifferentism."[77]

The response to Americanism also reflected sensitivity on the part of Rome, as well as the power held by the strongly conservative members of the hierarchy, to any threat to Rome's absolute authority. While the so-called "Americanist" crisis is now long over, the questions of that time continued to plague the Church throughout the twentieth century and remain visible in the polarization in the Church in the first two decades of the twenty-first century. As ecclesiology struggled to do then, it continues to struggle now in a different context: to understand and define the balance between the supremacy of Roman authority and jurisdiction and the autonomy and sacramental power of local bishops in diocesan, regional, and national churches. Ironically, the American Church at the end of the nineteenth century provided one of the few liberal alternatives to the official Roman Church of political, cultural, and intellectual reactionaries.

[76] Bokenkotter, *A Concise History of the Catholic Church*, 386–91. See also, Oskar Köhler, "The Condemnation of Americanism," in *The History of the Church*, 9:331–34.

[77] Hales, *The Church in the Modern World*, 177. Hales seems too harsh in his criticism of "Americanism."

7.

THE TWENTIETH-CENTURY CHURCH: FROM MODERNISM TO VATICAN II

7.1 The Modernist Crisis

Twentieth-century Roman Catholic ecclesiology had its origins in the confusion and reaction to Modernism, a controversial pattern of thought within Catholicism. Modernism, itself, had developed in response to liberal Protestantism in the nineteenth century. Liberal Protestantism was grounded in the thought of the philosopher Immanuel Kant (d. 1804) and the theologian and biblical scholar Friedrich Schleiermacher (d. 1834), often called the father of modern theology. Both thinkers were suspicious of the supernatural as a distinct category and turned to a more anti-dogmatic, humanitarian, and experiential form of Christian faith. This was exemplified in the subsequent works of systematic theologian, Albrecht Ritschl (1822–1889), who sought, following Kant, to move Christianity from the doctrinal to the moral spheres; and, likewise, Adolf von Harnack (1851–1930), who was best known for his achievements in theology and church history but was also a major force in German scientific circles, serving as a member of the Prussian Academy of Sciences and other major scientific institutes. Harnack was indeed an intellectual giant of Protestant thought at the end of the nineteenth and first decades of the twentieth century.

Catholic "Modernism" is ambiguous both theologically and historically. Did it serve more as a Catholic intellectual counterpart and expression of liberal Protestantism, or were early Modernists reacting to liberal Protestantism?

Modernism involved both a change in theological method and a shift in the content of doctrinal and biblical thought. The term "modernism" itself does not refer to a single school of theology or theologians but to a spectrum of approaches to an interpretation of the faith united by one common thread: a fundamentally different understanding of the relationship between the church and the world from the reigning post-Tridentine theology of the institutional church. Modernism, unlike the defensive and static theology of previous centuries, emphasized the importance of history and the developing social sciences in the reception and explanation of divine revelation. Modernism, instead of beginning with *a priori* truths, used human experience and historical method as the starting point for doing theology and interpreting God's revelation and Scripture.

Like Modernism itself, historical interpretations of the movement are quite diverse. Some consider so-called Modernism—given its name by the Roman Curia that condemned it—a heresy, the "mother of all heresies." Others interpret the movement of thought positively and see in it the beginning of Catholic theology's openness to post-Enlightenment historical and critical thinking. Some place the crisis that surrounded Modernist ideas as the last great battle for the soul of Catholicism in the nineteenth century; others view Modernism as the first of many conflicts that would afflict the Church and its theology in the twentieth century. Certain Modernists with more extreme ideas were condemned by the official Roman institution; others remained faithful to the authority of Rome. In any case, the impact of Modernism on twentieth-century ecclesiology was significant and unfortunate: the strong, authoritarian reaction to it stifled creative theology for decades, perpetuated the ultramontane spirit in the Church, and maintained an adversary relationship between the Church and world until the beginning of the Second Vatican Council.

Within the Roman Catholic Church at the beginning of the twentieth century, two intensely polarized approaches to theology and church existed side by side: first, the neoscholastic theologians and officials with power in the Roman Curia who believed the church was the perfect society, its truth above history, and its fullness of authority visibly manifest in the infallible Bishop of Rome; second, the reformers and liberals who were sensitive to history, the emerging social and natural sciences, a half century of biblical scholarship in the Protestant tradition, and the growing emphasis on human experience as a factor in the interpretation of dogma.[1] The first group of theologians and churchmen, commonly called Integralists, were unequivocally opposed to any form of cultural and religious pluralism and adaptation to the thought of the modern world. In contrast, the second group, from which so-called Modernists emerged, recognized the impact of mass culture and the growing diversity in interpreting the faith and attempted to adapt the classical Catholic understanding of the church and its doctrinal tradition to this situation.

As expressed in the writings of several of its proponents, Modernism was not without ideas which, understood in the context of their time, could be suspected of heretical thought. In a broader sense, however, the Modernist movement reflects the inevitable reaction of many intellectual Catholics to a century in which the Church under siege protected itself by its isolation from the great advances in languages, history, and natural sciences. While some scholars consider Modernism the most serious of attacks on Church authority, a "heresy which cut right at the root of the Christian revelation and the deposit of faith,"[2] others believe that Modernism was no more than "a loose coalition of scholars linked together only by their somewhat vague aspiration of narrowing the gap between Catholicism and modern culture."[3] Regardless of one's perspective, Modernism's impact on ecclesiology lay in the simple fact that, in John Dwyer's words, "It delayed for more than fifty years Catholic rapprochement with the modern world."[4] Because of the Church's reaction to the Modernist crisis, Catholic ecclesiology present in official Church documents and in the theology of many seminaries remained frozen for decades after the worst of the crisis had itself subsided. This meant that the idea of the church in the middle of the twentieth century, just before the beginning of the Second Council of the Vatican, remained in both traditional theological circles and in the popular imagination very much the same as it had been at the close of Vatican I—a perfect society with a strict pyramidal and hierarchical structure.

Modernist thought is most closely associated with the thought of Alfred Loisy (1857–1940) whose famous work *L'Evangile et L'Eglise* (The Gospel and the Church), published in 1902, became the "chief manifesto of

---

[1] For a history of Scripture scholarship, see Stephen Neill, *New Testament Interpretation 1861–1961* (New York: Harper and Row, 1962).

[2] Hales, *The Catholic Church in the Modern World*, 177.

[3] Bokenkotter, *A Concise History of the Catholic Church*, 377.

[4] Dwyer, *Church History*, 362.

Modernism."[5] Loisy's original intention was exemplary: to construct a Catholic refutation of the great liberal Protestant Adolf von Harnack's *Das Wesen des Christentums* (The Essence of Christianity). Unfortunately, the purpose of Loisy's work was lost in the storm of protest from the neoscholastic theologians in his own Roman Catholic tradition. As a historian and exegete, Loisy attempted to ground the Gospels in their historical context, suggesting that Jesus, like all other human persons, must himself be limited by his own historical and cultural place and understood and interpreted in light of his historical situation. Thus, he concluded that Jesus could not have imparted the ultimate truths of God.[6] He also affirmed that the church, especially the Catholic hierarchy, did not fit some pre-conceived divine plan that Jesus himself knew and was simply commissioned by his Father to carry out. Rather, the Christian community was grounded, like every other human society, in history and, therefore, was inevitably a product of evolution and development. On the basis of historical and Scriptural scholarship, Loisy called into question the classic, transhistorical blueprint theory of the church's origin. He affirmed that, although the church is based on what he said and did in his lifetime, Jesus himself did not directly establish the church. In Loisy's words

> The Church today resembles the community of the disciples neither more nor less than a grown man resembles the child he was at first. The identity of the Church or the man is not determined by permanent immobility of external forms, but by continuity of existence and consciousness of life through the perpetual transformations which are life's condition and manifestation.[7]

While these words are hardly shocking to the theologians and Scripture scholars in the half century after Vatican II, the neoscholastic theological worldview in 1903 that was insensitive to history saw the situation quite differently. Loisy's detractors could only equate the fact that, if the church is historically conditioned, so are all of the doctrines and moral laws of the Catholic tradition relative. This view, in their minds, was very dangerous to their self-contained and absolutist system of thought. Realistically, it would be hard to imagine that the Church, with such a closed mind at the beginning of the twentieth century, would be capable of recognizing change and development

[5] Dwyer, 360.

[6] Hales, *The Catholic Church in the Modern World*, 182.

[7] Alfred Loisy, *The Gospel and the Church* (New York: Charles Scribner's Sons, 1909), 172; quoted in Gratsch, *Where Peter Is*, 195.

as intrinsic and necessary to its understanding of the Gospel; it was unable to apply change and development to its own nature as the Christian community, to the truths of dogma and the moral law, and most of all, to its hierarchical authority.[8] This failure unfortunately isolated the Church from a world in which historical consciousness, scientific method, and the social sciences had become dominant over the older static metaphysical worldview. As one Jesuit of the time put it: "The Catholic Church has shut herself up in a far corner of a deserted country and now we think that we are invincible because no one worries about us or even knows us."[9]

Politically, this isolation was particularly true in the Church's struggle in France, highlighted by the infamous Dreyfus affair. After the establishment of the French Third Republic in 1875 following the conclusion of the Franco-Prussian War, the efforts of the new government to secularize education and to ban religious orders led to a hostility between the government and secularized masses on one side, and the Catholic establishment and people on the other. As one French official said in 1885: "Dominated or dominating—there is no middle of the road for the Catholic Church."[10] In 1905, the French government revoked the Concordat of 1801 between Napoleon and the Holy See and put Church property into the hands of lay associations.[11] In addition to complete political isolation, the Church was also unfortunately estranged from modern society intellectually and philosophically. Its reigning philosophy and theology, neoscholasticism, was indeed a "far corner of a deserted country" in the intellectual climate of the fin de siècle period and shortly after the turn of the century. In this context, Alfred Loisy's intention was to defend the rich tradition of Catholicism, using the historical and critical methods of his Protestant and secular contemporaries. Many of his conclusions perhaps were questionable, leading to the condemnation of his writings by Rome, but his historical-critical method was gradually vindicated in the decades after the First World War. Now the historical-critical method pioneered by Loisy is presumed in virtually every contemporary theological work, with the exception of fundamentalists of every Christian persuasion.

In addition to Loisy, Modernism was also associated with the Irish Jesuit

---

[8] Schoof, *A Survey of Catholic*, 31.

[9] Cited by E. Poulat, *Histoire, dogme et critique dans la crise moderniste* (Tournai: Casterman, 1962), 205.

[10] Quoted in J. Gadille, "The Failure to Reconcile Catholics and the Republic in France," in *The History of the Church*, 9:99.

[11] Gratsch, *Where Peter Is*, 191.

and convert, George Tyrrell (1861–1909), the German layman Friedrich von Hügel (1852–1925), the Italian Romolo Murri (1870–1944), and, to a lesser degree, the French philosopher mentioned earlier, Maurice Blondel (1861–1949). To this list one should add a woman, Maude Petre (1863–1942), the grand lady of modernist thinking.[12] These thinkers were both a challenge and a threat to the Church of their day. They challenged the Church to rethink its theology and place it in a more subjective, historical, and immanentist perspective. Tyrrell, for example, distinguished the reality of the church from both the papacy and hierarchy, understanding it as "the community of those who hearkened to the presence of God and who, in this process, achieved a deeper understanding of themselves and their task."[13] The Modernists also appeared as a threat to Church authority by the sheer speed in which their ideas demanded dramatic change in thought patterns, so long presumed and unquestioned in the neoscholastic Church. Add to this picture a lack of prudence on the part of many Modernists in dealing with Church authorities, together with a compulsive urge to destroy the established form of truth on the part of a few.[14] Since many bishops and the Roman Curia found Modernist ideas outside of their scholastic categories of understanding the world, they could only judge them as a serious threat to the traditional faith in all its aspects.

By their acceptance of a historical-critical interpretation of Scripture, the Modernists appeared to threaten the foundation of the Church's authority. Historical research into the life of Jesus of Nazareth and his community of disciples reached very different conclusions about the foundations of the church and the origins of the sacraments than the timeless and deductive truths of the neoscholastic tradition. Unfortunately, the emerging scientific scholarship employed by the Modernists was sometimes cynically presented and shocked those Catholic faithful whose fundamental principles had not changed since the Reformation. The Modernist view sought to understand Jesus as a human being within history and, perhaps most threatening of all, to place ecclesiastical hierarchy and papal primacy in a similar historical, and, therefore, relative, context. For the Modernist, Christian truth no longer simply existed *a priori*, something objectively given in revelation and held immutable in the "deposit of faith." Instead, this truth was historical,

[12] On Blondel, see Gregory Baum, *Man Becoming: God in Secular Language* (New York: Herder and Herder, 1970), 1–37.

[13] Dwyer, *Church History*, 363.

[14] Bokenkotter, *A Concise History of the Catholic Church*, 363.

discoverable through the evidence, and open to subjective interpretation in its reception. Even more earthshaking to the neoscholastic mind, the subjective reception of the truth of revelation was an intrinsic part of the truth itself.[15]

The Vatican's response to Modernism was swift and severe. Although many of the works of the Modernists were ironically written not to disrupt Catholic teaching but to refute the ideas of Liberal Protestants, Rome, with irony and tragedy, reacted quickly after the death of Leo XIII in 1903. With the succession to the papal throne of Pius X, the last signs of any effort on the part of the Church to meet the modern world halfway seemed to vanish. Quite the opposite, Pius X wished to take the Church back to the time of his namesake, Pius IX, who died in 1878.[16] Loisy's books were placed on the Index of Forbidden Books in 1903, and in 1907, the decree *Lamentabili Sane Exitu* (A Truly Lamentable Departure) was promulgated by the Holy Office, which was the successor to the Office of the Inquisition; now this office is called the Congregation for the Doctrine of the Faith. *Lamentabili* condemned sixty-five propositions, mostly attributed to Loisy and Tyrrell. In the same year, Pius X, in his encyclical *Pascendi Dominici Gregis* (Feeding the Lord's Flock) rejected a composite of ideas from a number of authors that the pope labeled as guilty of "Modernism," describing it as "the poisonous juice of all heresy."[17] In retrospect, some of the Modernist writers, given the climate of the Church at the time, went too far and too quickly. At the same time, the encyclical unfortunately was unable to distinguish between "reasonable progressivism and this 'rendezvous of all heresies' based on agnosticism and immanentism."[18] In this second encyclical, Pius X schematically reconstructed both, without recognizing the profound differences between them. As one commentator suggests, over the years it has become evident that Modernism, as a clearly defined theological program with the diabolical intention to harm the Church, never existed outside of the minds of Pius X and his curial advisors.[19] Rather, Modernism as a unified system of thought was more an invention of the Holy Office which uncritically attacked and condemned all those who favored historical research and who stood in opposition to the Church's

[15] This position was also held by the twentieth-century Lutheran theologian, Paul Tillich, in "Part I: Reason and Revelation," of his *Systematic Theology*, 1:71–105.

[16] Schoof, *A Survey of Catholic Theology*, 65.

[17] Hales, *The Catholic Church in the Modern World*, 186.

[18] Roger Aubert, "Intervention of Ecclesiastical Authority and the Integralist Reaction," in *The History of the Church*, 9:459.

[19] Dwyer, *Church History*, 364.

marriage between its teaching authority and neoscholastic patterns of thought. When the Biblical Commission in 1906 affirmed that Catholics must believe that Moses was the author of the entire Pentateuch (ludicrous in today's scholarship, especially given the fact that Moses's death is described in Deuteronomy 34!), Baron Friedrich von Hügel (d. 1925), the Austrian and English lay theologian and writer, proclaimed the decision as another victory for the "neoscholastic, utterly unhistorical, uncritical minds" in Rome.[20]

The tragedy of Modernism for the Church and its ecclesiology lay more in the conservative reaction of Pius X and the Holy Office than in the theology of the Modernists themselves. In addition to the condemnation of Loisy, Tyrrell, and other prominent figures, something of an ecclesiastical witch hunt took place for anyone with the slightest tendency toward Modernist ideas. Under the inspiration of Monsignor Umberto Benigni (1862–1934), the organized suppression of anyone suspected of Modernism continued from 1907 until the end of Pius X's reign in 1913. This excessive zeal was condemned by Cardinal Ferrari, Archbishop of Milan, as early as a few months after the appearance of *Pascendi Dominici Gregis* in 1907 but with little effect. One of the zealots, Abbate Cavallanti, condemned what he called semi-Modernism and compared it to semi-Pelagianism and semi-Jansenism after their condemnation. This semi-Modernism, he said, was "much more deceptive and insidious" than pure modernism because it proposes to be the "synthesis of all heresies."[21] Hence, an Integralist hunt for "modernistic tendencies" and the "modernistic mental constitution" took place in major seminaries and among the faculty of pontifical universities. This search had a chilling effect on Catholic theology for decades to follow, severely limiting its openness to history and the social sciences. Even notable places such as the École Biblique in Jerusalem, the theology faculty of Fribourg in Switzerland, and L'Institut Catholique of Paris suffered anti-modernist polemics. In 1910, Pius X established the famous "Oath against Modernism" in his motu proprio (on his own impulse) *Sacrorum Antistitum*, to be taken by all those teaching Catholic theology as well as all priests and seminarians; the oath was to be renewed annually.[22] This oath was finally rescinded on 17 July 1967 by the Congregation for the Doctrine of the Faith, headed at the time by the notorious

---

[20] See Friedrich von Hügel, cited in Bokenkotter, *A Concise History of the Catholic Church*, 63.

[21] Quoted in Aubert, "Intervention of Ecclesiastical Authority and the Integralist Reaction," 9:466.

[22] Aubert, 9:468.

Cardinal Alfredo Ottaviani, with the approval of Pope Paul VI.

Churchmen zealously opposed to Modernism were labeled "Integralists" because they wished to affirm "the integrity of their Romanism" at all costs. Their search for traces of Modernist thought took on the character of a "sacred crusade," or a witch hunt. Often, they lumped liberal thinkers of any kind and Modernists together, failing to distinguish between authentic progressive research and a few isolated ideas that might realistically threaten the faith. Anyone accused of watering down the faith, that is, interpreting the faith in historical rather than neoscholastic terms, incurred their wrath and, with the encouragement and support of Pius X, were often summarily relieved of their seminary or university teaching positions. Clandestine efforts, even espionage, were used to ferret out professors and priests tainted with Modernist thought; subsequent investigation often found them innocent. Men, sometimes the most loyal to the Church and the tradition, found themselves slandered and their reputations and careers ruined overnight.[23] One such victim in America was Father Francis P. Duffy, Professor at Saint Joseph's Seminary of the Archdiocese of New York, in Dunwoodie (part of Yonkers, just north of New York City), and editor and moving spirit of the New York Review (1905–1908), the finest American theological journal of the time.[24] After his dismissal from his position during the purge, he turned to pastoral work and became an army chaplain; today his statue stands in Times Square, New York, honored as the priest of the "Fighting Sixty-Ninth" Regiment in World War I. Like Duffy, many Modernists, regardless of their dismissal or condemnation, remained loyal to the Church. After George Tyrrell died in 1909, many efforts were made by his friends to obtain an official Catholic burial for him, but all were denied. After internment in a small Anglican parish cemetery, Maude Petre, the most notable woman in the Modernist movement, always a loyal daughter of the Church and Tyrrell's close friend, made this memorable ecclesiological comment: "Now some wonder why we worked so hard to obtain a Catholic funeral. I venture to think it was our duty to do so. Not to have done so would have been to give the lie to his life and to accept the notion that official, sectarian, ultramontane Catholicism was true Catholicism."[25]

---

[23] Aubert, 9:468–76; Dwyer, *Church History*, 364.

[24] James J. Hennesey, *American Catholics: A History of the Roman Catholic Community in the United States* (New York: Oxford University Press, 1981), 217.

[25] Quoted in Clyde F. Crews, *English Catholic Modernism: Maude Petre's Way of Faith* (Notre Dame: University of Notre Dame Press, 1984), 55.

The reaction to Modernism, especially in its extreme Integralist form, hindered theological research and deadened the soul of ecclesiology and research on the church in Scripture, the patristic era, and contemporary theology for decades. Any effort to understand the origins of the church and the formation of its hierarchical power in historical, and therefore "relative," terms was soundly condemned. The Integralist movement, of course, must be seen against the background of the enormous changes taking place in the intellectual world, changes which would inevitably force the Church to understand itself differently. These changes were threatening to some not only because they suggested different theological conclusions but wholly new theological starting places and vastly different sets of interpretative categories. The Integralists were the fundamentalists of their day, the "neo-orthodox," in sociologist Peter Berger's terms, who knew the world was changing but refused to acknowledge that such change was taking place.[26] Hence, they retreated into the safe but unrealistic harbor of the nineteenth-century Church where the truth was clear and provided security without question and without doubt. The excesses of the Integralist hunt for heretics reached its zenith in 1912 and 1913 when any theologian accused of any semi-Modernist thinking was dismissed from his position. Inevitably, this produced a strong reaction, with resistance taking place both among some high-level prelates deeply concerned for the Church, and in the writings of a number of French and German Jesuit theological journals.[27] With the death of Pius X and the election of Benedict XV as pope in 1914, the heavy-handed and overzealous tactics of Benigni and other Integralists finally ended. Regardless of the blame for the whole situation—and both sides must share in the responsibility—the Modernist crisis was a catastrophe for the Church. Theology became even more cautious and sterile. Ecclesiology, protective and narrowly focused for centuries, was further trapped, like a cornered animal, in the defense of the Roman Catholic orthodoxy of the time. In the end, the fury of the Modernist debate only made the animal tamer, more out of touch with the forces of twentieth-century thought swirling about it. The Oath against Modernism survived until 1967!

In addition to the disaster for the church of Modernism and its Integralist reaction, the pontificate of Pius X must also be remembered for more than ecclesiastical intrigue and a battle with a heresy of some dubious validity.

[26] See Peter Berger, *The Heretical Imperative: Contemporary Possibilities for Religious Affirmation* (New York: Doubleday Anchor, 1980), 89.

[27] Aubert, "Intervention of Ecclesiastical Authority and the Integralist Reaction, 9:479.

Surprisingly, a very significant event for twentieth-century ecclesiology took place during his reign. Pius was a man of great devotion to the liturgy and the Eucharist. Inspired by the music of the monks of Solesmes (a Benedictine Abbey in France), he revived liturgical music and considered Gregorian chant as "the perfect model of Church music," strongly encouraging its adaptation as the norm for all liturgical music. He is perhaps most remembered for his decree of 1905 that advocated frequent, even daily, reception of Holy Communion. The Eucharist had fallen into disfavor by a kind of theological and moral rigorism that believed that all premeditated venial sins must be removed before approaching the altar. In strongly rejecting this opinion, Pius agreed with the statement of Monsignor de Ségur that affirmed that the Eucharist is not "a reward for achieved virtue, but on the contrary, the means of achieving virtue." As an admirer of John "Don" Bosco (d. 1888), founder of the Salesians to help poor children in the Industrial Revolution, Pius believed that "Jesus [was] meant to be the daily remedy and the daily food for our daily shortcomings."[28] In spite of the sterility and defensiveness of the Church's formal ecclesiology, the ecclesial importance of the Eucharist was re-established and the inner life of the faithful was renewed by the efforts of this deeply spiritual man who was canonized a saint in 1954 during the pontificate of Pius XII. Pius X was also a significant influence on the liturgical movement that began shortly after his death and was a major factor in the renewal of ecclesiology later in the century.

7.2 World War I and the Development of Protestant Ecclesiology

7.2.1 World War I. The most important event for all the Christian churches in the first part of the twentieth century, and therefore for the history of ecclesiology, did not take place inside the churches themselves but in the broader and wider world in which the churches of Christ lived. This event, of course, was the First World War. With the twentieth century, any trace of the older medieval world where church and state, in spite of their battles, were inseparable, was eradicated. Now the world was free to be itself, to be world,

[28] Quoted in Roger Aubert, "Eucharist Decrees and Liturgical Renewal," in *The History of the Church*, 9:403–4.

that is, to be thoroughly "secular," in spite of the grand illusions of standing behind, or in front of, the Christian symbols.[29] The church, once all powerful in establishing the reigning norms of culture, was now one player among many in the competition to structure the human personality and organize human life politically and socially in a meaningful way. The controlling set of cultural, legal, and moral symbols characteristic of the medieval church had been in decline since the late Middle Ages. The de-Christianization and secularization of Europe, which had begun in earnest in the nineteenth century, gave both Protestant and Catholic churches a very different role in the twentieth-century marketplace for warm bodies and eager souls. With the emergence of science and technology and the enormous growth of attractive secular values in competition with one another, the churches' primary role in guiding and directing the culture and its people was displaced for all time by a symbol system whose primary goal was not transcendence but immanent and successful life in this world. In short, modernity and secularity defined contemporary life, not allegiance to the Christian symbols of Bible, church, worship, and moral values.

The war itself was true to its name—both a world war and a worldly war, with religion and the churches no longer a significant factor in its origin or outcome. While Pius X spoke openly about the danger of war during the last years of his reign, it also seems clear that he and his Secretary of State, the Spanish Cardinal Raphael Merry del Val, a fascinating character in church history in any century, favored Austria-Hungary and the old Emperor, Franz Joseph—apparently for no other reason than Austria was the last large Catholic country in Europe and the only one capable of supporting the older political order where the Church remained dominant. As war was imminent, "the Pope did not raise the voice of a prophet condemning war, but merely confined himself to a somewhat meek appeal to all peoples to pray."[30] In the period of increasing nationalism and a growing threat of conflict, the reaction of Catholic groups in different nations was also disappointing. On the contrary, "ecclesiastical groups as well as the faithful themselves joined more and more openly in the glorification of national feeling."[31] This chauvinism unfortunately prefigured the enthusiasm with which Catholics on both sides supported the fighting once it broke out. Pope Benedict XV's attempts to

[29] The Latin *seculum* means world or age.

[30] Roger Aubert, "The Outbreak of World War I," in *The History of the Church*, 9:523.

[31] Aubert, 517.

bring this "useless slaughter" to an end met a deaf ear among both Catholics and Protestants in Europe.

This "war to end all wars" suggested a different kind of fragmentation in the Body of Christ that history had not known before. Protestants and Catholics, instead of fighting each other, fought beside one another against their brothers and sisters in a hostile country. This suggested that newer national and secular loyalties had become much deeper than the older commitment to the Christian churches and a universe structured and ordered by institutionally religious principles and politics. It also revealed that the Christian message of peace and justice was little heeded by many self-proclaimed Christians, and for many, the message was viewed as irrelevant and unnecessary. In Protestant churches, the war rendered completely obsolete any vestiges of liberal Protestant thought and its humanist idealism of human progress that had flourished at the end of the nineteenth and beginning of the twentieth centuries. The war also changed the focus of Catholicism from its intra-ecclesial battle over Modernism and institutional conflicts to more realistic and inclusive concerns, involving an outside world in a great political struggle and the loss of the majority of the lower and middle classes of proletariat Europe who were Catholic in name only.

7.2.2 Karl Barth. Since the time of the Reformation, we have examined, almost exclusively, the path of Roman Catholic ecclesiology. Now it is time to examine the two most important Protestant theologians of the twentieth century, Karl Barth and Paul Tillich. Inspired by the war, and in reaction to the loss of transcendence in liberal Protestantism, the Swiss Protestant theologian, Karl Barth (1886–1968) uttered his great "No" to any theology that began with human history and faith in human progress. For Barth, the controlling idea and the center of all Christian theology could be found in the simple words, "Dominus dixit," that is, "the Lord has spoken." Barth's theology was a theology of crisis and of decision: the absolute revelation of God in confrontation with the crisis of the world and the human situation. Barth radically separated God from the human person, splitting heaven and earth, creator and creature, time and eternity, into two distinct orders. He rejected any confusion between the divine and the human as well as any "irreverent assimilation" of God and human persons. In his mind, an absolute separation exists between the divine and the human—a "desert barrier" and "polar zone," as he called it—and no bridge or community of any kind can overcome this abyss. Barth sought to let God be God and insisted that God's Word alone is the central issue of theology. God is superior and human beings inferior; the sinful nature of the human person must be overcome.[32] In this light, the church exists primarily on the human and inferior side of the divine-human equation. Barth sharply criticized the church as the culmination of human sin and weakness. For him, the Christian community remains always an "ambiguous fact," yet one that is inescapable given the human condition. In a powerful image, he suggests that the church is like a tabernacle or tent "wandering in the desert." He warns that it must never be turned into a temple or a pagoda, and affirms that, "[a] Church which is truly in earnest is itself bound to detonate the dynamite which blows up the pagoda."[33]

Barth's *Der Römerbrief* (Epistle to the Romans) of 1918 and later his massive *Kirchliche Dogmatik* (Church Dogmatics), begun in 1932, embodied Protestant neoorthodoxy, defined as a return to God and God's sacred Word as the starting point and foundation of all theology.[34] Barth's "dialectical" theology—so-called because the vast distinction between God and humanity serves as the source of their union at the same time—in one way or another influenced much of the theology, both Protestant and Catholic, for the rest of the twentieth century; he is still read and studied today, one hundred years since his first important book, *The Epistle to the Romans*, was published.[35]

Barth's theology inspired other important Protestant thinkers between the wars, including Friedrich Gogarten, Emil Brunner, and Rudolf Bultmann in Germany, and Reinhold Niebuhr in America. Although these theologians often disagreed with Barth, they also shared his search for a new theological starting point, a fresh approach to the understanding and proclamation of the Christian message in order to answer the crisis of the time. These Protestant theologians were not unlike their counterparts in the Catholic Church after World War I. Just as Protestants broke with their liberal, humanitarian roots in the decades before the war, Catholics began to emerge out of their rigid and static neoscholastic philosophical and theological framework and period of uncreative and static theology that followed the Modernist crisis. Both traditions, in their own ways, re-examined the meaning of the church both in

---

[32] Heinz Zahrnt, *The Question of God: Protestant Theology in the Twentieth Century* (New York: Harcourt, Brace and World, 1966), 19–26.

[33] Quoted in Zahrnt, 37.

[34] Karl Barth, *Epistle to the Romans*, trans. Edwyn C. Hoskyns (New York: Oxford University Press, 1933); Karl Barth, *Church Dogmatics*, trans. Edwyn C. Hoskyns (Edinburgh: T&T Clark, 1936–1962). For a brief presentation of Barth, see his *Dogmatics in Outline* (New York: Harper Torchbooks, 1959).

[35] Zahrnt, *The Question of God*, 24–25. See Berger, *The Heretical Imperative*, 61–86.

the light of the new historical situation of the modern world after World War I and the ancient sources of theology in Scripture and the tradition of the Fathers.

While Barth was much more of a "church theologian" than Paul Tillich was, his criticisms of the church were often deep and profound, and similar to Tillich's, although coming from a very different starting point that we will consider. Barth's ecclesiology is not easy to find if one were to look at the *Church Dogmatics* and search for such a heading. First, he prefers the term Christian community (*Gemeinde*) to church (*Kirche*), and his ecclesiology is implicit rather than explicit in many sections of the *Church Dogmatics*. If it is true that "for Barth theology is Christology," then this especially holds true for ecclesiology. For Barth, ecclesiology is Christology. The church emerges with the people elected by Christ into the community of the saved.[36] While he places his ecclesiology in the context of the Holy Spirit, his pneumatology is itself Christ-centered. Some scholars have suggested that a "lack of distinctiveness in Barth's pneumatology" leads to a kind on Binitarianism, where only two, not three, Persons of the Trinity matter.[37] As Barth writes: "All ecclesiology is grounded, critically limited, but also positively determined by Christology."[38] The primary image of the church for Barth is the Body of Christ, almost to the exclusion of other New Testament images and subsequent theological models. The vocation of the church is witness, not mediation or cooperation between the Gospel and world.[39] The church's true task is to attest to the reconciliation of the world accomplished solely by Christ; this work of Christ in reconciliation and redemption requires no supplementation. Because Christ is present, not absent, no mediation by the church is needed to make him present.[40] For Barth, the church is a *creatura verbi*, the direct creation of the Word. Barth "advocates a vision of the community, living in radical dependence on the written Word, continually testing its witness

---

[36] Kimlyn J. Bender, *Karl Barth's Christological Ecclesiology* (Hampshire: Ashgate, 2005), 3.

[37] James J. Buckley, "A Field of Living Fire: Karl Barth on the Spirit and the Church," in *Modern Theology* 10, no. 1 (1994), 84–85.

[38] Karl Barth, *Church Dogmatics*, vol. 4 (New York: Bloomsbury, 1955), 3, 786.

[39] Bender, *Karl Barth's Christological Ecclesiology*, 278.

[40] Bender, 279.

by this norm."[41] Barth discusses the Christian community in the concrete—he moves from the particular to the universal and affirms that, "we cannot move from the general to the particular, but only in the opposite direction."[42] Understanding Barth's ecclesiology means to discern his "controlling Christological logic" at the core of all he understands to be church.[43]

As one can see, Barthian ecclesiology is faithful to Calvin's vision of God, human nature, and the church. Paul Tillich's Protestant ecclesiology is quite different from Barth's. In Tillich's view, Barth's theology could be summed up in the first commandment: "Any teaching that draws God into the sphere of human possibility is rebellion against the first commandment."[44] Thus, any connection or interaction between divine activity and a church or Christian community seems impossible, or at least very tenuous, in Barth's thought. Since most twentieth-century Protestant churches were closer to Barth's theology than Tillich's, it is little wonder that Protestants and Catholics had little in common in their understanding of the church and starting point for ecclesiology, at least not until Vatican II.

7.2.3 Paul Tillich. Among Barth's contemporaries, Paul Tillich (1886–1965), a Lutheran theologian and chaplain in the German army, was, like Barth and his followers, deeply influenced by World War I. Tillich's theological roots are similar to Barth's in their early reaction to the excesses of liberal Protestantism, but after becoming an emigré from Nazi Germany to New York in 1933, Tillich's theology took a very different direction. In his autobiographical reflections, he wrote of his war service: "The experience of those four years of war revealed to me and to my entire generation an abyss in human existence which could not be ignored."[45] Tillich vividly understood that World War I had shattered the world of the nineteenth century, bringing "a harsh end to the optimistic spirit of progress and the civilized individualism

[41] Joseph Mangina, *Karl Barth: A Theologian of Christian Witness* (Louisville: Westminster John Knox, 2004), 48.

[42] Quoted in Nicholas M. Healy, "The Logic of Karl Barth's Ecclesiology: Analysis, Assessment, and Proposed Modifications," *Modern Theology* 10, no. 3 (1994): 255.

[43] Healy, 270.

[44] Paul Tillich, "What is Wrong with Dialectical Theology?" *The Journal of Religion* 15, no. 2 (1935), 129.

[45] Paul Tillich, *The Interpretation of History* (New York: Charles Scribner's Sons, 1936), 35. This chapter, comprised of his autobiographical reflections, is reprinted separately as *On the Boundary* (New York: Charles Scribner's Sons, 1966).

with which the liberal theologians had associated Christianity."[46] The war inspired Tillich to question both his liberal theological roots and his middle class evangelical piety; it served as a catalyst for the creation of what he called an "answering theology," that is, one which seeks to answer the ultimate questions of human existence in ways comprehensible and acceptable to modern persons, especially those in existential confusion, suffering, and despair.[47] Tillich believed that the theological answers came not from the human situation and from human need but from God's free and transcendent Revelation. Unlike Barth, however, he insisted that the theological answers cannot, in very caustic words, be "hurled at persons like stones." Instead, according to his method of correlation (considered in detail in chapter one of this volume), the answers must be correlated with the human condition and expressed in the same form in which persons pose their ultimate questions of existence and meaning. For Tillich, it is the function of the church to give answers, not only to itself but also to those outside in the culture.[48] He recognized that the Christian churches had failed to respond to the development of the modern thought and conditions of injustice in the nineteenth-century. Now after World War I, he believed it was imperative for the churches to address contemporary persons in their situation of confusion and loss of faith and hope.

In Tillich's theology, the question of the church is part of his complex system of ontology, or the study of being. This ontology, aptly described by a devoted former student and scholar as a "mystical ontology," reflects the worldview of Plato, Augustine, the medieval Franciscans such as Bonaventure, the Protestant mystic, Jakob Böhme (1575–1624), and the nineteenth-century idealist philosopher, Friedrich Schelling (1775–1854).[49] For Tillich,

[46] Schoof, *A Survey of Catholic Theology*, 78.

[47] In an interview before his death, Tillich looked back on his life's work this way: "My work is for those who ask questions and for them I am here." Quoted by Kenneth Bagnell, "Paul Tillich: An Interview," *The United Church Observer* 27, no. 15 (November 1965), 24.

[48] Tillich, *Theology of Culture*, 49. Tillich agreed with Barth that a new starting point for theology was necessary after the war, but, unlike Barth, he never gave up his intellectual roots in liberal Protestantism and remained, at least in part, sympathetic to Schleiermacher, Ritschl, Harnack, and Troeltsch. In 1935, just after arriving in America, Tillich strongly criticized Barth's ideas in "What Is Wrong with Dialectical Theology?," 127–45.

[49] Carl Braaten, "Paul Tillich and the Classical Christian Tradition," in *Perspectives on Nineteenth and Twentieth Century Protestant Theology*, by Paul Tillich, ed. Carl Braaten (New York: Harper and Row, 1967), 19.

God is Being-itself who does not exist, that is, "stand out" of being, but simply is. God is the answer to the human question of being. Jesus is the New Being who answers the question of human estrangement, overcoming the gap between the ideal, essential self and the estranged, existential self. This New Being is actualized in life as the Spiritual Presence that brings salvation or the unambiguous life. The Spiritual Presence is revealed historically in three ways: in all of humankind as a preparation, in the central manifestation of the Divine Spirit in the Cross and Resurrection of Jesus, and in the Spiritual Community.

Tillich's understanding of the church, like his anthropology and Christology, must be framed in the context of his split between essence and existence—whenever "the ideal is held against the real, truth against error, good against evil."[50] This split, he says, serves as the "backbone of the whole body of theological thought" and "must be elaborated in every part of the theological system."[51] Essence is that which makes a thing what it is; but the appearance, the actualization of what is, always has the quality of imperfection and distortion when contrasted with its essential nature. Essence both "empowers and judges that which exists."[52] Anthropologically, Tillich affirms, "what man is in his essential, spiritual and heavenly nature and what he is in his existential, material and earthly nature is the main problem of theology in general and of Christology in particular."[53] Rendered ecclesiological, the dual nature of the church is translated from an invisible/visible, divine/human structure to an essential/existential one.[54] Tillich makes a clear distinction between the ideal and essential church and the historical churches that live under the conditions of estrangement. He employs the term "Spiritual Community" for this essential or ideal church, a designation employed only in the Systematic

---

[50] Tillich, *Systematic Theology*, 1:202.

[51] Tillich, 1:204.

[52] Tillich, 1:203.

[53] Paul Tillich, "A Reinterpretation of the Doctrine of the Incarnation," *Church Quarterly Review*, 147, no. 294 (January–March, 1949), 138–39.

[54] See Paul Tillich, *Systematic Theology*, vol. 3 (Chicago: The University of Chicago Press, 1963), 162–65.

Theology.[55]

The Spiritual Community mediates the Spiritual Presence; it is the community of the New Being, the place "where the New Reality which is Christ...moves into us and is continued by us."[56] The church's nature is ontological, standing "for the power of being-itself." Its function is soteriological (the doctrine of salvation): mediating "a courage which takes doubt and meaninglessness into itself."[57] It is the place where the "reunion of man to man is pronounced and confessed and realized," where this reunion becomes an "actual event" in space and time.[58] Healing, the process of participating in the transcendent union, was pre-formed in a person's essential nature, disrupted in existential estrangement, and recreated and made actual in the Spiritual Community by the power of the Spiritual Presence.[59] The Spiritual Community is not so much established by the Spiritual Presence, as it is an intrinsic part of what it means to say that the Spiritual Presence is manifest in history because the Spiritual Presence embraces the human spirit in social groups so that "all the functions of the human spirit—moral self-integration, cultural self-creativity, and religious self-transcendence—are conditioned by the social context of the ego-thou encounter."[60] Personal life presupposes encounter with other persons in a community, and community itself has no meaning without the historical dimensions of past and future.[61] The church as the Body of Christ was, for Tillich, the Spiritual Community, the essential church "as it should be."[62] It was a "strictly theonomous symbol" (a symbol completely transparent for the presence of God), representing the community of people participating in the transcendent unity of the Spiritual Presence.[63] The Spiritual Community is also a community of love; it possesses agape, the perfect love of God, which serves both as the criterion of the variety of love relations possible within it, and as an "anticipation of the perfect union in Eternal

[55] Tillich, 3:152–54.

[56] Tillich, *Theology of Culture*, 212–13.

[57] Paul Tillich, *The Courage To Be* (New Haven: Yale University Press, 1952), 188. Reprint, with an introduction by Peter Gomes (New Haven: Yale University Press, 2001).

[58] Paul Tillich, *The New Being* (New York: Charles Scribner's Sons, 1955), 24.

[59] Tillich, *Systematic Theology*, 3:157.

[60] Tillich, 3:139.

[61] Tillich, 3:135.

[62] Tillich, 1:148.

[63] Tillich, *The Protestant Era*, 62.

Life."[64]

Tillich refused to identify the Body of Christ with the churches themselves. Tillich understands the relationship between the Spiritual Community and the historical church in this way: the Spiritual Community is the "inner telos" (end or goal), the dynamic essence, of the churches, and the "source of everything that makes them churches."[65] Churches share in all the ambiguities of life, and of religion in particular. The churches live in the "yes and no" of the world: they reveal the Spiritual Presence that creates their essence; they also conceal and distort this essence through the profanization and demonization of religious life.[66] There are not two churches but two aspects of one church (*Doppelgestalt,* double form), of "essentiality determining existence and being resisted by existence."[67]

The Spiritual Community is comprised of all those healed by the power of the New Being and empowered to overcome their estrangement from their essential selves and from God as the Ground of their Being. One must state again that the Spiritual Community or Church is not to be simply equated with the historical churches. The Spiritual Community is the essential Church, the dynamic essence at the heart of the historical and sinful churches. While the historical churches participate in the salvific life of the Spiritual Community, they also exist under the conditions of estrangement, and thus both genuinely reveal and tragically conceal their essence as the Spiritual Presence and transforming grace in the human community.[68]

Tillich's ecclesiology, because it greatly understated the importance of the historical Christian community, was considered too universal, too mystical, too invisible by the majority of Catholic theologians, as well as by many theologians within his own Protestant tradition.[69] Yet, his idea of the church as the Spiritual Community was ironically not parochial but truly catholic. In his theology, this Spiritual Community or the Church can be latent or manifest as well as visible or invisible, depending on its relationship to the historical

---

[64] Tillich, *Systematic Theology*, 3:156.

[65] Tillich, 3:162–64.

[66] Tillich, 3:165.

[67] Tillich, 3:163.

[68] Tillich, 3:151ff.

[69] For example, see the harsh criticism from one of Tillich's lifelong friends, Nels F. S. Ferre in "Three Critical Issues in Tillich's Philosophical Theology," *Scottish Journal of Theology* 10 (1957), 225–38; and in "Tillich's View of the Church," in *The Theology of Paul Tillich,* rev. ed., ed. Charles Kegley and Robert Bretall (New York: Pilgrim Press, 1982), 284–301.

criterion of the Cross. Whenever the power of the New Being is present through faith and love, the latent Spiritual Community exists. Before Jesus of Nazareth, all historical expressions of the Spiritual Community were latent, though they could be visible in so far as the Spiritual Presence was at work in temples and cults and religious movements of all kinds. After the Cross, the Spiritual Community became manifest and visible.

In spite of major differences, certain similarities between Tillich's idea of the church and Catholic ecclesiology are also clear. Although Tillich placed the idea of a latent Spiritual Community or Church in the essential world that informs existence, it is close to the more mystical and universal understanding of church in Catholic theology. Such ecclesiology finds expression in the Shepherd of Hermas's venerable old woman who existed before creation or in Yves Congar's church that has existed from Abel or the first just human person.[70] Tillich's mistake in the mind of his critics was his desire to preserve the eternal church from the sinful reality of the churches. He believed, for example, that Catholic theology was always tempted to substitute the historical church for God Godself; this he considered an idolatrous action or, in his term, heteronomous, ("heteros" or other and "nomos," law or rule) in which ultimate authority comes from another finite reality.[71] At the same time, his mystical and ontological approach to the church moved Tillich's ecclesiology closer to the Catholic ecclesiology that was to blossom between the wars and take official form at the Second Vatican Council.

Tillich's concept of the latent and manifest church also opens up the question of the role of the church in universal salvation and the relationship between the Christian church and other world religions. For unlike Barth and other Protestants, Tillich places the church as Spiritual Community closer to God than to human beings, divinizing it in the way that is more Catholic than Protestant. Although, in his Platonic fashion, he proceeds to separate the Spiritual Community or Church as the ideal from the churches as sinful historical communities, such a dialectic is not foreign to a truly Catholic understanding of the church. Indeed (as we will see below), it has its counterpart in the dual nature of the church in classic Catholic ecclesiology and in the sacramental ecclesiology that became prominent just before and during the Second Vatican Council. Put differently, Tillich's accusation that Catholic

---

[70] Yves M. -J. Congar, "Ecclesia ab Abel," in *Abhandlungen über Theologie und Kirche*: *Festschrift für Karl Adam* (Essays on Theology and Church: Writings in Honor of Karl Adam) (Dusseldorf: Patmos Verlag, 1952).

[71] Weigel, *Catholic Theology in Dialogue*, 24–25.

ecclesiology tends to put the Church in place of God is partially true and partially false—it all depends upon what you mean by church.[72]

Most important for Catholic ecclesiology was Tillich's sense of what he called the "Catholic substance," that is, community, doctrine, and liturgy—the sum of the visible sacramental elements in which the invisible, transhistorical spirit of Christ can be grasped, comprehended, and accepted by persons in concrete historical forms. Tillich proposed three aspects of this Catholic substance: first, sacramentalism or the sacramental presence of grace; second, unity in a community of love; third—and surprisingly for the Protestant Tillich—authority.[73] For Tillich, God's grace must take human and historical form, what he called a Gestalt of grace, no matter how fragmented and incomplete such form may be. Tillich was deeply concerned about the objectified and authoritarian structure of grace in the Roman Catholic Church, as he saw it; but he was equally concerned about a Gestalt-less or unstructured and interior Protestantism on the other. His sacramental understanding of the church was not unlike that which was to develop in Catholic ecclesiology before and after World War II. Tillich's appreciation of the more romantic and interior sense of Catholicism was also quite similar to Catholicism's own rediscovery of a more spiritual and mystical understanding of the church and Catholic identity that developed between the World Wars (which we will consider below). In a 1929 work, Tillich expressed both his understanding of the post-Modernist Catholic Church he rejected and the deeper meaning of Catholicism he admired and embraced:

> The Catholic Church…has manifestly been able to preserve a genuine substance that continues to exist, although it is encased within an ever hardening crust. But whenever the hardness and crust are broken through and the substance becomes visible, it exercises a peculiar fascination; then we see what was once the life substance and inheritance of all of us and what we have now lost, and a deep yearning awakens in us for the departed youth of our culture.[74]

7.2.4 A Catholic Perspective on Barth and Tillich. Both Barth's and Tillich's

---

[72] Weigel, 25.

[73] In 1951, Tillich gave a lecture in Germany on the Protestant Principle and Catholic Substance published as *Der Mensch im Christentum. Protestantische Vision: Katholische Substanz, Protestantisches Prinzip, Sozialistische Entscheidung* (The Person in Christianity. Protestant Vision: Catholic Substance, Protestant Principle, Socialist Encounter) (Düsseldorf: Ring Verlag, 1953). No English translation exists.

[74] Tillich, *The Protestant Era*, 194.

ecclesiologies have much to offer twenty-first-century Catholic ecclesiology that is both faithful to the tradition and open to a full reception of the documents of Vatican II. Their ecclesiology, however, must be read against the backdrop of the most dramatic shift in Catholic theology since Trent in the sixteenth century. As students of theology, Tillich and Barth were raised with the authoritarian spirit and ultramontane attitude of Catholic ecclesiology in the post-Tridentine and Vatican I Church. Ecclesiology at Vatican I was reduced to the study of the power of the hierarchy, especially the bishop of Rome—ecclesiology became "hierarchology."[75] Barth's and Tillich's understanding of Catholicism was fundamentally Tridentine, and it is not clear whether or how far they moved beyond this position. Neither lived to see whether the reforms of Vatican II were "received" by the church, in the formal theological meaning of the term, and to what extent and in what manner such reception took place.[76] Both had an inkling that much was afoot in Catholicism, and since Barth lived three years longer than Tillich did, he witnessed the crucial years after the Council. After his trip to Rome as an invited guest at Vatican II, he wrote a brief appraisal of the Council in a book, *Ad Limina Apostolorum* (To the Threshold of the Apostles), in which he mentioned that he was pleased to see the liturgical reforms in place.[77] Tillich, in the introduction to the third volume of his Systematic Theology, acknowledges the similarity of his work with that of the French Catholic paleontologist, Pierre Teilhard de Chardin and calls on Protestant theology to "take into consideration the present, more affirmative relation between Catholicism and Protestantism," describing it as a "kairos, a moment full of potentialities, in Protestant–Catholic relations."[78] Yet, neither could see the impact the Council had on the theology and the life of the church.

While it may have been simple for Catholic theologians to criticize Barth's and Tillich's ecclesiology—Tillich's church was too above history and Barth's church had too little to do in history—a more ecumenical approach is clear in retrospect. Vatican II took Barth's and Tillich's theology seriously, and whether consciously or not, the ecclesiology that emerged from the Council was much closer to Tillich's and Barth's church than any of the

---

[75] Congar, *Lay People in the Church*, 58–59.

[76] For a definition of "reception," see J. M. R. Tillard, "Vatican II: Did We Receive It?" *One in Christ* 21 (1985): 276–83.

[77] Karl Barth, *Ad Limina Apostolorum: An Appraisal of Vatican II*, trans. Keith R. Crim (Louisville: John Knox Press, 1968), 13.

[78] Tillich, *Systematic Theology*, 3:6.

Fathers at Vatican I could have imagined; for that matter, it was closer than Tillich and Barth themselves could have anticipated during the Pian era of Catholicism before John XXIII. Neither, of course, would accept the most Catholic of statements from St. Thomas: "Since therefore grace does not destroy nature but perfects it, natural reason should minister to faith as the natural bent of the will ministers to charity."[79] Both would witness the beginnings of a very different Catholicism open to their own fundamental theological positions.

Let us begin with Tillich. At Vatican II, I suggest that Catholic ecclesiology became more Tillichian that Barthian. It had been Barthian in this sense: Barth was to the Word as Catholicism was to the ecclesia. Both existed above history and were of divine origin. Becoming more Tillichian suggests more than the obvious affinities of Tillich to Catholic ontology and sacramentality, though these elements are noteworthy. The substance of Tillich's method of correlation, in which theology must answer the philosophical questions rising out of human experience, was embraced by the Council and in subsequent Catholic theology. *Gaudium et Spes* was a careful examination of the human person and culture in the modern world. In the famous text:

> To carry out such a task [that is, like Christ, of serving not to be served], the Church has always had the duty of scrutinizing the signs of the times and of interpreting them in the light of the Gospel. Thus, in language intelligible to each generation, she can respond to the perennial questions which men ask about this present life and the life to come, and about the relationship of the one to the other.[80]

The Second Vatican Council, in breaking with the static, neoscholastic way of doing theology, heralded two important changes in Catholic thought: the shift to historical consciousness and the primacy of experience. In neoscholastic patterns of thought, truth existed *a priori*, free from the whims of history or experience. Now, like Tillich, Catholic ecclesiology fostered a church that explored the human condition in all its complexity, so the Gospel message could meet the needs of a modern culture. Furthermore, the starting point of theology was human experience, very much a Tillichian and not a Barthian idea. For one Catholic theologian, theology became "a way of 'testing' the contributions of the experience" and applying it to various theological

---

[79] Thomas Aquinas, *Summa Theologica*, Part 1, Question 1, Article 8, Response to Objection 2.

[80] *Gaudium et Spes*, art. 4.

disciplines.[81] Another says that theology is "about life, the experience of life in all of its spiritual implications, especially those that point to God at the center of life itself."[82] One is reminded here of Tillich's concept of Revelation as "reason in ecstasy."[83]

Barth himself was aware of this new openness to experience and examining the signs of the times, and he saw its inherent danger. He asks Catholicism: "Is it so certain that dialogue with the world is to be placed ahead of proclamation to the world?"[84] If, Barth says, the renewal of the church at Vatican II was not "a theoretical and practical understanding of itself in light of the revelation on which it is founded" but "a renewal of her thinking, speaking, and acting today in light of the modern world," then he warns that the resulting danger for Catholicism would be "an undesired repetition of the errors committed in modern Protestantism." Had he lived to read Avery Dulles's 1977 book, *The Resilient Church: The Necessity and Limits of Adaptation*, Barth would have clearly been on the side of limiting adaptation. For Barth, the church was a witness to Christ's redemption, a herald to a sinful world, and dialogue and adaptation with the culture would threaten its primary role.

As early as 1974, a certain reaction was taking place to the movement of the Council to be open to the world, not unlike the criticism of some that Tillich's method of correlation was surrendering the autonomy and the transcendence of the theological answer. A group of American thinkers, including Avery Dulles, issued the Hartford Appeal, decrying a world that was closed to transcendence; the Appeal insisted that the church must establish an agenda for the world, not the world for the church.[85] Barth would have been an enthusiastic supporter of this document. And Barth would have laughed in agreement at the line of Philip Rieff, sociologist of Freud, who in a 1971 lecture said, "Experience is a swindle; the experienced know that much."[86]

7.2.5 The Protestant Principle and the Catholic Substance. Perhaps the most profound change at Vatican II, in Tillich's terminology, was the recovery of the Protestant principle within the Catholic substance. For Tillich, the

---

[81] Thompson, 14.

[82] Lane, *The Experience of God*, ix.

[83] Tillich, *Systematic Theology*, 1:111–13.

[84] Barth, *Ad Limina Apostolorum*, 27.

[85] Peter Berger, "For a World with Windows," in *Against the World and For the World: The Hartford Appeal and the Future of American Religion*, ed. Peter Berger and Richard John Neuhaus (New York: Seabury, 1976), 8–19.

[86] Philip Rieff, *Fellow Teachers* (New York: Harper and Row, 1972), 8.

Protestant principle guards the Transcendent, insisting that no specific manifestation of the Holy can be identified with the Holy itself, whether it be a book, a church, a government, or a philosophy of life. Ecclesiology as the study of the *societas perfecta* left no room for a prophetic element. If the church were perfect, how could it change? Why would it change? In the theology from Trent to Vatican II, the Catholic Church tended to divinize its institutional structure against all criticism. Hence, in his Syllabus of Errors of 1864, Pius IX condemned anyone who said that, "the Church is not a true and perfect society, entirely free—nor is she endowed with proper and perpetual rights of her own, conferred upon her by her Divine Founder."[87] The documents of Vatican II brought a different vision of the Catholic Church: no longer is the church a perfect society but a "stranger in a foreign land," a "pilgrim church"; "the Church already on this earth is signed with a sanctity which is real although imperfect."[88] By characterizing herself as the "universal sacrament of salvation," the church implies, since all sacraments both reveal and conceal, that she is the sacrament of Christ's presence as well as his absence, until he returns in glory.[89] Too much emphasis has been placed on the "Catholic substance" of sacramentality, that is, its visibility, and not enough on the "Protestant principle." In every sacramental form, we have only the sign and the reality together, or what the medieval theologians called the *res et sacramentum*, the finite form (*sacramentum*) and the infinite reality to which it points (*res*); we do not have the eschatological reality of the *res tantum*, where God will be all in all.[90] This is why the penultimate chapter of *Lumen Gentium* considers the eschatological nature of the church. Karl Barth agrees enthusiastically: "Where the Church is, there it has an aim, the Kingdom of God." This goal must incite restlessness, not a sense of comfort in its members. The church, says Barth, "runs like a herald...not a snail...to deliver the message....The church lives by its commission as a herald."[91] For Tillich, the churches are "tools of the Kingdom of God" and should become "vehicles of

---

[87] Pius IX, *The Syllabus of Errors*, 1864, https://www.papalencyclicals.net/pius09/p9syll.htm, error 19.

[88] *Lumen Gentium*, chap. 1, art. 8; chap. 7, art. 48.

[89] *Ad Gentes*, art. 1.

[90] See Frederick Parrella, "Tillich's Understanding of Symbol and Contemporary Catholic Sacramentality," in *Internationales Jahrbuch für die Tillich–Forschung*, ed. Christian Danz (Münster: LIT–Verlag, 2006), 114.

[91] Barth, *Dogmatics in Outline*, 147. Barth was a perfect fit for Avery Dulles's model of the Church as Herald; see Dulles, *Models of the Church*.

history's movement towards its aim."[92] At the same time, the churches are part of the scandal of history, for in existence they are often poor tools and inadequate vehicles for God's Kingdom.

At the Council, Catholicism admits this inadequacy by affirming that the Church in the present is like all other human societies. "The Church, embracing in its bosom sinners, at the same time holy and always in need of being purified, always follows the way of penance and renewal."[93] While this is a long distance from "perfect society," it would not be enough for Tillich, or for that matter, Barth. While Catholicism locates the Spiritual Community in both the real and ideal world, at least it has come to admit human imperfection, acknowledging a church of sinners, even if not a sinful church. As the *Decree on Ecumenism* states, "Christ summons the Church to continual reformation as she sojourns here on earth. The Church is always in need of this, in so far as she is an institution of men here on earth."[94] The documents and all subsequent official statements fail to call the Church herself "sinful," but there is no shortage of Catholic theologians willing to do so. Augustine, after all, acknowledges that the church is the *corpus permixtum*, and as Michael McCarthy writes of Augustine: "Any reference to the purity of the Church is located within an ongoing Christological narrative, where purity is the result of Christ's action and humble self-giving and cannot be claimed as a property of the Church itself."[95] Barth would agree completely, and for that matter, Tillich too. Perhaps the Catholic Church's magisterium in the twenty-first century should reread Augustine.

Given the sacramental reality of the Church, many Catholics after the council have affirmed that the institution, more particularly its teaching authority, must also be understand sacramentally, not literally. As Kenan Osborne says: "Hierarchy shares in the symbolic fabric of the religious dimension of life, and consequently hierarchy shares in both the advantages of the symbolic and the temptation of the symbolic to be demonic."[96] Here Tillich would certainly admit that Catholic theology, even if not the magisterium itself, was

---

92 Tillich, *Systematic Theology*, 3:376. See also Tillich, "What is Wrong with Dialectical Theology?," 134–35.

93 *Lumen Gentium*, chap. 1, art. 8.

94 *Unitatis Redintegratio*, chap. 2, art. 6.

95 Michael McCarthy, S.J., "Religious Disillusionment and the Cross: An Augustinian Reflection," *Heythrop Journal* 48 (2007): 561.

96 Kenan Osborne, "Tillich's Understanding of Symbols and Roman Catholic Sacramental Theology," in *Paul Tillich: A New Catholic Assessment*, ed. Raymond F. Bulman and Frederick J. Parrella (Collegeville, MN: The Liturgical Press, 1994), 99.

taking a less heteronomous position with regard to ecclesial authority and that all symbols, when taken literally or as absolute, can become demonic. Furthermore, by failing to fully identify the church with the Roman Catholic Church, and by acknowledging the positive value of other Christian churches, of other world religions, and of the secular order, the Catholic Church implicitly acknowledged Tillich's idea of a latent Spiritual Community, or whenever the power of the Spiritual Presence is at work in communities outside the organized church, "in which the unexpressed church would be a living reality."[97] As the Council says: "It follows that the separated Churches and Communities as such...have been by no means deprived of significance and importance in the mystery of salvation. For the Spirit of Christ has not refrained from using them as means of salvation."[98]

Turning to Barth and the Roman Catholic theology, Barth was surely pleased that the Council placed the Word of God at the center of Revelation and emphasized the importance of the Word in understanding the church. Even in the title of the Dogmatic Constitution on Divine Revelation, *Dei Verbum* or "The Word of God," Catholic theology signaled a new direction on the role of Scripture in the foundation of the church. As the Council says: "This teaching office is not above the Word of God, but serves it, teaching only what has been handed on, listening to it devoutly, guarding it scrupulously and explaining it faithfully in accord with a divine commission and with the help of the Holy Spirit, it draws from this one deposit of faith everything which it presents for belief as divinely revealed."[99] With the exception of chapter two of the document, which Barth describes as a "painful weakness" because of its emphasis on both Scripture and tradition "flowing from the same divine wellspring,"[100] he agrees with the spirit of the document. He praises chapter six for its "Barthian" language: "The Church has always venerated the divine Scriptures just as she venerates the body of the Lord."[101] Again, he views *Dei Verbum* and its "trend to the Bible" as "unmistakably foreign to Trent and Vatican I," and asserts that Vatican II was truly a "reforming council."[102] Just as Catholic theology acknowledges that the Eucharist makes the

---

[97] See Paul Tillich, "Kirche und humanistische Gesellschaft," in *Gesammelte Werke*, vol. 9 (Stuttgart: Evangelisches Verlagswerk, 1967), 60–61. Originally published in *Neuwerk*, vol. 13 (1931): 4–18.

[98] *Unitatis Redindegratio*, chap. 1, art. 3.

[99] *Dei Verbum*, chap. 2, art. 10.

[100] Barth, *Ad Limina Apostolorum*, 50–51.

[101] *Dei Verbum*, chap. 6, art. 1.

[102] Barth, *Ad Limina Apostolorum*, 47, 54.

church as well as the church the Eucharist, so too does the Word of God truly make the church. The centrality of Word for church is central to Barth; those who believe in Christ are sent out: He writes: "'Go and preach the Gospel!' It does not say, 'Go and celebrate services!' 'Go and edify yourselves with the sermon!' 'Go and celebrate the Sacraments!' 'Go and present yourselves in a liturgy, which perhaps repeats the heavenly liturgy!'"[103] In short, the church has only one true mission: witness to Christ by preaching His Word.

Catholic life and Catholic liturgy is founded on and nourished by the Word of God. As the Constitution on Sacred Liturgy states, "[Christ] is present in His word, since it is He Himself who speaks when the holy scriptures are read in the Church."[104] The Catholic Mass has two equal parts: the liturgy of the Word and the liturgy of the Eucharist; one cannot exist without the other. Here, the theological reception of this truth has not been fully realized in the Church's life; the unity of Word and sacrament needs greater acceptance. Would that Catholic clergy were as devoted to preaching the Word as their Protestant brothers and sisters are! Furthermore, *Dei Verbum*, the Dogmatic Constitution on Divine Revelation, makes it clear that, "easy access to Sacred Scripture should be provided for all the Christian faithful."[105] This is a fundamental change from the attitude of the Tridentine Church. Barth's *Dominus dixit* was truly heard at the Second Vatican Council.

Thus, we can see the beginning of the "century of the Church" taking shape, not only in the great rise of Catholic ecclesiology, which began between the world wars, but also in two of the most significant names in Protestant theology in the first half of the twentieth century. The older antagonisms between the two traditions in Western Christianity also began to mellow in light of World War I and the human carnage that took place between nominally Christian nations. The ecumenical movement began to take greater shape in a world where the human situation and the rise of secularism became larger issues than the centuries-old conflict between the churches. Granted official status and recognition in Catholicism at the Second Vatican Council, ecumenism was born again after the First World War in the writings of those theologians, both Catholic and Protestant, who were weary of centuries of dispute. They recognized that the churches were facing a much deeper challenge than their old intra-ecclesial arguments: the presence of secular, modern

---

[103] Barth, *Dogmatics in Outline*, 146–47. See Waldron Scott, *Karl Barth's Theology of Mission* (Exeter: Paternoster Press, 1978).

[104] *Sacrosanctum Concilium*, chap. 1, art. 7.

[105] *Dei Verbum*, chap. 6, art. 22.

consciousness which often held the Christian message in disdain or at best viewed it as irrelevant to their existential experience in contemporary society.

7.3 Catholic Ecclesiology after World War I

In the decade after World War I, a new concern with human solidarity, a new consciousness of a wider world, was taking form in Western culture both politically and intellectually. In the political order, the League of Nations was formed, with limited success, to protect the world from future wars. Philosophically, there was a general shift from interpreting reality in individualistic and subjective categories towards a more objective and communal understanding, typified in the thought of Edmund Husserl (d. 1938), the father of phenomenology, Martin Heidegger (d. 1976), the existentialist philosopher and metaphysician, Gabriel Marcel (d. 1973), the Catholic existentialist philosopher, and Max Scheler (d. 1928), the philosopher and phenomenologist, who influenced both Heidegger and the Jewish scholar, Martin Buber (d. 1965). In Catholicism, the effect of the First World War on Catholic theology was also significant, but it did not produce "that epochal radical change that occurred on the Protestant side" through the works of Barth and the other "theologians of crisis." Change took place in Catholic theological circles not in "dialectical leaps but in a continuous development and in positive progress."[106] The Great War marked the slow demise of neoscholasticism as the dominant approach to theology in Catholicism. No longer could official Catholic theology neglect human history when history itself was torn apart by war among Christian nations now in a desperate search for healing.

In the decades between the World Wars, Catholic theology was given fresh life and spirit. Much attention was given to ecclesiology, stimulated by reflection on the war itself and dissatisfaction with the one-sided ecclesiology that dominated the static and institutional Catholic theology since the Council of Trent. Theologians sought to redress the imbalance in the Church's apologetic, defensive approach in its self-understanding by the creation of a more biblical and dogmatic appreciation of church. Renewed interest in the church as mystery opened up questions concerning the inner and invisible life of the church, the relation of church and the Kingdom of God, the intention

[106] Leo Scheffczyk, "The Main Lines of the Development of Theology between the First World War and the Second Vatican Council," in *History of the Church,* vol. 10, *The Church in the Modern Age*, ed. Hubert Jedin, Konrad Repgen, and John Dolan (New York: Crossroad, 1981), 260.

of Jesus to establish a church, and the relationship between the church and universal salvation—some of the very questions raised by the Modernists several decades earlier.[107] This regeneration took place not only in formal doctrinal theology but also in the broader arena of Catholic life that produced a fresh Catholic consciousness of faith. In sum, after a half-century of dormancy, the theology of the Church between the wars experienced a period of new life and became "more holistic and vital."[108] Ecclesiology was evolving from the hierarchology of the First Vatican Council to a more expansive and inclusive theological discipline, dramatically shifting its focus in response to Catholicism's renewed sense of an inner life of mystery. This romantic, spiritual sense of the Catholic tradition was so aptly described by the German national romantic art historian and philosopher, Julius Langbehn (1851–1907), as the "spirit of the whole."[109]

Between World War I and World War II, the significant change in Catholic theological research was spurred by a return to the theology's original sources: the Bible, the liturgy, and the writing of the Fathers.[110] Each in its own, interconnecting way renewed the face of Catholic theology in general and ecclesiology in particular. Catholics, especially in Germany, were aware that the shift in the intellectual climate towards a more unified sense of the world brought secular patterns of thought closer to the enduring strengths of the Catholic tradition. With the collapse of progressive, individualistic culture after the First World War, there was a new openness to the transcendent, and much talk was heard in Catholic circles about "the Catholic man," the "Catholic view of the world," and the "essence of Catholicism"—all suggesting a more reflective, experiential, and inner-directed understanding of the Catholic experience.[111]

Two significant names in German Catholic theology in the 1920s were Romano Guardini (1885–1968) and Karl Adam (1876–1966). In different

---

[107] Gratsch, *Where Peter Is*, 198–99.

[108] Weigel, *Catholic Theology in Dialogue*, 12.

[109] Scheffczyk, "The Main Lines of the Development," in *The History of the Church*, 10:261–62.

[110] For a treatment of the key names in French theology, see James M. Connolly, "The Theology of the Sources," in *Voices of France: A Survey of Contemporary Theology in France* (New York: Macmillan, 1961), 30–69.

[111] Schoof, *A Survey of Catholic Theology*, 78–80; Erwin Iserloh, "The Movements Within the Church and Their Spirituality," in *The History of the Church*, ed. Hubert Jedin, vol. 7, *The Church between Revolution and Restoration* (New York: Seabury, 1980), 299.

ways, both were giants and two of the twentieth-century fathers of Catholic theology. Guardini, an Italian by birth, was raised in Germany and ordained a priest there. Sympathetic to Saint Augustine and the Augustinian tradition, his doctoral dissertation examined the work of the medieval Franciscan Saint Bonaventure. Thus, Guardini stood outside the neoscholastic tradition when he accepted the chair in Catholic Philosophy at Berlin in 1923. Guardini was a philosopher, a theologian, a literary critic, an artist, a spiritual writer, and a pioneer in the revival of the liturgy. One of his earliest works, *Vom Geist der Liturgie* (On the Spirit of the Liturgy) of 1918, was a trailblazer in the liturgical movement (which we will consider below). In his first important ecclesiological work, *Vom Sinn der Kirche* (On the Meaning of the Church), he states that "a religious movement of incalculable import has begun: the Church is awakening in the souls."[112] He believed that "the Church is the one great power which makes possible a perfect community when members are genuine personalities."[113] Since Guardini was, strictly speaking, outside the sphere of systematic theology and therefore less open to official scrutiny in the decades after the Modernist crisis by church authorities, his many popular and literary works were free from curial examination and able to prepare the way for the theological breakthrough that would come later.[114] His work, *Der Herr: Betrachtungen Uber Die Person Und Das Leben Jesu Christi* (The Lord: Reflections on the Person and the Life of Jesus Christ) is, according to historian Roger Aubert, a work that does not fit with precision into any scholarly category but is without a doubt one of the great books of the epoch.[115] In his writings, Guardini continually emphasized that Christianity was not "an ethic" or "a systematic interpretation of the world" but a "participation in the same existence of Christ himself."[116] By his vision of the church not as a visible and perfect society but a mystery of common life shared in the Holy Spirit, Romano Guardini was a major figure in the restoration of ecclesiology after the war and one of the first harbingers of Vatican II.

---

[112] *Vom Sinn der Kirche* was first published in Mainz, Germany in 1922. It was later translated into English as *The Church and the Catholic* and published in London in 1935 and New York in 1953. It is quoted in Iserloh, "The Movements Within the Church and Their Spirituality," 305.

[113] Iserloh, 305.

[114] Schoof, *A Survey of Catholic Theology*, 84.

[115] Romano Guardini, *Der Herr: Betrachtungen über die Person und das Leben Jesus Christi* (Würzburg: Werkbund Verlag, 1937).

[116] Roger Aubert, *La théologie Catholique au milieu du XXe siècle* (Tournai: Casterman, 1954), 81–82.

Karl Adam was likewise a post-World War I pioneer in Catholic ecclesiology, especially in his 1924 work, *Das Wesen des Katholizismus* (The Essence of Catholicism).[117] The starting point and guiding thread for his ecclesiology was the Pauline symbol of the church as the Body of Christ. This heralded a sharp break with the nineteenth century's understanding of the church as the Kingdom of God. Here the Kingdom was understood not in the New Testament sense as the eschatological life of God present to us but, just as Robert Bellarmine affirmed in the sixteenth century, a sovereign society comparable to the Kingdom of France or the Republic of Venice. Unlike human kingdoms or societies, the church was the perfect society or perfect Kingdom. Originally accepted not as formal theology but a kind of spirituality, this idea of the Body of Christ as the matrix of ecclesiology was received very slowly and with considerable resentment by some theologians in the 1920s and early 1930s who saw it as an attack on their own theology.[118] For Adam, the experience of the church was not so much of an institution or agent of salvation as it was the living fruit of salvation; the church was a community of life and love whose center and foundation is Christ himself. In his interpretation of Paul, Adam states that "the Body of Christ is and must be an organic body, that it works by its very nature in a manifold of functions, and that this manifold is bound together by the one Spirit of Christ into an inner unity."[119] For him, "Christ the Lord is the real I of the Church."[120] Adam's ecclesiology was a significant step in the shift of the theology of the church from the older defensive apologetic framework to a deeper understanding based on solid dogmatic principles. Above all else, in retrieving the biblical image of the Body of Christ, Adam restored the long submerged and sometimes lost emphasis on a "mystical understanding of the essence of Catholic Christianity and the Church."[121]

7.4 Ecclesiology in France

In France, the renewal of the church after World War I moved more slowly

---

[117] Karl Adam, *Das Wesen des Katholizismus*, (Düsseldorf: Patmos, 1924). Later references are to the 1954 Doubleday Image edition.

[118] Weigel, *Catholic Theology in Dialogue*, 12–13.

[119] Adam, *The Spirit of Catholicism*, 37.

[120] Quoted by Iserloh, "The Movements Within the Church and Their Spirituality," 306.

[121] Scheffczyk, "The Main Lines of the Development" in *The History of the Church*, 10:265.

than in Germany. The problem in the French Church had been the ongoing political and social conflict between the church and the state since the end of Pius IX's pontificate in 1878. The French *church* was itself split: on one side, some wished to make an accommodation to the "laicists" or the advocates of secularization and separation of church and state; on the other, Catholic traditionalists continued to oppose the French Republic and supported the *ancien régime*. The traditionalist movement, called the Action française (French action), comprised primarily of members of the French aristocracy and the army, advocated a return to the monarchy and the traditional values of the Greco-Roman culture and the Catholic faith. (Action Française was also the name of a daily newspaper, published from March 21, 1908, to August 24, 1944, which expressed and circulated the group's ideas.) After World War I, the movement became an unfortunate and serious obstacle to reconciliation between the French government and the Vatican. This fact compelled Pius XI (1922–1939), the successor of Benedict XV, to condemn the Action française in 1926. This condemnation, although a stunning blow to the traditionalists in the French Church, at last freed the church in France from its political questions and permitted it to focus on the problem of the enormous de-Christianization that had occurred in the last half century. A "long-delayed spring" burst upon Catholic life in France, beginning with new literary life through the writings of Georges Bernanos (1888–1948), who was a devout Catholic with monarchist leanings, probably most famous for his 1936 novel, *Diary of a Country Priest* (1936), made into a movie in English in 1951; François Mauriac (1885–1970), a devout Catholic, French novelist, dramatist, critic, poet, journalist, and member of the Académie française and winner of the Nobel Prize in Literature; and Emmanuel Mounier (1905–1950) probably best known for his philosophy of Personalism and the Catholic Worker Movement that offered a new vision of nonviolent revolution to change the social order.

In philosophy, both Etienne Gilson and Jacques Maritain made important contributions to the general renaissance of Catholic intellectual life, the renewal of French theology, and the revitalization of the Catholic spirit. Much like the revival in German Catholicism, there was a search for an integral, mystical sense of the Catholic faith.[122] Gilson (1884–1978) began his work on Descartes but became an avid scholar and proponent of the philosophy of Thomas Aquinas. Maritain (1882–1973) was an agnostic before

[122] Schoof, *A Survey of Catholic Theology*, 93–97; Pierre Blet, "The Catholic Church of France," in *The History of the Church*, 596.

converting to Catholicism in 1906. An author of more than sixty books, he also helped to revive Thomas Aquinas for modern times and was influential in the development and drafting of the Universal Declaration of Human Rights. (Both Gilson and Maritain were common names in the classrooms of Jesuit universities in the United States in the 1950s and early 1960s.)

The crucial names in the renewal of French theology and ecclesiology after 1930 are these: Emile Mersch, S.J. (1890–1940); Yves Marie-Joseph Congar, O.P. (1904–1995); Cardinal Henri de Lubac, S.J. (1896–1991); Marie-Dominique Chenu, O.P. (1895–1990); Cardinal Charles Journet (1891–1975); and Cardinal Jean Daniélou (1905–1970). The fact that half of these great theological innovators were named Cardinals of the church by the pope suggests the high respect in which they were held, not only by theological faculties and fellow theologians but also by the institutional church, which, ironically, often criticized and called into question their writings.

Like Karl Adam, Emile Mersch's two works on the Mystical Body restructured ecclesiology and grounded it on a theme fundamentally foreign to the neoscholastic approach to theology. *Le Corps mystique du Christ: Études de théologie historique* (The Mystical Body of Christ: Studies from Historical Theology) and *La théologie du Corps mystique* (The Theology of the Mystical Body) were based on both the New Testament and the Fathers, not on static, abstract, neoscholastic themes.[123] Mersch, a Belgian Jesuit, devoted his entire theological career to restoring the concept of the Mystical Body to a central place in ecclesiology. He carefully distinguished two aspects of one church: a visible society of baptized believers under the hierarchy, and the Mystical Body formed in the unity of those who live in the life of Christ.[124] Instead of the scholastic tendency to deal with the relationship of Christ and the church in terms of Western philosophical categories of cause and effect, Mersch used the anthropology of the Eastern Fathers as a lens for his ecclesiology. Cyril of Alexandria, for example, described the unity of Christ and Christians as the "physical and organic unity between head and members" within the church. In Mersch's view, just as Christ is the ground of the human soul and one's other and truer self, so too Christ acts upon the church not from without as a

[123] Emile Mersch, *Le Corps mystique du Christ: Études de théologie historique* (Paris: Desclée de Brouwer, 1933–1936); published in English as *The Whole Christ*, trans. John R. Kelly (Milwaukee: Bruce, 1938). Emile Mersch, *La théologie du Corps mystique* (Paris: Desclée de Brouwer, 1944); published in English as *The Theology of the Mystical Body*, trans. Cyril Vollert (St. Louis: B. Herder, 1951).

[124] Dulles, *Models of the Church*, 47–48.

merely external efficient cause but from within as the source of the community's life and being, as the genuine soul and Spirit of the church.[125]

The theology of the church as the Mystical Body, popular in both German and French Catholic thought between the wars, encountered considerable opposition by two other strands of the theological tradition. First, a number of conservative theological manuals continued to work out of the neoscholastic approach, exemplified in Timoteo Zapelena's *De ecclesia Christi: Pars apologetica* (The Church of Christ: Apologetic Part),[126] Joachim Salaverri's "De Ecclesia Christi," (On the Church of Christ) in *Sacrae theologia summa* (A Compendium of Sacred Theology),[127] and Sebastian Tromp's *Corpus Christi quod est ecclesia* (The Body of Christ that is the Church).[128] These works remained faithful to the spirit and often the letter of Counter-Reformation Catholic ecclesiology that identified the visible church with the Kingdom of God on earth and continued to examine the church in an extrinsic and non-historical perspective. As Tromp says: "The Church is the juridical and ethical continuation of the mission of Christ, in the manner of a true and perfect society, hierarchically constituted, universal and perpetual."[129] So while a mystical, spirit-centered ecclesiology, properly in step with the ancient church, was developing, Tridentine ecclesiology continued to exist and flourish beside it. This pattern of theological bifurcation can also be found as late as in the documents of the Second Vatican Council. As contemporary Catholics will attest, remnants of this polarization endure well into the twenty-first century.

Corresponding to and in line with the emerging Mystical Body theology, a second, more progressive school of thought grounded its understanding of the church in the ancient biblical image of the Hebrew People as the People of God. Part of this movement resulted as a reaction to a certain ecclesiological mysticism in an ecclesiology based on the Mystical Body that tended to be exaggerated and perhaps unhealthy. By demonstrating so forcefully the

---

125 Avery Dulles, "A Half Century of Ecclesiology," *Theological Studies* 50 (1989), 421–22.

126 Timoteo Zapelena, *De exxlesia Christi: Pars apologetica* (Rome: Gregorian University, 1940); rev. ed., 1950.

127 Joachim Salaverri, "De Ecclesia Christ," in *Sacra Theologia summa*, 2nd ed. (Madrid: Biblioteca de Autores Cristianos, 1952); 5th ed., 1962.

128 Sebastian Tromp, *Corpus Christi quod est ecclesia*, 4 vols. (Rome: Gregorian University, 1937); rev. ed. 1946–1972.

129 Quoted in Richard McBrien, *Do We Need the Church?* (New York: Harper and Row), 1969, 105–6.

intimate unity of head and members within the Body, theologians sometimes blurred the distinction between Christ and Christians. For example, the work of Karl Pelz, *Der Christ als Christus* (The Christian as Christ), which was placed on the Index of Forbidden Books in 1940, went so far as to say that the hypostatic union between the divine and human natures in Christ is in some ways extended to all Christians.[130] This would mean that God became incarnate in every person in the same manner as God was incarnate in Jesus. By contrast, the concept of the church as the People of God placed greater emphasis on the church's biblical foundation, its continuity with the Jewish people, its historicity, and its eschatological destiny. Among those supporting an ecclesiology based on the church as the People of God were Alfred Wikenhauser,[131] Robert Grosche,[132] and Mannes D. Koster. In his 1940 work, *Ekklesiologie im Werden* (Ecclesiology in the Making), Koster boldly called the concept of the Mystical Body metaphorical and pre-theological.[133] The theological debate was settled in 1943 when Pius XII issued his encyclical, *Mystici Corporis* (The Mystical Body), in which he called the Mystical Body of Christ the noblest and most sublime way of describing the church.[134] Unfortunately, by identifying the Mystical Body of Christ with the Roman Catholic Church alone, Pius attempted to maintain complete harmony within the encyclical with post-Tridentine ecclesiology, especially Bellarmine's definition of the church as a visible society. In spite of this serious limitation, the encyclical, *Mystici Corporis*, was a major breakthrough in the ecclesiology of the first half of the twentieth century.

At the same time, a number of Scripture and patristic studies after the encyclical continued to demonstrate the centrality of the People of God both in the Bible and in the writings of the Fathers. The French theologian Lucien Cerfaux showed that the Jewish idea of the People of God is at the core of Paul's theology of the church, since followers of Christ were heirs of the

---

[130] Karl Pelz, *Der Christ als Christus* (Berlin, 1939. Dulles, *Models of the Church*, 48.

[131] Alfred Wikenhauser, *Die Kirche als der mystische Leib Christi nach dem Apostel Paulus* (The Church as the Mystical Body of Christ According to the Apostle Paul) (Münster Westfalen, 1937).

[132] Robert Grosche, *Pilgernde Kirche* (Pilgrim Church) (Freiburg, Matthias - Grünwald Verlag, 1938).

[133] Mannes D. Koster, *Ekklesiologie im Werden* (Paderborn: Schönigh, 1940).

[134] Dulles, "A Half Century of Ecclesiology," 422–24.

promise and God's true people.[135] The Benedictine scholar, A. Schaut, also pointed out the frequency of the references to the church as the People of God in the Roman Missal. In the spirit of *lex orandi, lex credendi*, that is, the rule of prayer is the rule of belief, Schaut concluded that, "it appears to us that the designation, people of God, offers a starting point for the understanding of both the spiritual, invisible side as well as the visible juridical side of the Church."[136] It would take *Lumen Gentium* (The Light of the Nations), the Constitution on the Church of the Second Council of the Vatican, to employ the term "People of God" as the primary image of describing the church; this document also refined and developed the ideas of *Mystici Corporis*. Most important, *Lumen Gentium* and the other documents of the Second Vatican Council broke with the traditional identification of the Body of Christ with the visible Roman Catholic Church.[137]

7.5 The Liturgical Revival in the Twentieth Century

A significant factor in the transformation of ecclesiology from the paradigm of the church as a perfect society to a mystical, interior, and spiritual understanding of the church as Body of Christ and People of God was the liturgical movement. This movement was not only theological but also spiritual and practical.[138] The revival of liturgy was, as Charles Davis says, "a movement of pastoral renewal, intimately connected with the biblical and catechetical revivals" taking place at the same time. Liturgical studies were supported by "historical scholarship of the highest quality, in no way lacking critical

---

[135] Lucien Cerfaux, *La théologie de l'Eglise suivant Saint Paul* (Paris: Les éditions du Cerf, 1947); published in English as *The Church in the Theology of Saint Paul*, trans. Geoffrey Webb and Adrian Walker (New York: Herder and Herder, 1959); Gratsch, *Where Peter Is*, 215.

[136] Quoted by Gratsch, *Where Peter Is*, 215–16, taken from an article by the Benedictine, Schaut, "Die Kirche als Volk Gottes: Selbstaussagen in römische Messbuch," (The Church as the People of God: Self Understanding in the Roman Missal) *Benediktinische Monatsschrift* 25 (1949), 187–95.

[137] Dulles, *Models of the Church*, 48. See Karl Rahner, "Membership of the Church According to the Teaching of Pius XII's Encyclical *Mystici Corporis Christi*," in *Theological Investigations*, vol. 2 (Baltimore: Helicon, Press, 1963), 1–88.

[138] Charles Davis, *Liturgy and Doctrine: The Doctrinal Basis of the Liturgical Movement* (New York: Sheed and Ward, 1960), 23. See also *How Firm a Foundation. Leaders of the Liturgical Movement*, comp. and ed. Robert L. Tuzi (Chicago: Liturgical Training Publications, 1990).

vigor."[139] The origins of the liturgical movement go back as far as the romanticism of the early nineteenth century with its anti-rational sense of mystery and its rediscovery of transcendence. Although the theologian Johann Adam Möhler was not concerned directly with practical questions of liturgical restoration, his theology of the church, grounded in the Spirit and the Incarnation, became one of its most significant inspirations of the twentieth-century liturgical revival, especially in Germany. With so much theological attention in the life of the church given to its organizational, institutional, political, and cultural questions during the second half of the nineteenth century, the rediscovery of liturgy was at first limited to monastic communities. Two of the most prominent were the Benedictine monastery at Solesmes in France, founded by Dom Guéranger (1805–1875), and the monastery at Beuron in Germany, established by the Wolte brothers, Benedictine priests from Cologne, some years later. The elder brother, Dom Maur Wolte, was a prolific scholar in both Scripture, especially the Psalms, and the writings of the Fathers.[140]

The liturgical movement continued in Belgium in the first decade of the twentieth century under Dom Lambert Beauduin (1873–1960), Belgian monk who founded the monastery now known as Chevetogne Abbey in 1925. As early as 1909, at the Catholic Conference at Malines, he put forth his program of a pastoral renewal of the Christian life with the liturgy as its primary source and central focus.[141] Pius X, as mentioned above, was an active supporter of the Eucharist and frequent participation in Holy Communion during this same period. Between the wars, the movement continued through the work of the famous Austrian Augustinian priest, Pius Parsch (1884–1954), who presented a much clearer understanding of the Church through its liturgy. Parsch, whose goal was to "bring the Church's worship to the simple folk," published twenty-five million texts of the liturgy in the 1920s.[142] In

---

[139] Davis, 23.

[140] See "Dom Maur Wolter et son œuvre," (Dom Maur and his Work) *Revue Bénédictine* 7, 377–86; The Communities of Saint-Severin of Paris and Saint-Joseph of Nice, *The Liturgical Movement* (New York: Hawthorne, 1964), 12–14.

[141] Davis, *Liturgy and Doctrine*, 14–15.

[142] Iserloh, "The Movements Within the Church and Their Spirituality," 302. Parsch was a voluminous writer and founder of several journals. Most of his works, all in German, became available to an American audience through the Benedictines of Collegeville, Minnesota. Two works of note: *The Church's Year of Grace*, 3 vols., originally published in 1926, 4th ed. published 1952–1958; and *The Liturgy of the Mass*, 3rd ed. (London: B. Herder, 1957).

France, the liturgical journal *La Maison-Dieu* elaborated the foundations of an apostolate based on ecclesiology and liturgy.[143] Through the revitalization of the liturgy that took place in monastic communities and in scholarly and popular journals, the first connections between liturgy and a theological understanding of the church itself became prominent.

At the center of much of the liturgical revival between the wars was the famous Benedictine monastery of Maria Laach in Southwest Germany, near Koblenz and Andernach.[144] The monastery became an important center of the liturgical revival after the election of Idelfons Herwegen as Abbot in 1913. The same year, Herwegen published the first of numerous essays, "Das Kunstprinzip der Liturgie" (The Artistic Principle of Liturgy). In 1914, he established the first liturgical week in Germany with the Katholic–Akademiker–Verband (the Association of Catholic Academics), and after World War I, such weeks continued from 1919 to 1939. The Abbot encouraged his monks to publish works on the liturgy in common; *Die Betende Kirche* (The Praying Church) appeared in 1924, a large volume on the liturgy in all its forms intended for Christians at large. More important was the journal, *Jahrbuch für Liturgiewissenschaft* (Yearbook for the Study of the Liturgy), first published in 1921, reaching fifteen volumes by 1939; resurrected after the Second World War under the title, *Archiv für Liturgiewissenschaft* (Archives for the Study of the Liturgy), the journal had reached twenty-three volumes by 1981.[145]

In 1918, Herwegen began the famous series *Ecclesia Orans* (The Church at Prayer), the first volume of which was Romano Guardini's *Vom Geist der Liturgie* (The Spirit of the Liturgy). Guardini's impact on the liturgy and spirituality was no less than that on ecclesiology. This particular book "remained the great herald of liturgical enthusiasm through its twenty editions which were translated into virtually every modern language by the end of the second war, the last being issued in 1962."[146] As a leader of the spiritual life, Guardini was without peer. One of the monks of Maria Laach, Dom Damasus Winzen, describes Guardini in his memoirs as "our leader...our most understanding helper and counselor." In moving words, the spirit of what was best in early twentieth-century Catholicism finds expression in this touching description

[143] P. Stanislaus Jáki, *Les tendances nouvelles de l'Ecclesiologie* (Rome: Casa Editrice Herder, 1957), 61–64.

[144] Aubert, *La théologie catholique*, 37–38.

[145] See Burkhardt Neunheuser, "Towards a History of Maria Laach Between the Wars," *Monastic Studies* 13 (1982), 217–26.

[146] Neunheuser, 223.

of Guardini:

> He was too complex, too sensitive, too truly catholic, to sell us simple solutions and slogans....In the daily celebration of the holy mysteries and by way of the living Word, Guardini showed us the unity in the seeming contradictions of life. He put us on the way to inner recollection. He opened to us the radiant beauty of true friendship and genuine love. He made us aware of the dignity of conscience, of the inner world of the self. He interpreted to us the sacred symbols of the cult and led us into the world of the liturgy, even into the most hidden recesses of the responses with which the praying church answers the word of the holy readings.[147]

In addition to Guardini, the name that perhaps dominates all the others in the development of a theology of liturgical mystery was the monk of Maria Laach, Dom Odo Casel (1886–1948).[148] Born Johannes Casel, he lived the second half of his life as a chaplain to a Benedictine convent; fittingly, he died on Holy Saturday after intoning the Lumen Christi (Light of Christ) at the liturgy. His important work is *Zur Idee der liturgischen Mysterienfeir* (Liturgy as the Celebration of Mystery), published in 1923; it has been translated as *The Mystery of Christian Worship* and remains readily available today.[149] Casel broke with the traditional neoscholastic interpretation of the church's sacramental acts, especially the Eucharist, in which the ritual is effective primarily in an extrinsic way, that is, where the effects of the saving ritual come to the

[147] Damasus Winzen, *A Monk of Two Worlds*, ed. Anne V. Winter and Johannes Lind, privately circulated manuscript (Pine City, NY: Mount Savior Monastery, 1974), 50–92. This work contains reflections on Maria Laach. Afraid that the Nazis would close the monastery, Herwegen asked Father Damasus to come to America in 1939 and establish a Benedictine community. In 1951, Mount Saviour Monastery was founded in Pine City, New York, a small village outside of Elmira. Father Damasus served as the first Prior from 1951 until 1968. He died in 1970. For a recent biography of Father Damasus, see J. Madeleva Roarke, *Father Damasus and the Founding of Mount Saviour* (Pine City, NY: Madroar Press, 1998).

[148] For the details of his life, see H. A. Reinhold, "Timely Tracts: Dom Odo Casel," *Orate Fratres* (now *Worship*) 22 (1948), 366–72. A good survey of Casel's life and work can be found in the issue of the French liturgical journal, *La Maison-Dieu* 14 (1948), which was dedicated to Casel.

[149] Dom Odo Casel, *Zur Idee der liturgischen Mysterienfeir* (Freiburg: Herder Verlag, 1923).

believer from the outside.[150] Rather, by the individual's visible participation in the mysterious action itself, the saving reality should make itself present in mystery through and under the veil of symbols within the believer's very being. Put differently, by the symbolic action of the community, the saving grace of God in Christ, Paul's hidden mystery of God from all ages, is made mysteriously present and effective in the heart and soul of the Christian. Hence, the bond between the Christian and Christ is not primarily juridical nor moral but mystical and ontological. Each person actually participates in the very life of Christ by participating in the symbols that make this life effective in the core of the person's being. Liturgy is the supreme action of the church because it expresses the innermost nature of the church itself—the meeting point between God and human persons, between eternity and time, between the source of all hope and human despair, and between grace and sinfulness. According to English Dominican, Aidan Nichols, Casel should be accounted "a giant among theologians of the Liturgy and a figure raised up by Providence to salvage from perils the worship of the Church…one of the great fathers, I would say the great father of the twentieth-century liturgical movement."[151]

Martin Boler, O.S.B., Father Damasus's successor as prior, was also attuned to the Maria Laach tradition. He explained the liturgy of the Easter vigil this way.[152] At the beginning, we are in the darkness of the crypt, but since the external and visible symbol expresses the inner reality, the darkness is in us. When the light of the paschal fire and candle is lit, the flame symbolizes the light of Christ present to Christians; through faith, this light becomes mysteriously their own light living within them, healing and transforming their lives. As Christ was transformed from death to life by the power of God, so too is this power of transformation present and effective within those present at the liturgy by their mysterious participation in the symbolic words and actions of the entire community. What is transformed is the small and petty self and all that brings death to the image of God hidden within each person. This transformation is captured in the ancient prayer of the church in the Easter Vigil uttered immediately after the paschal candle is lit: "May the Light of Christ, rising in glory, dispel all the darkness from our

---

[150] Scheffczyk, "The Main Lines of the Development," *The History of the Church*, 267.

[151] Aidan Nichols, *Looking at the Liturgy: A Critical Review of its Contemporary Form* (San Francisco: Ignatius Press, 1996).

[152] Martin Boler, O.S.B., successor to Damasus Winzen at Mount Saviour Monastery, in an Easter Vigil homily, April of 1969.

hearts and minds." Through the external ritual, the power that heals the inner self, rescuing the individual from whatever brings death, comes to life and is real and effective within the believer. In the liturgy, as the Exultet, the prayer of the church on Holy Saturday, says, the things of heaven and those of earth are truly united. In ecclesiological terms, liturgy creates and realizes, in Yves Congar's insightful words, "a synthesis between the exterior and the interior, between hierarchy and community, between the primacy of Christ's action and human participation, between present reality and eschatological vision, between earth and heaven."[153]

Odo Casel's theology of mystery, which became prominent in the 1930s and 1940s, was one of the sources of inspiration of Pius XII's 1947 encyclical on the liturgy, *Mediator Dei.* The pope emphasizes the importance of worship as both exterior and interior actions of the church that are "intimately linked with each other." While exterior worship "reveals and emphasizes the unity of the Mystical Body....The chief element of divine worship must be interior."[154] Obviously, if liturgy truly reflects the nature of the church, then the church must be more than the perfect visible society; it must also be the mystery of interior grace. At the same time, the pope, ever faithful to post-Tridentine theology and discipline, criticized some of the liturgical experimentation common at that time, such as Mass in the vernacular, the restoration of the altar to primitive table-form, and the elimination of black as a liturgical color. (In less than two decades, the Second Vatican Council would take care of all of these issues.) Since the pope was concerned about Protestant ideas, he also warned that participation by the faithful in the Eucharist did not mean that they themselves are endowed with priestly power.[155] Not until the Second Vatican Council was the liturgical movement and Odo Casel's theology of mystery officially acknowledged and proclaimed in *Sacrosanctum Concilium*, the Document on the Sacred Liturgy. In this document, the liturgy is described as "the summit toward which all the activity of the Church is directed" and "the fountain from which all her power flows."[156] In sum, the liturgical movement throughout the first half of the twentieth century was much more than just a transformation and updating of rubrics; it signaled a general

---

[153] Yves Congar, *L'Eglise de Saint Augustin à l'époque moderne,* 461.

[154] Pius XII, *Mediator Dei*, 20 November 1947, arts. 23–24.

[155] Pius XII, arts. 60–62, 82–84. Many of these liturgical experiments, of course, were officially accepted by Vatican II less than twenty years later.

[156] *Sacrosantum Concilium* in *The Documents of Vatican II,* ed. Walter Abbott (New York: America-Guild Press, 1966), art. 10.

spiritual renewal of the life of the church and profoundly changed the church's self-understanding. It marked the definitive end of the exaggerated institutionalism that had been the mark of ecclesiology for centuries. The ecclesiology that both underlies and emerges from liturgical studies remains with us today as one of the most important sources of hope for the future of the church.

7.6 Theologians as Harbingers of Vatican II: Congar and de Lubac

In addition to the liturgical movement in Germany, a greatly rejuvenated French theology also played a vital role in the development of a theology of the church. In the years between the significant work of Emile Mersch on the Mystical Body (1933ff) and the call for Vatican II in 1958, the most important ecclesiological work took place at two French theological centers, Le Saulchoir of the Dominicans, reestablished in Paris in 1937, and Fourvière, the Jesuit house of studies at Lyons. Among the Jesuits, Henri de Lubac and Jean Daniélou established the series *Sources chrétiennes* (Christian Sources) for scholarly texts and translations of the writings of the Fathers of the Church. De Lubac, who began his teaching career at Lyons in 1929, was fluent in the entire Christian theological tradition from the Fathers through medieval theology to the fundamental questions of his own time. He delved into many of the scholastic disputes of the day, and his exceptional learning allowed him to relate these scholastic questions to their underlying patristic and historical sources.[157] He was asked by Congar to write a monograph for the new series devoted to the study of the church, *Unam Sanctam* (One and Holy) and he responded with his first book, *Catholicisme: Les aspects sociaux du dogme* in 1939.[158] The significance of this particular work lies in both its breadth and its substance. It is a Catholic and catholic synthesis of the Christian faith, including the fundamental questions of persons and society, transcendence and eternal life, doctrine and sacraments. Most of all, it is a work of ecclesiology that differs radically from the neoscholastic institutional model of the church as a perfect society. De Lubac restores an awareness of the church as mystery, confined yet free of time and history, visible and invisible, both the

[157] Schoof, *A Survey of Catholic Theology*, 111–13.

[158] Henri de Lubac, *Catholicisme: Les aspects sociaux du dogme* (Paris: Les éditions du Cerf, 1939); published in English as *Catholicism: A Study of Dogma in Relation to the Corporate Destiny of Mankind*, trans. Lancelot C. Sheppard (New York: Sheed and Ward, 1950).

goal and way, the saint and sinner. Without divinizing the church, he reasserts the spiritual unity between the divine and the human within the one mystery of church, a mystery so profound that "it is deeper still, if that were possible, than the mystery of Christ." The Church is the sacrament or mystery of God made present in history: "If Christ is the sacrament of God, the Church is for us the sacrament of Christ; she represents him, in the full and ancient meaning of the term, she really makes him present."[159] And the Catholic Church is, true to its name, universal. As he writes:

> She is the Catholic Church...Nothing authentically human, whatever its origins, can be alien to her...She wishes at the same time to satisfy and more than satisfy the yearnings of each soul in every age; to gather in everything for its salvation and sanctification...There is nothing good which Catholicism cannot claim for its own...Catholicism is religion itself. It is the form humanity must put on to finally be itself. It is the only reality which by its existence involves no opposition...the very opposite of a closed society....Catholicism is at home everywhere and everyone should be able to feel himself at home in the Church."[160]

In this significant work, de Lubac may have come closer to the genuine ecclesiological spirit of the Fathers than anyone since long before the Reformation. The restoration of this mystical, sacramental, and universal view of the church was "a theological blueprint for the dynamic French Church of the period."[161] This blueprint was to become the soul of the ecclesiology of Vatican II.

Another significant contribution to ecclesiology from the Jesuit school at Lyons came from an often underrated theologian, Yves de Montcheuil, whose works became popular after World War II. A professor at the Institut Catholique in Paris, he was active in Catholic Action groups before and during World War II. His writings on the church both reflect and embody his pastoral experience and the many conferences he gave to different Catholic groups. After his death at the hands of the Nazi Gestapo in 1944, his finest work, *Aspects de l'Eglise* (Aspects of the Church) was published posthumously in 1948 as one of the *Unam Sanctam* (One and Holy) series of Congar.[162] The

---

[159] De Lubac, 42–43.

[160] De Lubac, 159–60.

[161] Schoof, *A Survey of Catholic Theology*, 113.

[162] Yves de Montcheuil, *Aspects de l'Eglise* (Paris: Les éditions du Cerf, 1948); published in English as *Aspects of the Church* (Chicago: Fides, 1955). De Montcheuil's

book examines the interior life of the church and its relationship to the world and human persons. On the inner nature of the church, de Montcheuil explores its biblical foundation, emphasizing the images of the new Israel and the Kingdom of God; he then examines the church as the Body of Christ, the interior life of the church, the catholicity and sanctity of the church, the role of the hierarchy, and the place of the Christian within the ecclesial community. In an ecumenical spirit, he evaluates the role of the Catholic Church and the separated churches, the relationship of the church to the salvation of non-believers, the work of the church in the temporal order, and finally, the role of the church's missionary activity. De Montcheuil's ecclesiological approach, far from the neoscholastic manuals popular in seminaries of his day, was a virtual outline of the topics covered in the key documents of the Second Vatican Council. In his chapter on the interior life of the church, he prefigures the first chapter of the Constitution on the Church more than a decade before the Council was called. He writes:

> The Church is, in short, a community of love. That is the culminating point of her interior life.... This love does not spring forth on the human plane—it comes from the Trinity itself. In her visible organization, by her sacraments, rich in spiritual efficacy, the Church is the implanting on earth of the unifying love by which the Trinity lives. In her, this love comes down to earth in the midst of a mankind whose members are isolated, opposed, in order to reconcile them to each other in order to bring them back to God.[163]

In his discussion of the church and universal salvation, de Montcheuil places great importance on salvation in and through the church by desire, what has been called in classical terminology, the *votum ecclesiae* or desire for the church. He writes: "Therefore, not only is no one ever saved except by a grace which is bound up with the existence of the church, but too, no one is ever saved except with relationship to this unique church because without knowing it, one lives by her and for her as best he can."[164] While not considered a great speculative theologian, de Montcheuil's sense of Catholicism was both deep and expansive. For him, the church "is not something all completed, something static; she is a growing reality whose goal is to spread out

---

name was often mentioned with admiration while I was a graduate student in the 1960s by my professors who had studied in Europe after World War II.

[163] De Montcheuil, 61.

[164] De Montcheuil, 159.

even to the very dimensions of mankind."[165] In sum, de Montcheuil's personal and pastoral ecclesiology was most influential in French theology from the end of World War II until the Second Vatican Council.[166]

In this rejuvenated French Church of the pre- and post-World War II period comes perhaps the most influential ecclesiologist of the twentieth century, the Le Saulchoir Dominican, Yves M. -J. Congar. His groundbreaking work, volume one of Unam Sanctam series, *Chrétiens désunis: Principes d'un oecuménisme catholique* (Christians Ununited: Principles of Catholic Ecumenism), "marked the first public expression of a new theological orientation towards the ecumenical movement."[167] Congar's ecumenical ecclesiology has been characterized as a "prophetic anticipation of the teaching of Vatican Council II."[168] His other early works which embody most of his major ecclesiological insights include *Esquisses du mystère de l'Eglise* (Sketches on the Mystery of the Church),[169] *Vraie et fausse réforme dans l'Eglise* (True and False Reform in the Church),[170] and *Jalons pour une théologie du laïcat* (Guidelines for a Theology of the Laity).[171] For Congar, the church is the continuing mystery of God within human persons, the very "dwelling of God in the faithful. All personally, all together, in their very unity, are the Temple of God because they are the Body of Christ animated by his Spirit."[172]

In his important early work, *The Mystery of the Church*, which was not

---

[165] De Montcheuil, 157.

[166] Connolly, *Voices of France*, 97–98.

[167] Yves M. -J. Congar, *Chrétiens désunis: Principes d'un oecuménisme catholique* (Paris: Les éditions du Cerf, 1937); published in English as *Divided Christendom: A Catholic Study of the Problems of Ecumenism*, trans. M. A. Bousfield (London: G. Bles, 1939); Connolly, *Voices of France*, 98.

[168] Dulles, "A Half Century of Ecclesiology," 424.

[169] Yves M. -J. Congar, *Esquisses du mystère de l'Eglise* (Paris: Les éditions du Cerf, 1942); published in English as *The Mystery of the Church*, trans. Geoffrey Chapman (Baltimore: Helicon, 1960).

[170] Yves M. -J. Congar, *Vraie et fausse réforme dans l'Eglise* (Paris: Les éditions du Cerf, 1950). A substantial amount of this originally controversial book was translated and made available in *Cross Currents* 1 (1951): 80–102; and *Cross Currents* 3 (1953), 358–65.

[171] Yves M. -J. Congar, *Jalons pour une théologie du laïcat* (Paris: Les éditions du Cerf, 1953); published in English as *Lay People in the Church*, trans. Donald Attwater (Westminster, MD: The Newman Press, 1965).

[172] Yves M. -J. Congar, *The Mystery of the Temple: The Manner of God's Presence to His Creatures from Genesis to the Apocalypse* (Westminster, MD: The Newman Press, 1962), 281.

translated into English until 1960, eighteen years after its first French edition, Congar cites five important movements, deeper than the level of abstract theology, operative in the renewal of the church's life: liturgical, mystical, missionary, communal apostolic, and theological. These movements, he believed, "like a great stirring in the depths of the sea," were transforming the actual life of the church and radically changing its ecclesiology. In considering the implicit theology of the church in Thomas Aquinas, Congar states that the Catholic tradition is characterized by three marks: first, the church is a Spirit-centered reality, as the body whose soul and principle of unity is the Holy Spirit; second, the church is contemplated in Christ just as Christ is contemplated in the church; third, the inward church of the Spirit cannot be separated from the outward church in its social, hierarchical, and sacramental nature.[173] In his chapter on the Mystical Body, Congar claims that the Body of Christ is not our work but the gift of Christ continuing and prolonging himself in human beings. The Body is the ongoing, historical recreation of humanity in the image of Christ.[174] In his treatment of the hierarchy, Congar carefully distinguishes between the church as an Event and the church as an Institution, a duality, he states, which is relative but quite real.

In discussing the church as an institution, Congar employs the anthropological principle that the Holy Spirit, as the active center of the world of grace, is so interior to the life of the person that the Spirit's action is virtually indistinguishable from individual visible actions in a human life. This principle, when applied to the community as a whole, helps to establish the key Catholic foundation for the hierarchy of the church and its authority. Like the Spirit active within the person's soul, the actions of the hierarchy must be founded on depths of the Spirit's life hidden within the church. In the tradition of Johann Adam Möhler a century earlier, Congar suggests a life-centered ecclesiology that is Spirit-centered, and a structure-ecclesiology which is centered in Christ's Incarnation. In a Spirit-ecclesiology, the church is formed not from the outside and above, but from the inside, from the Spirit of love that wishes to "embody [her] self." In a Christ-centered ecclesiology, the church owes its visible structure to the actions of Christ in human form and is, thus, a Christological mystery. The Body of Christ is built up not only by functional and hierarchical mediation but also by those unpredictable

[173] Congar, *The Mystery of the Church*, 73–74.
[174] Congar, 90.

events and happenings of grace offered by the Spirit to those who accept them. For Congar, the Spirit "remains transcendent to the Church [she] dwells in; [she] is not just a divine force giving supernatural efficacy both to the ministry and the sacraments, but a Person sovereignly active and free. [The Spirit] is not made use of by others but [she] [her]self directs events."[175]

In sum, Congar sought to recover the life-giving Spirit and spirituality of the first thirteen hundred years of Christianity, before the church became so involved with questions of social, political, and institutional power. Of course, he was aware of how necessary such involvement was for the life and the autonomy of the church. Grounded in both the modern historical-critical school of theologians and in the finest tradition of the scholastics who served as his theological starting point, Congar was in many ways a quiet revolutionary who worked to accomplish what other theologians from Möhler in the early nineteenth century onward had attempted to do—to restore to the church its sense of mystery, to begin the study of the church by returning to the New Testament and to the Fathers from the first to the sixth centuries; finally, to create an ecclesiology which moves from the inner creative reality of the divine presence within the community to external form and structure. To paraphrase Elmer O'Brien's words, Yves Congar possesses a magnificent theological gift because he, without abandoning Thomistic categories, has thus managed to speak so meaningfully of and to the church in our day.[176] As Avery Dulles expresses it: "Congar evidently felt that the earlier centuries could provide better models for the transition into the present age, when the Church had ceased to dominate society and culture, and was obliged to rely again on its [own] power to attract hearts and minds."[177] And again, in his final tribute to Congar after his death in 1995, Dulles writes:

> In ecclesiology, Congar tried to overcome excessive concentration on the papacy, the hierarchy and jurisdiction that he regarded as characteristic of the second millennium. He cherished the writers of the early church for their intense spirituality, their prayerful listening to the voice

[175] Congar, 137; see also 132–45.

[176] Elmer J. O'Brien, "Theology in Transition," in *Theology in Transition: A Bibliographical Evaluation*, ed. Elmer J. O'Brien (New York: Herder and Herder, 1965), 247.

[177] Dulles, "A Half Century of Ecclesiology," 425.

> of their Lord, and their openness to conversion and reform. The Church, for Congar, was essentially communal and conciliar....In his impact on official Catholic teaching and on interchurch relationships, he perhaps surpasses every other theologian of our century.[178]

Yves Congar, along with Henri de Lubac, Jean Daniélou, Emile Mersch, Karl Adam, Romano Guardini, and many others, are names that mark the end of one era and the beginning of another. Major historical changes are imperceptible to the very people who helped bring them to life. As philosopher and writer Antoine St.-Exupéry says, "we lack perspective for the transformations that go deep."[179] The pioneering Catholic theologians in the years between World War I and the end of the 1950s could never have imagined that the fruit of their work would take form in an ecumenical council called by Pope John XXIII in 1958. The Council, like the theologians who prepared for it in the preceding decades of theological research and writing, also marked the end and a beginning. Post-Tridentine Catholicism—at its worst, defensive, abstract, triumphalist, and isolated from the movement of modern experience—was disappearing before everyone's eyes, but few people knew it. As Wilhelm Neuss said on the eve of the Reformation: "Life had undergone a profound change which had been long in coming—only nobody knew it. In its appearance, life had been Catholic, but it was an illusory picture."[180] So, too, life in the sheltered Catholic worlds, often called "Catholic ghettos"—both intellectual and geographical—in the first half of the twentieth century was coming undone. The forces of modern life—held at bay at the gates of

[178] Avery Dulles, "Yves Congar: In Appreciation," *America* 173, no. 2 (July 15–22, 1995): 6–7.

[179] Antoine St.-Exupéry, *Wind, Sand and Stars* (French title: *Terre des hommes*) is a memoir by the French aviator and writer, Anoine de Saint-Exupéry. It was first published in France in February 1939 and was then translated by Lewis Galantière and published in English by Reynal and Hitchcock in the United States later the same year. The French and English versions of this book differed significantly; Saint-Exupéry removed sections from the original French version he considered inappropriate for its targeted US audience, and added new material specifically written for them, and Lewis Galantière translated the revised book into English. Translation, "An Appreciation" was added to later printings, contributed by Anne Morrow Lindbergh and earlier published in *The Saturday Review of Literature* on 14 October 1939.

[180] Quoted in Lortz, *How the Reformation Came,* 32.

the church in the so-called Modernist crisis—would have their say in the self-understanding of church in the final third of the twentieth century and well into the early decades of the twenty-first century.

8.

VATICAN II AND ITS AFTERMATH

8.1 Catholic Ecclesiology: Trends before the Council

In 1940, the European theologian, Mannes D. Koster, who championed the image of People of God over Body of Christ in the immediate years preceding Pius XII's encyclical *Mystici Corporis*, coined the phrase that ecclesiology was "in the making."[1] As we have seen, the same could not be said about other areas of Catholic theology. Trinitarian theology, Christology, and sacramentology, for example, all had detailed treatises dating back to much earlier epochs in the life of the church. Not even the Reformation and the Council of Trent in the sixteenth century produced a formal treatise, *De Ecclesia*, on the church. Only in the twentieth century did the Christian community find the *kairos*, or the "right time," to meditate upon, and to communicate, its own inner life and nature, and its outer role in culture, in a more thorough and structured manner. In the twentieth century, ecclesiology came into its own; indeed, this was "the century of the church."[2]

The twentieth century can be called "the century of the church" on two

---

[1] Mannes D. Koster, *Ecclesiologie im Werden*. He was also mentioned in chapter seven.

[2] This phrase is attributed to the Lutheran bishop Otto Dibelius, *Das Jahrhundert der Kirche*, (Berlin: Furche-Verlag, 1927; and the Catholic theologian Romano Guardini, *Vom Sinn der Kirche*, 1922. It should be understood only in a descriptive sense. The fifth century, for example, was clearly "the century of Christology," since the Council of Chalcedon in 451 established the *one* person, *two* natures doctrine.

levels. *First*, objectively, the church became the dominant theme in much theological speculation following the First World War. This is a direct result of a number of factors: the disruption of the Western world as a result of the "war to end all wars"; a new freedom and a growing individuality in both the church and society in general; a different interaction and tension between the sacred and the secular; a sharply altered understanding of the church as a sociopolitical entity and its function within an ever-growing secular culture; and finally, an awareness that theology inevitably had to confront modern thought. In Protestantism, Karl Barth uttered his resounding "No" to liberal Protestantism and the reigning worldview of Harnack, Ritschl, and Troeltsch, among others, where the human person, not God's revelation was the starting point of theology. In Catholicism, theology, which had been relatively dormant for the half century from the end of the reign of Pius IX to the end of World War I (1878 to 1914), began a slow rejuvenation. A principal reason for this theological "malaise" was surely the Modernist crisis and the anxiety in the Rome about anything new in speculative theology. Thus, the ecclesial rejuvenation was inspired by the call of a world that had been slowly abandoning the church for many years. This renewal following World War I, as we have seen, was the theological precursor of the Second Vatican Council.

Second, the twentieth century was also a time of the church in a subjective sense. Christians began to acknowledge that the church was, as mentioned earlier, the "meeting place of all mysteries."[3] For both positive and negative reasons, the Church made itself the center of its own theological reflection—not simply that the church became an object of faith, but that faith somehow discovered its roots and its foundation in an ecclesial milieu. Theology, therefore, whose ongoing task is to articulate the meaning and reasonableness of faith, became more than in other periods, in M. D. Chenu's phrase, an "ecclesial science."[4]

Why was there no formal document or treatise in ecclesiology before the last century, and what were the circumstances that permitted the church to concentrate on itself in those years before, during, and immediately after the Second Vatican Council? The first question involves us in the whole history

---

[3] Henri de Lubac, *The Splendour of the Church* (New York: Deus Books, 1962), 14. This point is explained theologically by M. -J. Le Guillou in "Ecclesiology," in *Sacramentum Mundi*, 1:317.

[4] M. D. Chenu, "Theology as an Ecclesial Science," *Concilium* 21 (New York: Paulist Press, 1967), 95–106.

of ecclesiology we have been discussing in these pages.[5] As we have considered, little was written about the nature of the church in the patristic and early medieval era since the *ecclesia* was primarily a subjective and mystical reality closely identified with God, Christ, and the sacraments. The first formal treatises on the church, which appeared at the beginning of the fourteenth century, were ad hoc and narrow answers to specific political and social forces challenging the church's visible and hierarchical authority. A certain tragic pattern in ecclesiology developed since that time, a pattern that has persisted until the mid-twentieth century. Emphasis was almost always placed *not* on the whole mystery of the church but on its visible and political role in the world and its nature as a hierarchical society. This situation was dictated by the necessity of defending the visible church and its powers against a variety of antagonists: the kings of France, such as Philip the Fair at the beginning of the fourteenth century; the spiritualists and Conciliarists in the fourteenth and fifteenth centuries; Luther, Calvin, and other Protestant reformers from the sixteenth to the twentieth century; Jansenism and Gallicanism in the seventeenth century; Rationalism, which denied the supernatural, in the eighteenth century; and finally, liberalism, nationalism, and sometimes undisciplined romanticism in the nineteenth century. The mystical and transcendental aspects of the church, dominant in the implicit ecclesiologies of the early centuries, never found their way into subsequent formal ecclesiologies.

When the "Mystery of the Church" became the first chapter of *Lumen Gentium*, the Dogmatic Constitution on the Church at the Second Vatican Council, all the dimensions of the complex reality of church were presented for the first time in two millennia. The church had encountered its own nature in a way it had not succeeded in doing before.[6] Of course, this breakthrough in ecclesiology at the Second Council of the Vatican did not have the unanimous support of the bishops present! A strong faction of traditionalists was led by a long-time director of the Holy Office (of the Inquisition)—the name was changed to the Congregation for the Doctrine of the Faith by Pope Paul

---

[5] As an excellent reference, see Jaki, *Les tendances nouvelles de l'ecclesiologie*; Yves Congar, *L'Eglise de Saint Augustin de l'epoque modern*; Gustave Weigel, "Catholic Ecclesiology in Our Time," in *Catholic Theology in Dialogue*, 8–19; and Richard McBrien, "The Development of a Church-Centered Ecclesiology," in *Do We Need the Church?* (New York: Harper and Row, 1968), 100–150.

[6] See A. C. Outler, "A Response," *The Documents of Vatican II*, ed. Walter Abbott (New York: America-Guild Press, 1966), 102.

VI—Cardinal Alfredo Ottaviani. He fought tirelessly to maintain the institutional status quo and all of the theological and canonical documents that supported it. In his view, *Lumen Gentium* should have begun with chapter three, "The Hierarchical Structure of the Church with Specific Reference to the Episcopate," not chapters one and two, "The Mystery of the Church," and "The People of God."

The developments in Catholic ecclesiology in the twentieth century from World War I up until Vatican II, many of which were looked at with suspicious eyes by the conservatives at the Council, were the results of the theological forces we have already considered: the liturgical revival, the return to theological sources in the study of the Church Fathers, and the biblical movement that created a historical-critical understanding of both God's Word and God's people. In addition—and this point should not be underestimated—the development of an educated laity in the Church, especially in Western Europe and North America, between the World Wars and particularly after World War II, was a harbinger of things to come. Finally, the Counter-Reformation sense of Catholicism—the belief that the church was a society organized like a state, in a pyramid structure with the pope at the top and the Roman central authority directly beneath him—was at long last eroding. This "fortress mentality" or pyramidal society was less a community given life by the Spirit, and more, as Congar says, "an organization where Christ intervened at its origin as the founder, and the Holy Spirit as the guarantee of its authority."[7]

Different theological images of the church were also rediscovered from biblical and sacramental sources to understand the church—primarily, the Mystical Body of Christ and the People of God. Perhaps more importantly, theological presuppositions were being changed. Scholasticism and neoscholasticism, with its abstract and unhistorical theories of knowledge that had dominated theology in some form since the thirteenth century, were called into serious question. This epistemology lacked sensitivity to time and history; it was closed to adaptation and development except in logical forms; it used the biblical tradition and the patristic writings as tools to prove *a priori* theological theses rather than as rich experiential sources of life and tradition. Neoscholasticism, for all of its theological richness, could not create, no matter how some theologians tried to do so, an eternal philosophy that disregarded history and human experience. It could no longer survive as the reigning paradigmatic framework of theology in light of the twentieth-century world. The

[7] Congar, *L'Eglise du Saint Augustin à l'epoque moderne*, 382–83.

reality of a secular and scientific worldview made the reality of God and the church in human affairs more and more suspect or irrelevant to the lives of many people. Then, the scientific world became the technological world almost overnight. Now, in the third decade of the twenty-first century, how could people live without their laptops and their iPhones? Let us recall the wonderful insight of theologian Piet Schoonenberg, which is worth repeating here: "Theology exists in history, not in eternity." In other words, theologians who were unaware of the intrinsic historical nature of the Christian faith, those who thought their theology would last for all time, prove the very point they were implicitly denying; for they were part of a historical time and a theological enterprise unaware or insufficiently aware of its own historicity.[8]

Like all genuine reform, the movement for change had to come from inside the tradition, the institution, the structure itself. The beginning took place with the growing realization that the neoscholastic system of thought could not be the exclusive and definitive form in which divine Revelation was to be understood, embodied, and interpreted. Other philosophies—existentialism, phenomenology, interpersonalism, and logical positivism, among others—the growth of historical research and the other social sciences, especially sociology, along with the powerful influence of Freud, Jung, and modern psychology, could no longer be neglected by theologians in their work. The church was now understood in sociological, not mystical, categories. The Second Vatican Council marked the final break of the teaching church with neoscholasticism as the only, or even the primary, way of doing theology.[9]

This break heralded two positive changes in Catholic theology: the shift to historical consciousness and the primacy of experience. The extent of the shift in formal theology from a static to a dynamic perspective is exemplified in the simple statement in article five of *Gaudium et Spes*: "The human race has passed from a rather static concept of reality to a more dynamic evolutionary one."[10] Richard McBrien (1936–2015) firmly believes that "the implications of this sentence cannot easily be exaggerated."[11] Another commentator calls this statement the "modern Church's sudden and belated discovery

---

[8] Schoonenberg, *Man and* Sin, 192.

[9] See Schoof, *A Survey of Catholic Theology*, 146–51. One sees the last hold of neoscholastic thought in the so-called "new theology" of the 1940s and in Pius XII's encyclical, *Humani Generis* of 1950.

[10] *Gaudium et Spes*, art. 5.

[11] Richard McBrien, *Church: The Continuing Quest* (New York: Newman, 1970), 28.

of human historicity and 'sociality'—the discovery that being-man-in-the-world involves possessing a political nature both in tune with and capable of transforming history and himself."[12] The starting point of theology was no longer metaphysical and rational theses about the essential and abstract order but concrete and historical situations in which human beings live. The church was no longer conceived as the "perfect society" that transcended history and possessed the eternal truths necessary for salvation. With Vatican II, the church recognized itself as a "pilgrim in a foreign land," conscious of her origin in Christ and her destiny in Christ's return.

The church's attitude toward the world changed dramatically, too. No longer did the church possess grace in the face of a graceless humanity, but rather it served as a sacrament of grace offered and made present to all the world. The church became aware of her primary mission of preaching, community, and service, not self-survival. Significantly, such a mission must consider the concrete and diverse experience of being individuals in this world. Likewise, the church is not a community that takes God's place but is God's servant; thus the church itself was capable of criticism and recognized itself as a church of sinners, an *ecclesia semper reformanda* (a church always in need of reform), capable of changing and developing historically as everything human does.[13] As the Council Fathers state, again in *Gaudium et Spes*: "It will be increasingly clear that the People of God and the human race in whose midst it lives render service to each other. Thus, the mission of the church will show its religious, and by that very fact, its supremely human character."[14]

Catholicism, therefore, dramatically shifted its own ecclesial self-awareness as a result of the deliberations and the documents promulgated at the Second Vatican Council. The church ceased to be the institution of salvation that was a product and a slave of the Tridentine system. By entering into its deepest mystery, the church became aware of its reality as the sacrament of Christ and the world's salvation; it understood itself as the dynamic sociohistorical People of God with its eschatological destiny. The church no longer equated itself as the only real and true church and became a participant in the ecumenical movement by acknowledging the ecclesial reality in other

[12] A. A. Bolado, "Reflections on Ambiguities in the Use of the Word 'Church,'" *Concilium* 66 (New York: Herder and Herder, 1970), 70.

[13] See Karl Rahner, "The Church of Sinners," and "The Sinful Church in the Decrees of Vatican II," in *Theological Investigations*, vol. 6 (Baltimore: Helicon, 1969), 256–94.

[14] *Gaudium et Spes*, art. 11.

Christian communities.[15]

8.2 Catholic Ecclesiology: Trends after the Council

Vatican II in hindsight was hardly the end of developments in Catholic ecclesiology. The conservatives and the progressives at the time of the Council were both victims to a certain ecclesiological naïveté—the former by refusing to admit that there were any problems in the church in need of candid discussion and solution, the latter by believing all problems would and could be solved by simple reform. The Council was as much or more a symptom of the crisis in the church and in its mission as it was a solution. The sessions in Rome revealed, above all else, that the church could not be separated from the world, and hence, precisely as church, it had to participate in a communal reexamination of culture and society. Simple ecclesial reforms could not put the church on the right path when humanity itself was confronting a crossroads in its destiny.

The Council gave the church the conceptual tools to encounter and deal with the massive problems of human growth and human suffering in a global multicultural world. At least, it laid the groundwork for the continual reform and development. The church learned that human destiny and the destiny of the church were intimately linked; that the order of redemption was to embrace, envelop, and carry the order of creation; that grace was boundless and inclusive as transcendent mystery but also immanent in historical forms and human processes beyond its merely institutional structures. The era of the Church as a "perfect society," dominant as an image in nineteenth century, appeared to be gone forever.

Thus, ecclesiology after Vatican Council II was in a dilemma. The study of the church, as the German political theologian Johannes Metz (1928–2019), said more than a half century ago, required more than the "tactical expression of how the present situation might be changed."[16] At the same time, to go beyond this point seemed to imply voiding the basic substance of ecclesiology, an implicit denial that the church is a mysterious entity in itself and worthy of study.[17] This means that the church could not study herself without examining all of human destiny and that for which she is a

[15] See McBrien, *Church: Continuing Quest*, 23–41.

[16] Johannes Metz, "Editorial," *Concilium* 66 (New York: Herder and Herder, 1970), 7.

[17] See Yves Congar, "Do the Problems of Our Secular World Make Ecumenism Irrelevant?" *Concilium* 64 (New York: Herder and Herder, 1969), 19–20.

sacrament—the Kingdom of God. Karl Rahner, in his little monograph at the end of the Council, justifies the church's inquiry into her own nature at Vatican II this way:

> In the first place, man, historical man, in view of the manner in which he considers himself both as an individual and part of the cosmos, is always in the end the ultimate problem; that is, no problem is finally solved, no perspective insured of its place, until the problem of man is resolved. The same is true of the Church. In any dialogue or discourse, the Church must always consider herself the first and last problem. The very obviousness with which ecclesiology became almost automatically the key theme of the Council shows, therefore, how much man and the church, with all their ability of reflection and all their responsibilities towards others, uncannily consider themselves to be the ultimate problem.[18]

Two new ideas were proposed in answer to this dilemma: a new definition of ecclesiology and a new focal point in understanding the church. These ideas emerged as a natural development out of the reasons that the church made herself the object of study at the Council in the first place.

In more recent decades, theologians were writing about the "turn to the subject," and philosophers and scholars have been "deconstructing" reality in postmodernity. Much has been written about this now firmly established "postmodern world." This turn began at the Council—an awareness that human beings, as persons and as subjects, cannot be separated from the objective mystery of the church; and human beings as church cannot be separated from other subjects and persons in society. So, Gregory Baum could redefine ecclesiology shortly after the Council as "not simply the study of the Christian Church [but]...rather the critical study, based on divine revelation, of what happens in human society."[19] Thus, the boundaries of ecclesiology were broadened after the Council in a way no one before could adequately predict:

---

[18] Karl Rahner, *The Church After the Council* (New York: Herder and Herder, 1966), 40.

[19] Baum, *Man Becoming*, 68. Gregory Baum was a theologian and professor emeritus of the faculty of religious studies at McGill University. During Vatican Council II he was an appointed *peritus* at the Secretariat of Christian Unity, responsible for the conciliar draft documents on ecumenism, religious liberty, and the Church's relation to Judaism and other world religions. He was born of Jewish and Protestant parents and converted to Catholicism after World War II in 1946. He served as the editor of *The Ecumenist* for over thirty years.

in Edward Schillebeeckx's phrase, the boundaries between church and humanity, church and world, have been blurred.[20]

This broader understanding of ecclesiology also meant that the focal point of the church's self-understanding had also been broadened and significantly expanded. The Catholic Church could no longer understand itself as a distinct, separate, and isolated entity, but that of which she is a sacrament and a herald, that which she embodies yet can only point to in hope—the Reign of God. According to Richard McBrien, a kind of post-conciliar "Copernican revolution" took place in Catholic ecclesiology. Just as Copernicus moved from a geocentric universe to a heliocentric one, so too the church could no longer be understood as the center of God's plan of salvation. The real center is the message of Jesus himself, the Kingdom of God.[21] The church is the sacrament of the Kingdom, but she herself cannot be the focal point of God's plan or the most inclusive category in which salvation is to be accepted and interpreted. We "need the church," McBrien says, in so far as we are "willing to relativize the church for the sake of the reign of God."[22] Catholicism could no longer understand itself as the one, true church, the exclusive possessor of the grace of salvation; it could not equate itself with the Kingdom of God on earth. While the church is the sacrament of the Kingdom, as *Lumen Gentium* clearly pointed out, it has come to see that its eyes could not only be cast inward on itself as visible sign, but it must also be focused beyond itself, on the Kingdom as its eschatological destiny.[23] The church could no longer consider itself as the center of the mystery of salvation; rather the true focal point is salvation revealed in Jesus.

This ecclesiological "Copernican revolution" was one of the most important developments in Catholic ecclesiology after the Second Vatican Council. Some Catholic theologians were less at home with this new terminology, sensing a threat to the continuity of the tradition and anxious about the world's setting the agenda for the church and not the other way around. Such a group signed the "Hartford Appeal for Theological Affirmation" in 1974. Their statement took issue with the most popular liberal fashions of the decade since the end of Vatican II, including the idea of a secular Christian and political eschatology. Rev. Richard Neuhaus, conservative Lutheran

---

[20] See Edward Schillebeeckx, "The Church and Mankind," in *The Church and Mankind, Concilium* 1 (New York: Paulist Press, 1965), 95.

[21] Consult the main thesis of McBrien's *Do We Need the Church?*

[22] McBrien, *Church: The Continuing Quest,* 84.

[23] *Lumen Gentium*, chap. 1, art. 3.

editor of *First Things* (later a convert to Catholicism), and Lutheran Peter Berger, author and sociologist at Rutgers, were the originators of the Hartford protest. Exasperated by what they considered a church sellout to such man-made ideologies as scientific rationalism and socialism, they wrote the original draft of the statement in 1974. Among the signers who were able to agree on the protest with surprising alacrity were Jesuit theologian Avery Dulles, Eastern Orthodox Seminary Dean Alexander Schmemann, Lutheran theologians George Forell and George Lindbeck, Yale Chaplain William Sloan Coffin Jr., and Presbyterian and Evangelical theologian Lewis Smedes of Fuller Theological Seminary.[24] They believed that such a theory of the church could only deprive it of its credibility and make it vulnerable to the world and its secular values.[25] In the biblical and eschatological perspective of the Kingdom, the

---

[24] The specific theses that the churchmen condemned as "false and debilitating" were these: (1) Modern thought is superior to all past forms of understanding reality and is therefore normative for Christian faith and life. (2) Religious statements are totally independent of reasonable discourse. (3) Religious language refers to human experience and nothing else, God being humanity's noblest creation. (4) Jesus can only be understood in terms of contemporary models of humanity. (5) All religions are equally valid; the choice among them is not a matter of conviction about truth but only of personal preference or lifestyle. (6) To realize one's potential and to be true to oneself is the whole meaning of salvation. (7) Since what is human is good, evil can adequately be understood as failure to realize human potential. (8) The sole purpose of worship is to promote individual self-realization and human community. (9) Institutions and historical traditions are oppressive and inimical to our being truly human; liberation from them is required for authentic existence and authentic religion. (10) The world must set the agenda for the Church. Social, political and economic programs to improve the quality of life are ultimately normative for the Church's mission in the world. (11) An emphasis on God's *transcendence* is at least a hindrance to, and perhaps incompatible with, Christian social concern and action. (12) The struggle for a better humanity will bring about the Kingdom of God. (13) The question of hope beyond death is irrelevant or at least marginal to the Christian understanding of human fulfillment.

[25] This was the basic wisdom of the Hartford Appeal of 1974. At the center of the appeal was the fear that the world would set the agenda for the Church, not vice versa. Almost a half century ago *Time* magazine published its report "The Hartford Heresies," that is no less relevant for contemporary pressing theological issues. (*Time*, February 10, 1975, 33). A group of eighteen Christian thinkers of nine denominations, after a weekend at the Hartford Seminary Foundation in Connecticut, joined in a dramatic warning that American theology had strayed dangerously far afield.

church discovers its true being as a sign of God's presence, a promise of salvation, and the embodiment of Christic grace, as it is the Body of Christ. This understanding of the church is a development and clarification of the concept of the church as sacrament proposed at Vatican II. Such development took place naturally when implications of the church as sacrament were more thoroughly explored in light of history and eschatology, membership in the church, and the problem of *extra ecclesiam nulla salus*, or "outside the church, there is no salvation."

8.3 The Church as Sacrament: Foundational Theology

The concept of the church as sacrament results from the integration of several decades of ecclesiological research: the theology of the Mystical Body that developed after 1925, the concept of the People of God of the 1930s and 1940s, and the more recent theology of the church as the sign of Christ that developed after World War II, especially in Germany.[26] The theological evolution of the church as sacrament went in this manner: first, a reappraisal of the sacraments as part of the integral life of the church; second, a newfound

Their "Appeal for Theological Affirmation" condemned thirteen pervasive ideas, all of which undermine "transcendence," the essential truth that God and his kingdom have a real, autonomous existence apart from the thoughts and efforts of mankind. In 1,150 words, their statement took issue with some of the most popular liberal fashions of the past decades, especially secular Christianity, political eschatology, and the human potential movement. The specific theses the churchmen condemned as "false and debilitating." After each of these assertions the statement added a qualifying paragraph explaining why the idea is wrong, even though it might sound beguiling and contain an element of truth. The statement nowhere mentions the people who have promulgated these false theses, but the discussions at Hartford included references to Harvey Cox, author of *The Secular City*, Situation Ethicist Joseph Fletcher, and Britain's Bishop John Robinson, whose famous book, *Honest to God*, was in everyone's pocket or bookbag at the time. As for the pervasiveness of the thinking exemplified in the theses, the Jesuit Avery Cardinal Dulles affirmed that the ideas were widespread in the Roman Catholic Church, particularly among popularizers of the late Teilhard de Chardin and liberation theologians who give the Bible a Marxist interpretation. A professor from Manhattan's Union Theological Seminary, an influential Protestant school, said that these theses summarized general belief there.

[26] Charles Moeller, "The History of *Lumen Gentium's* Structure and Ideas," in *Vatican II: An Interfaith Appraisal* (Notre Dame: The University of Notre Dame Press, 1966), 125.

awareness of the relationship between Christ, his Eucharist, and his Mystical Body; finally, the awareness that the church was not just the church of sacraments but the church is herself the primal sacrament. The classic works already mentioned by Karl Adam, Emile Mersch, Yves Congar, and Henri de Lubac were essential for a sacramental understanding of the church. The basic thesis of the church as primal sacrament was expressed by Henri de Lubac as early as 1939: "If Christ is the sacrament of God, the church is for us the sacrament of Christ; she represents him in the full and ancient meaning of the term, she makes him present."[27]

The key names in the development of sacramental understanding of the church were the Dominican Edward Schillebeeckx and the Jesuits Otto Semmelroth and Karl Rahner. In 1952, Schillebeeckx published the first part of a projected two-volume work on the sacraments in St. Thomas Aquinas.[28] In 1960, he published his famous work, *Christ the Sacrament of the Encounter with God.* Schillebeeckx places the sacramental actions of God in the whole sweep of the history of salvation, restoring an essential perspective to writings on sacraments that had been lost in much post-Tridentine theology. Sacraments are not simply actions of the ordained clergy concerned with technical and legal conditions for their valid administration and reception; rather, they are administered as a sacred event and at a sacred time where one encounters the mystery of God's active love and transforming presence. The advent of "encounter" theology, more reminiscent of Martin Buber than the theology found in earlier neoscholastic manuals, placed sacraments in a personalist framework, and, like Dom Odo Casel's work on liturgy a generation earlier, restored a sense of mystery to the whole sacramental action. For Schillebeeckx, God reveals Godself through the unfolding of the divine mystery or sacrament in which sacrament could be defined as "a divine bestowal of salvation in an outwardly perceptible form which makes the bestowal manifest."[29]

---

[27] De Lubac, *Catholicism: A Study of Dogma in Relation to the Corporate Destiny of Mankind*, 43.

[28] O'Brien, "Theology in Transition," 237.

[29] Edward Schillebeeckx, *Christ the Sacrament of the Encounter with God*, with a foreword by Cornelius Ernst, O.P. (New York: Sheed and Ward, 1963), 15. Reviewed by Maurice Schepers, O.P. in *Dominicana* 49, no. 2 (1964), 164–68.

In 1953, apparently quite independently of the work of Schillebeeckx, Jesuit theologian Otto Semmelroth developed the foundational ecclesial dimension of sacrament—or perhaps more accurately, the sacramental dimension of the *ecclesia*—in his work, *The Church as Primal Sacrament*.[30] He insisted that the Church had to be understood as the foundational sacrament of God's presence or the seven sacraments would be cut off from their authentic source of life. Likewise, Karl Rahner, the most important Catholic theologian of the twentieth century, argues that the church is the sacrament of Christ in like manner. The key point is that the church is sacramental only in so far as it is Christocentric; in other words, and in a manner surprisingly akin to the Lutheran Paul Tillich, the mystery of the church is really the mystery of Christ.[31] Karl Rahner gives us the following definition of the church:

> Now the church is the continuance, the contemporary presence, of that real, eschatologically triumphant and irrevocably established presence in the world, in Christ, of God's salvific will. The Church is the abiding presence of that primal sacramental word of definitive grace, which is in the world, effecting what is uttered by uttering it in sign.[32]

This sacramental framework allows Catholic theology to understand the relationship of Christ and the church in a dialectical manner. While the church is incarnational in its deepest mystery, that is, it makes the incarnate God present in its preaching and its sacraments, the church must also be distinct from the Incarnation in its explicit meaning. In other words, the incarnational model cannot be applied to the church as it is to Christ. The divine and the human within the church is radically different from the divine and the human in the Christ. For this very reason, there is no effort in the documents of Vatican II to describe the church as the "prolongation of the Incarnation" or "Christ in time." Similarly, *Lumen Gentium*, the Constitution on the Church, makes it clear that no *communicatio idiomatum* or communication of idioms between Christ and the church is possible; that is, what is said of

---

[30] Otto Semmelroth, *Die Kirche als Ursakrament* (Frankfurt: Knecht, 1953); published in English as *The Church as Primal Sacrament*, (New York: Herder and Herder, 1965). See a recent book chapter by Dennis M. Doyle, "Otto Semmelroth, SJ, and the Ecclesiology of the 'Church as Sacrament' at Vatican II," in *The Legacy of Vatican II*, ed. Massimo Faggioli and Andrea Vicini S.J. (New York: Paulist Press, 2015).

[31] In Tillich's language, the churches are embodiments of the Spiritual Community that is given life by the power of the New Being.

[32] Karl Rahner, *The Church and the Sacraments* (New York: Herder and Herder, 1963), 127.

Christ's human nature can be said of his divine nature but the same cannot be said of the church in the same way it is said of Christ.[33]

8.4 Symbol and Sacrament

In order to understand the meaning of the church as sacrament, one must begin with the idea of a symbol. A symbol is a visible, sensate sign that reveals the inner, transempirical, and transcendent dimension of reality. All symbols are two-edged or two-sided—they point to something beyond themselves while at the same time participating in the power of the reality to which they point. Unlike signs, which are arbitrary and do not share in the reality of what is signified (for example, a full stop sign does not participate in the fact of stopping), symbols have the power of what is signified. Therefore, a flag or a ring has power because it shares in the reality of a nation or the relationship established by the gift of a ring. Symbols also grow and die naturally—they cannot be dismissed or legislated away. When a symbol ceases to have power, it will eventually die. (For example, the monarchy in Great Britain, while it is primarily ceremonial, still has some power over the British people; likewise, the vows in a wedding ceremony have power only as long as the love and the commitment between two people exists.) One cannot tamper with another's symbols without incurring a strong and often nonrational reaction. Symbols are always powerful in making and celebrating life's meaning and in transforming an individual experience of self and world.[34] For example, each generation has its own particular set of symbols—in its clothing, in its language, in its politics and its morals, in its taste in music and film, in the whole way in which it interacts with the world and friends and strangers within it.

Today, many traditional sacred symbols have been called into question. This fact does not mean that symbols cease to flourish and are not powerful in structuring and shaping people's lives. For many today, symbols are often secular and function in an implicitly religious context. Yet these same symbols remain religious in so far as they are connected to life's import and meaning for an individual or a community. An explicitly religious symbol might be to attend the Eucharist in a church or chapel; an implicit symbol might be to help a friend in need of physical, psychological, or spiritual support. A culture cannot survive without symbols, whether these symbols are connected to a

---

[33] See *Lumen Gentium*, art. 8; also, Alois Grillmeier, "The Mystery of the Church," in *Commentary on the Documents of Vatican II*, ed. A. Grillmeier (New York: Herder and Herder, 1967), 46.

[34] Tillich, *Dynamics of Faith*, chap. 3.

sacred religious tradition or are the secular products of the culture, the media, or government policy. People cannot function without symbols of some sort whether they are aware of their role and function or not. Contemporary secular symbols often serve as substitutes for older sacred or religious symbols. Many moderns, "freed from any suspicions of divinity," in the phrase of Freudian scholar Philip Rieff, often turn their work, their material possessions, or their drive for leisure and pleasure into gods whom they worship through the appropriate symbols.[35] Even the most superficial of symbols accomplishes an ordering and a structuring of life in one way or another.

All sacraments are symbolic actions of the church; that is, by visible signs, words, objects, and actions, an invisible and meaningful event takes place in the spiritual core of a person. The foundation of sacraments can be located in the anthropological fact of our physical and historical natures: God reveals God in the only way we as human persons can accept and understand, that is, in signs and symbols, in the concrete things of the earth that are human and corporeal. Church sacraments are symbols of God's healing presence in the world. In other words, with a sacrament, grace comes with the visible action.

Human rites of passage—birth, puberty, marriage, sickness, and death—have always been moments of special significance for people and have been celebrated in every human community. These are the special times and places in life where the community celebrates the reality of God—or the transcendent in some form—as present in the lives of individuals. The divine presence grasps individuals in order to purify them of isolation and sinfulness, and to prepare them for another stage of life.[36]

8.5 Jesus as Sacrament

The Creator engages persons in experience wherein a call to belief and trust is made is a sacramental form of revelation. In every such sacramental event, in any place and at any time in history since Jesus' life on earth, there is one sensate medium that the Creator uses for this revelation: the humanity, the bodiliness of Jesus. But because Jesus, in his human body, has already been drawn through death into communion with the Creator in the Resurrection, he has been removed from immediacy with every other living being. For about a thirty-five-year span in history, the Creator did act through the bodiliness of Jesus in its immediate presence to other human beings. This bodiliness of

[35] Philip Rieff, *The Triumph of the Therapeutic: Uses of Faith after Freud* (Chicago: The University of Chicago Press, 1987), 7.

[36] See Theodore J. Mackin, "Marriage as a Sacrament," unpublished manuscript.

Jesus was God's sacrament; God disclosed the divine presence within it and worked to implement the plan for the human race through it. Because of this, we know who God the Creator is through knowing the person Jesus.

Part of the Creator's case for our trusting in God is that God has been made visible in Jesus' human bodily form through death and the Resurrection. What these traditional terms mean is that in his humanity Jesus is placed at the point of contact between the Creator and creation. In St. Paul's interpretation of Jesus, God's act both holds all things in existence and calls them back through the humanity of Jesus. God wills us into existence through the human desire of Jesus; God calls us back to God through the attractiveness of humanity exemplified in Jesus. The church teaches that the creator has chosen to act upon people through their humanity, through their physical beings open to God's use. These people comprise the church, those called out to be a sacrament of God present in Jesus and in what God accomplishes through Jesus' Paschal mystery.

8.6 Vatican II on Church as Sacrament

The Second Vatican Council, to the surprise of many observers, used two principal images for the church: the People of God and sacrament. Four important conciliar texts of Vatican II describe the church as sacrament:

> By her relationship with Christ, the church is a kind of sacrament or sign of intimate union with God, and of the unity of all mankind (*Lumen Gentium*, art. 1).
>
> God has gathered together as one all those who in faith look upon Jesus as the author of salvation and the source of unity and peace, and has established them as the Church that for each and all she may be the visible sacrament of this saving unity" (*Lumen Gentium*, art. 9).
>
> Rising from the dead he sent his life-giving Spirit upon his disciples and through his spirit has established his body, the Church, as the universal sacrament of salvation (*Lumen Gentium*, art. 48).
>
> For it was from the side of Christ as he slept the sleep of death upon the cross that there came forth the wondrous sacrament which is the whole Church (*Sacrasanctum Concilium*, art. 5).

The sacramental image of the church suggests the relationship between Christ and the church in this way: the death of Christ and his resurrection means that he is no longer visibly present to us. Yet Christ must be alive as a present reality, even though not visibly present in himself. His heavenly body continues to fulfill the salvific function of his earthly body. The church is the sacrament of Christ in glory—of Christ's heavenly body now. As the salvation and healing power of Christ was once visibly present in Jesus in history, this salvation is now visibly present in the church as the symbol of Christ's invisible heavenly body. Christ died, in St. Paul's words, *ephapax*, once and for all.[37] The "making present" in history of Christ's sacrifice does not mean its repetition or its extension. It can be present now, in accord with human nature, only through sacramental forms. The sacrament is twofold: first, of *historical* time, the corporeal manifestation of the once and for all grace of Christ, and, second, of *vertical* presence, the heavenly Christ who is alive and the enduring source of that grace.

The fact that Christ is no longer visibly present to us, that he can be present only sacramentally, suggests that the church is the sacrament both of Christ's presence *and* of his absence, that the inner dialectic of a sacrament involves both a making present and a failing to make present. Like a symbol, a sacrament points to a reality beyond itself while participating in that reality at the same time. The church does embody Christ, and as such, it is truly the Body of Christ. But, correlatively, the church is not Christ in that it can only signify him, point him out, be a sign and a herald of his healing power. Christ's Passover is, in the same event, the complete salvific act on God's part and the rejection of that act on humanity's part. In Christ's death, humankind, in Schillebeeckx's words, "has banished from the world God's kingdom in Christ, and so has impelled it from the *communio* of persons."[38] The church itself, insofar as it is part of humankind, shares in this rejection. The profound contradiction of the Cross can only be understood and accepted in light of the Resurrection. But both events that form the one Paschal mystery imply that henceforth our salvation depends on someone who is absent from our experience. In Schillebeeckx's words:

> We may justly conclude from this that the final state of our condition as it was created by original sin is a situation in which the privation of supernatural grace can only be removed sacramentally, a situation in which man found himself ever since and because of the breach of the covenant with God, was made complete through man's rejection of Christ.[39]

---

[37] See Heb 9:25–27. The word appears five times in the New Testament, twice in Paul's Epistles, and three times in the Epistle to the Hebrews. See 1 Cor 15:6; Rom 6:10; Heb 7:27; Heb 9:12; and Heb 10:10.

[38] Schillebeeckx, "The Church and Mankind," 79.

[39] Schillebeeckx, 80.

8.7 The Church and the Holy Spirit

The other side of this "absence of Jesus" is the presence of the Holy Spirit. The coming of the Spirit is not to be understood as a substitute for Christ, nor are Christ and the Spirit separate and distinct. The Spirit of the Lord, the One who unites the Son and the Father in the Trinitarian life, is the One who comes and who remains with the church. The Council states that Christ "sent his life-giving Spirit upon his disciples and through this Spirit has established His Body, the Church, as the universal sacrament of salvation."[40] Pentecost is an Easter reality; put differently, at the *moment* Jesus dies on the Cross, he is alive with God and present *as* Spirit that he shares with the Father. Liturgically, these events are spaced over fifty days, but they are more than simple temporal moments because they have absolute and eternal significance. Jesus, in his humanity, is the sender of the Spirit through his establishment as Lord and Christ in his Passover. The sending of the Spirit is the sending of new life—for the world and the church—and is intrinsic in Christ's own passage from death to life. This "other side" of the Easter event is summarized by Schillebeeckx in this way: "Pentecost is the eternally continuing actuation or application of this mystery (or sacrament) in and through the Holy Spirit who now realizes and perfects in us that which was completed in Christ. Only through the Spirit whom Christ sends us does what is a reality in Christ—that in him all the faithful sit at the right hand of the Father become actual in ourselves."[41]

8.8 The Church as Sacrament and the Kingdom of God

The rediscovery of the concept of the Kingdom of God is one of the most significant developments in the Catholic ecclesiology at the Second Vatican Council. Just as in other areas of theology, the statements of the conciliar documents themselves are a kind of middle ground between Tridentine theology and the breakthrough of the "new theology" that can be found at the Council. It would be a mistake to see the documents of the Council in terms of what is all new; the Council did not make so radical a break with the past as early liberal commentators thought. Rather, the Council was a kind of a "halfway house," with a significant remnant of Tridentine theology embedded

[40] *Lumen Gentium*, art. 48.

[41] Schillebeeckx, *Christ the Sacrament,* 27–28; 40–44.

within the biblical-historical framework of the conciliar documents.[42]

The Kingdom or Reign of God is the biblical symbol that captures the historical and eschatological nature of the church. As Lutheran theologian Carl Braaten writes: "The quest for a fully developed doctrine of the church can be satisfied only when theology is recast in an eschatological mold, only when one thinks from the end toward the present, from the coming kingdom of God to the Church by way of the world."[43] Just as the distinction between person and nature provided a clue to the Christological problematic, so too the distinction between the Kingdom of God and the church may be a most important insight into the church's own quest for self-understanding.[44] In terms of Vatican II, *Lumen Gentium* reflects the beginning of change. If one were to read the document free of a Tridentine perspective, one would be struck immediately by the concrete and historical, rather than abstract and static, approach to the Church. The Kingdom or Reign of God is the fullness of God's mystery revealed to human beings. Jesus Christ, in his words, works, and presence, is God's Kingdom; the church is now, in *Lumen Gentium*'s words, "the Kingdom of Christ present in mystery."[45] Her goal as the visible People of God is the Kingdom of God, "which has been begun by God himself on earth, and which is to be further extended until it is brought to perfection by him at the end of time."[46] The church is a pilgrim church, "announcing the cross and death of the Lord until he comes," always on route and in search of her fulfillment in the eschatological Kingdom.[47]

The most important element in Vatican II's treatment of the Church and Kingdom is the clear distinction made between these two realities. While the theology of the conciliar documents is still very much church-centered rather than Kingdom-centered, as an analysis of *Lumen Gentium*'s chapter seven would indicate, a breakthrough has been made. *Lumen Gentium* makes it clear that the church here and now cannot be simply identified with the Kingdom

[42] See Richard McBrien, *The Remaking of the Church: An Agenda for Reform* (New York: Harper and Row, 1973). See section 8.1 of this volume.

[43] Carl Braaten, "Paul Tillich and the Classical Christian Tradition," introduction to Paul Tillich, *Perspectives on 19th and 20th Century Protestant Theology* (New York: Harper and Row, 1967), xv.

[44] See John Haughey, "Church and Kingdom: Ecclesiology in the Light of Eschatology," *Theological Studies* 29 (1968): 72.

[45] *Lumen Gentium*, arts. 5 and 3.

[46] *Lumen Gentium*, art. 9.

[47] *Lumen Gentium*, art. 9.

of God. The church is the seed of the Kingdom, the revealer of the Kingdom in history, and the sacrament of the Reign of God. As Christ's Body, however, the church is hardly complete and remains unfulfilled in its historical nature. While it is a sacrament of salvation, it is still a church of sinners. Augustine's mystical comment, mentioned earlier, captures the church's eschatological destiny perfectly: there will be one Christ loving himself (*unus Christus seipsum amans*). While present as sacrament now, the Kingdom is a future reality, fulfilled only at a time when God shall be all in all. The Body here and now is subject to its head and is ever seeking union with it. As *Lumen Gentium* notes: "He fills the church, which is his Body and his fullness, with his divine gifts, so that she may grow and reach all the fullness of God."[48] Because the church is only the seed of the Kingdom, incomplete as the sacrament of the Lord, it is the church which "embraces sinners in her bosom," which is both "holy and always in need of being purified," and which must constantly pursue "the path of penance and renewal."[49]

Thus, the Catholic Church understands and proclaims its relative nature between the two foci of her existence, the Kingdom revealed both here and now and the not-yet-fulfilled eschatological Kingdom at the Parousia.[50] In a mysterious way, the church makes the Kingdom of God present in time, yet *only* sacramentally, that is, through mystery and through symbols of hope and expectation. The sacramental concept of the church, then, is an ideal framework to correlate a theology of the Kingdom and the eschatological nature of the church. A sacrament is by its very nature, as Semmelroth says, "something eschatological," which means, "the eschaton, the heavenly salvation we have yet to reach, has already invaded the world in sacramental sign and is caught in an earthly element as in a seal."[51]

With the significant shift in Catholic ecclesiology in the relationship between the Church and the Kingdom of God, the concept of sacrament becomes an ideal model. Sacrament avoids the pessimistic view in the Calvinist tradition and in the free churches, in which church and Kingdom are too widely separated. Likewise, the dialectical relationship between Kingdom and church similarly avoids a Catholic triumphalism where church and Kingdom

---

[48] *Lumen Gentium*, art. 7.

[49] *Lumen Gentium*, art. 8.

[50] See Sabbas J. Kilian, "Dialogue in Ecclesiology," *Theological Studies* 30 (1969): 64.

[51] Otto Semmelroth, "Chapter Seven," *Commentary on the Documents of Vatican II*, ed. A. Grillmeier (New York: Herder and Herder, 1967), 282.

are too closely united and often indistinguishable. Sacrament thus moves the earthly church away from a pure "ecclesiology of glory," permitting it to see that the fullness of its glory lies in the coming Kingdom that will embrace both church and world. Its present glory is Christological, bound up in the mystery of the Cross.

Several advantages of the sacramental understanding of the church are clear. *First*, the church as Sacrament of the world's salvation opens a path to understand non-Christian faiths and the significant problem of "outside the church there is no salvation."[52] The problem of *extra ecclesiam, nulla salus* has been around since the Fathers of the Church. Of course, the issue can be reduced to your definition of "church" and "outside." In 1948, quite a stir was made by the Jesuit theologian Leonard Feeney, who took a strong literal interpretation of the term, excluding anyone but baptized Roman Catholics from salvation. Salvation comes only from God, not the church; salvation is God's free gift. Hence, other religions may be understood to have salvific power. What is unique about Christianity, to paraphrase Karl Rahner, is not that it possesses grace and other religions do not, but that this grace has become historical and definitive in Jesus; it is Jesus as the human face of God who is absolute, not the church.

Second, as discussed in the previous chapter, authority in the Church could be understood differently. The church's authority is itself a sacrament of the only true authority in heaven or on earth: God alone. When authority becomes absolute, it is always threatened with idolatry, since nothing finite can be equated with the infinite. *Third*, the idea of the church as sacrament allows for ecumenical discussion among other Christian congregations. God's grace is made concrete in the world through church—the Catholic pole of sacrament. The Protestant pole is also important: God's grace always transcends any one finite expression, be it in the church or the book. Paul Tillich calls these two poles Catholic substance and Protestant principle.

---

[52] The *Catechism* (once again quoting *Lumen Gentium*, art. 14), summarizes all this as follows: Basing itself on Scripture and Tradition, the Council teaches that the Church, a pilgrim now on earth, is necessary for salvation: the one Christ is the mediator and the way of salvation; he is present to us in his body which is the Church. He himself explicitly asserted the necessity of faith and baptism, and thereby affirmed at the same time the necessity of the Church which men enter through baptism as through a door. Hence they could not be saved who, knowing that the Catholic Church was founded as necessary by God through Christ, would refuse either to enter it or to remain in it. *Catechism of the Catholic Church*, part 1, sec. 2, chap. 3, art. 9, para. 3, no. 846.

8.9 Catholic Substance and Protestant Principle[53]

Paul Tillich's concept of the Catholic substance and Protestant principle helps the reader understand the two poles of Western Christianity, Catholicism and Protestantism. Catholic substance is the transparency of the finite to the infinite; in Tillich's description of God's grace through the Holy Spirit, the "Spiritual Presence cannot be received without a sacramental element however hidden the latter may be."[54] Protestant principle and Catholic substance describe the dialectical tension within finite symbols that mediate the divine grace. Catholic substance affirms that every person, place, or thing is capable of becoming a sacrament of the presence of the divine Spirit. In Protestant theologian André Gounelle's description of Catholic substance:

> [It] puts the accent on the reality of the presence of God in certain places. 'Place' should be understood in a broad sense: locality (sanctuary, pilgrimages), but also institutions (the Church, the papacy, the assembly of bishops, councils or synods), texts (the Bible, the doctrinal definitions, and confessions of ecclesiastical faith), ceremonies (rites, sacraments), objects (relics), images (icons). The nature and list of these religious 'places' varies according to specific tradition and situation. In those which are recognized, it is considered that the believers meet with the very being of God.[55]

Protestant principle, on the other hand, guards the Transcendent, insisting that no specific manifestation of the Holy can be identified with the Holy itself. "It considers as sacrilegious and blasphemous the sacralization of certain places, because God alone is divine and God has the monopoly of the sacred or the holy. Nothing can tie God down or 'fence him in,' as Calvin writes. God always remains supremely free."[56]

---

[53] This section appeared in much longer form in my "Tillich's Catholic Substance Today," *Dialog: A Journal of Theology* 36 (1997): 128–34.

[54] Tillich, *Systematic Theology*, 3:122.

[55] André Gounelle, "Paul Tillich: A Vision of Protestantism for Today," in *Spirit and Community: The Legacy of Paul Tillich's Thought*, ed. Frederick J. Parrella (Berlin and New York: Walter de Gruyter, 1995): 161–62.

[56] Gounelle, 162.

Although Tillich was a constant and vocal critic of the objectification and de-personalization of sacraments in the post-Tridentine Catholic Church, he was also alarmed by the decrease in sacramental thinking within Protestantism. "Sacraments have lost their spiritual power and are vanishing in the consciousness of most Protestants," he writes in *The Protestant Era.* This has also become the situation in Catholicism in recent years. When the Spirit cannot be mediated through visible signs or sacraments, when the unconscious dimension of a person cannot be touched, the power and vitality of the Christian message is concentrated in one's deliberate moral decision so that either the message or consciousness may suffer. According to Tillich, the Christ would be accepted as just another "religious personality and not as the basic sacramental reality, the New Being."[57] No wonder that more than a half century ago, Tillich could discern "the longing of youth for new symbols," symbols which unlocked the Eternal in the temporal order and created a world open to the transcendent.[58]

Catholic theologians obviously have appreciated Tillich's emphasis on Catholic substance, on the mystical and the sacramental dimension of religion. Once viewed by scholars in the 1940s and 1950s primarily through existentialist categories, Tillich's thought is now accepted much more in the spirit, as Thomas O'Meara says, of the "romantic-idealist systematician" he was.[59] A "mystical ontology" is one of the most important characteristics of Tillich's thought, rendered all the more significant because it stands in creative tension with his commitment to a prophetic and *kairic* interpretation of history. Tillich offers Catholics not just a formal theological system but an approach to the Christian's encounter with God and God's presence in the finite world that is intuitive, incarnational, universal, one that carries within it its own critical and prophetic principle. In Walter Leibrecht's words: "Tillich has been a mystical theologian in the classic sense of the phrase.…His is a theology of the spirit. It is a mystical experience, if we do not misconstrue the meaning of this word, which underlies all his theology."[60]

[57] Tillich, *The Protestant Era*, xix.

[58] Paul Tillich, *The Rediscovery of the Prophetic Tradition of the Reformation* (Washington, DC: Christianity and Modern Man Publications, 1950), 27.

[59] Thomas O'Meara, "Paul Tillich and the Catholic Substance," in *The Thought of Paul Tillich*, ed. James Luther Adams, Wilhelm Pauck, and Roger Shinn (San Francisco: Harper and Row, 1985), 300.

[60] Walter Leibrecht, "The Life and Mind of Paul Tillich," in *Religion and Culture: Essays in Honor of Paul Tillich*, ed. Walter Leibrecht (New York: Harper, 1959), 19–20.

Likewise, we must not forget the other side of Tillich's dialectic, the Protestant principle. Since the Second Vatican Council, it is this Protestant Tillich that is as much appreciated by Catholic scholars of Tillich as his emphasis on the Catholic substance. At Vatican II, Catholicism's emergence into the modern world involved a sudden loss of innocence about its timeless truths and ecclesiastical structures; inevitably, iconoclasm reigned unchecked for a short period. Catholicism was at last experiencing its own kind of reformation. What was enduring and what was transitory in its own Catholic substance had to be rediscovered under the power of the prophetic principle. The Council made the Roman Catholic Church a church not only of Catholic substance but also of Protestant principle. The church redefined itself not as a community above history but as a pilgrim church, even more a church of sinners. The formal reception of historical consciousness and the prophetic principle in the life of the Church has marked Catholic theology and Catholic life in the six decades since the Council. Ronald Modras writes of the present situation in Catholicism: "It is not Catholic efforts to restore orthodoxy and authority that are striking, however, but the widespread continuing existence and growth of Catholic self-criticism. What Tillich called the prophetic or Protestant principle continues to thrive in the Catholic Church, more, I would submit, than in most other Churches."[61]

The extent to which Roman Catholicism accepted the prophetic principle into its self-understanding is obvious in Tillich's own criticism, a half century ago, of the essays in *Paul Tillich in Catholic Thought* in light of the subsequent conciliar documents.[62] Tillich emphasizes his subjectivity against the Catholic theologians' objectivity, as well as his autonomy versus their position on Church authority or heteronomy. As Kenan Osborne observes, one finds in *Lumen Gentium* the "clear indication that the Light of the World is Jesus alone, and that the Church, including Church leadership, is thereby relativized." Only when the Church and its leadership is a sacrament of Christ is it truly Church. Likewise, *Gaudium et Spes* affirms "the inviolability of the human conscience, into which the Spirit of God speaks to a person." Finally,

[61] Ronald Modras, "Catholic Substance and the Catholic Church Today," in *Paul Tillich: A New Catholic Perspective*, ed. Raymond F. Bulman and Frederick J. Parella (Collegeville, MN: The Liturgical Press, 1994), 43.

[62] See Paul Tillich, "An Afterword: Appreciation and Reply," in *Paul Tillich in Catholic Thought*, ed. Thomas F. O'Meara and Donald Weisser (Dubuque, IA: Priory Press, 1964), 301–11. Keep in mind that while the book was published in 1964, most of the articles date from the 1950s.

Dei Verbum makes it clear that Scripture "confronts everyone in the Church with an accountability: all are under the word of God, Church authority included."[63]

One can only imagine Tillich's response to the reforms of Vatican II had he lived to grasp the full import of the Council. In 1963, Tillich was aware of the changes that Pope John XXIII and the Second Vatican Council could make in Catholic life and theology. The issue for Tillich at the time was the degree and the effectiveness of the revival of what he called the "principle of reformation" within Catholicism.[64] Tillich surely had an uncanny sense of the reforming spirit in the Roman Church: "It sometimes appears in these days that the Roman Catholic Church is more open to the demand for reformation than are the churches of the Reformation."[65] If Tillich were still with us today, he would be very pleased with the extent of Catholicism's incorporation of the Protestant principle. Without this principle of self-criticism, the Catholic substance, as Tillich certainly knew, could not discover new spirit and fresh life. In Thomas O'Meara's words: "The Protestant principle is not the critique outside the substance...but a flame within the spiritual presence."[66] In spite of new heteronomies today within the Church's institutional form, it is this very substance, invigorated and refreshed by the prophetic spirit, which continues to make Catholicism attractive to the secular world. It will continue to do so only in so far as it keeps the flame of the Protestant principle alive. One might argue that the neo-Tridentine attitude of the last two popes is an effort to remove the Protestant principle from the Catholic substance present in the Catholic Church. This means a return to the danger of idolatry against which Luther first protested.

8.10 Contemporary Models of the Church

One of the most important developments in the theology of the church after Vatican II was Avery Dulles's creation of an ecclesiology based on models. With the seeds of his work prepared by the ecclesiologists and theologians from World War I through the Council, Dulles suggests that six *models* unlock the mystery of the Church in a way that a *definition* could only block deeper insight. His book, *Models of the Church*, first appeared in 1974 with

---

[63] Osborne, "Tillich's Understanding of Symbols and Sacramental Theology," 104–5.

[64] Tillich, *Systematic Theology*, 3:168.

[65] Tillich, 3:4.

[66] O'Meara, "Tillich and the Catholic Substance," 304.

five models presented and discussed. A second edition and a final model, the community of disciples, appeared in 1987.[67] (Unfortunately, the second edition only added a chapter and did not integrate his final model into the discussion of the evaluation of the models and their relationship to one another.) A second weakness of the book lies in his excessive concern with only the Roman Catholic position on a number of issues, but given its time and place, the book made a very important contribution to ecclesiology. (Dulles's work is used in both Catholic seminaries and Protestant schools of divinity.) The book provides interpretive categories for Church that open discussion and provide both a unity and diversity in ecclesiology. Ideally, the book should be rewritten and revised from beginning to end while keeping the basic six models that he presents. Much more integration of non-Eurocentric, multicultural, and global interpretations of the Church should be included in this reworking of this seminal text.

Models function as symbols, and so unlock the mystery without attempting to capture it in any verbal formula. They are images that are used reflectively and critically to deepen one's theoretical understanding. In terms of the church, we have the biblical images of temple, vine, flock, and body, among many others. Other models are more abstract, such as institution, society, and community. Some models serve as paradigms or dominant models, those accepted as more inclusive and more fully adequate than other models. From the Council of Trent to the Second Vatican Council, the reigning Catholic model has been "institution," where Church was primarily understood in terms of its visible structures, especially the rights and powers of its officers. In the Protestant tradition, the reigning model has been predominantly herald, but with elements of other models, such as servant, community of disciples, and mystical communion.

Dulles proposes a practical or pragmatic norm for the verification of models: models are effective "by living out the consequences to which they point."[68] Thus, models should be judged not by their theological purity or adequacy but their impact on the life of the community at any given time. The shift from theoretical justification to practical and pastoral reasons for a model's effectiveness has been a significant change in recent theology. Put differently, how does the model resonate in the experience of the faithful? How does it assist in forming a community? How does it unlock the mystery of grace or church as, in Dulles's words, the "divine self-gift"? In addition to

---

[67] Avery Dulles, *Models of the Church*, rev. ed. (New York: Doubleday, 1987).

[68] Dulles, 24.

the model of the church as sacrament so prominent at Vatican II, let's briefly outline the five models Dulles offers us to understand the mystery of the church.

8.10.1 The Church as Mystical Communion. The model of the church as Mystical Communion deserves special attention. Dulles divides this model into two powerful biblical images, the Body of Christ and the People of God. These are the oldest images of the church. As we considered in chapter two, the People of God is derived for the Old Testament proclamation of "I will be your God and you will be my people." The term "people," *qahal* in Hebrew, was translated in the Septuagint, the Greek translation of the Hebrew bible, as *ekklesia*, *ecclesia* in Latin, the word Paul uses for the church. The advantage of this term, emphasized in the title of the second chapter of *Lumen Gentium*, is its ability to strengthen the ties between the Hebrew origins of Christianity and the subsequent gentile church. The Christian church is thus the new People of God, the new Jerusalem. The disadvantage of the term "People of God" is its lack of emphasis on the distinct difference Jesus the Christ makes in the emergence of Christianity from its Jewish roots.

The Body of Christ is the oldest term used by Paul to explain what this new People of God is. In calling the church Christ's body, Paul means much more than just a moral metaphor; he uses the term in a metaphysical sense. Body can have several meanings: first, a physical body of people united externally by common goals, such as a government body or a social club like the Lions or Shriners. Second, a family is a body united by the deeper ties of blood and genes as well as a common history. Finally, the Body of Christ is unique because it comprises people united in the deepest and most meaningful of ways, in the Holy Spirit. In Baptism, persons formally join this body in its historical expression, and they are united to others beyond all human ties and human appearances, even the appearances of disunity. It is a unity deeper than blood and deeper than the highest shared human aspirations.

8.10.2 The Church as Herald. The herald model, the most popular model in Protestant ecclesiology, is derived from the Greek *kerygma,* the message announced to the men of Athens, and later the word used for the earliest preaching of the Gospel message. (Preaching or *kerygma* was distinguished from teaching or *didache* in the early church. It is very difficult to rediscover the ancient *keryma*, with small fragments in the Pauline writings and in Acts.[69]) In this model, the church is established by both the preaching and the

[69] See C. H. Dodd, *The Apostolic Preaching and Its Development* (New York: Harper and Row, 1964).

hearing of the Word of God. In spite of the efforts of Vatican II to restore Scripture to a central place of Catholic worship and to unite word with sacrament, the concept of hearing the Word of God is lost on many in the pews. This issue is more cultural than theological. We live in a culture where the ritual of proclamation and hearing is not prominent, and most of our "words" are heard electronically or in typed form. The idea of not just listening to words but hearing the Word deep in our hearts, calling us to serve the Gospel message and to form a community, was the goal of the documents on revelation and liturgy at Vatican II. Much work still needs to be done to make the Word come alive and become an integral part of Catholic worship.

Along with problems in the proclamation of the Word, a second liability in the Catholic tradition has been preaching or homiletics. The history of preaching in the Catholic tradition differs widely from our Protestant brothers and sisters.[70] In 1969, in his revised ritual for the Mass, Pope Paul VI described the homily or sermon as one of "the elements that [has] suffered injury through the accidents of history."[71] Stephen DeLeers notes that in the "divorce" between the Protestants and Catholics in the sixteenth century, the "property settlement" was "unfortunate" for both sides: "Protestants got the Word and Catholics got the sacraments."[72] Although Trent recognized the importance of preaching—in no small part because the Reformers' success was due to their excellent preaching—the quality of Catholic preaching fell precipitously far behind the preaching of the Reformers. At the beginning of the twentieth century, Catholic preaching was, sadly, "optional…non-scriptural, and non-liturgical."[73]

The historical reasons for this must be noted. *First*, the connection between preaching, Sacred Scripture, and the liturgical action had all but been lost. Trent itself characterized preaching the Gospel of Jesus as "teaching [the people] what is necessary for all to know with a view to salvation…the vices they must avoid and the virtues they must cultivate so as to escape eternal

[70] The following section is based on my paper, "The Theologian as Preacher: Paul Tillich and the Roman Catholic Homiletic Tradition," in *Paul Tillich: prédicateur et théologien pratique*, ed. Jean Richard, Mac Dumas, and Mireille Hébert (Berlin: LIT Verlag, 2007).

[71] Paul VI, *Apostolic Constitution Approving the Roman Missal*, quoted in Stephen V. DeLeers, *Written Text Becomes Living Word: The Vision and Practice of Sunday Preaching* (Collegeville, MN: The Liturgical Press, 2004), 1.

[72] DeLeers, 2.

[73] DeLeers, 6.

punishment and gain the glory of heaven."[74] The tone of this statement of Trent sounds more Gnostic and Pelagian than truly Gospel-centered. In sum, Protestant and Catholic ministers "took preaching in the opposite direction" from each other.[75] A *second* reason for poor Catholic preaching was the stilted theology taught in seminaries. Theology was apologetic and ahistorical, interested in speculative questions and neglectful of its "pastoral and kerygmatic" dimensions. Preaching in this context was often reduced to a "vulgarization of theological tracts" taught in seminaries.[76] A *third* reason was the neglected state of Catholic biblical scholarship until after World War I. Pius X, in his attack on Modernism, also attacked, in the strongest of terms, "agnostic, immanentist, and evolutionist" biblical scholarship.[77] Not until after the war did a renewal in Catholic theology and biblical scholarship take place. Finally, in his encyclical, *Mediator Dei* of 1947, Pius XII embraced historical-critical biblical scholarship and encouraged scholars to continue their work.

A *fourth* and final reason for the quality of Catholic preaching was the dominant image of the priesthood from Trent to Vatican II. Trent reformed the priesthood by the creation of seminaries, which placed the primary emphasis on the holiness of the priest's life instead of his ministry and service to the community. While Vatican II expanded this concept of priesthood considerably, from one ordained to consecrate the Eucharist to a priest who shares in the three offices of Christ as priest, prophet, and king, secular or diocesan priests for centuries were trained to be "mini-monks," in pursuit of a life of holiness. Before Vatican II, the *cura animarum* (care of souls) and the role of preaching within this ministry was understood as secondary in the priest's life and subordinate to his primary quest for sanctity.[78]

An ecclesiological sea change took place with the documents of renewal at the Second Vatican Council: a renewed emphasis on the liturgy of the Word and the importance of preaching. The sermon or homily at Sunday

---

[74] The Council of Trent, Fifth Session, in Norman P. Tanner, ed., *Decrees of the Ecumenical Councils*, vol. 2 (Washington, D.C: Georgetown University Press, 1990), 669.

[75] DeLeers, *Written Text Becomes Living Word,* 4.

[76] Domenico Grasso, *Proclaiming God's Message: A Study in the Theology of Preaching* (Notre Dame: University of Notre Dame Press, 1965), xxvii.

[77] *Pascendi Dominici Gregis,* quoted in DeLeers, *Written Text Becomes Living Word*, 5.

[78] See Kenan Osborne, "Priestly Formation," in *From Trent to Vatican II: Historical and Theological Investigations*, ed. Raymond F. Bulman and Frederick J. Parrella (New York: Oxford University Press, 2006), chapter 7.

Mass was made a requirement, along with an effort to teach priests to base their sermons in the Scriptural readings of the day. Josef Jungmann, S.J. (1889–1975) was perhaps the most significant name in the revival of kerygmatic theology, in which the message of salvation is proclaimed as it was in the ancient church. The goal of preaching is not truth in the scientific sense but life and holiness.[79] At the same time, preaching or kerygmatic theology remained very much theology. As Michael Schmaus says, "Every scientific theology must in some way also be a theology of preaching unless it wants to run the risk of ceasing to be scientific theology."[80]

Many of the documents of Vatican II could be cited in the restoration of the prominence of the Word of God in the liturgy and the importance of preaching on this Word. As the Decree on Ministry and Life of Priests clearly states, "Priests have as their first charge to announce the Gospel to all." Preaching is intimately connected to the entire liturgy: "Preaching of the Word is necessary for the administration of the sacraments, since they are the sacraments of faith, which is born and nourished by hearing the message."[81] Luther might not have said it better! Furthermore, after the Council, both Pope Paul VI and Pope John Paul II promulgated numerous documents referring to the homily, and no less than twelve of the congregations within the Roman Curia have likewise issued documents on preaching in the decades after Vatican II.[82] Of course, the quality of preaching as well as its reception by Catholics from the end of the Council until today are both other matters, but the decline of preaching from Trent to Vatican II is finally over and the restoration of the Word to a role equal to sacrament appears fully under way. One positive indication that such a restoration of the proclamation of the Word is succeeding comes from a scientific survey published in 2000 that affirms that Protestants and Catholics are now in agreement that the component of the service most important to one's spiritual life is the sermon. It is no

---

[79] Jungmann's most famous work is *Die Frohbotschaft und unsere Glaubensverkündigung* (Regensberg: Pustel, 1936; published in a synoptic English translation as *The Good News and Its Proclamation* (New York: Sadlier, 1961); see also his "Le probléme du message à transmettre ou le probleme kerygmatique," *Lumen Vitae* 5 (1950); cited in Grasso, *Proclaiming God's Message*, xxvi-xxvii.

[80] Michael Schmaus, preface to *Katholische Dogmatik*, vol. 2 (München: Max Hüber 1962); cited in Grasso, *Proclaiming God's Message*, xxix.

[81] *Presbyterorum Ordinis,* chap. 2, in Tanner, ed., *Decrees of the Ecumenical Council*, 1046–47.

[82] For a listing of official Roman Catholic documents concerning preaching from 1963 to 1994, see DeLeers, *Written Text Becomes Living Word,* 195–200.

wonder that Catholics, at least in the United States, seek out churches that have both good preaching and good music.[83]

8.10.3 The Church as Servant. The servant model of the church emerged in the social revolution of the 1960s, but its roots, of course, go much further back in church history. Avery Dulles contends that the model of servant cannot be found in the New Testament; often this is difficult to understand from our vantage point today. For the early community of Jesus' followers—the Nazarenes or "People of the Way"—the expectation of the Lord's return was the dominating factor in their experience. They were not involved in the world because they saw Jesus' return as imminent. For this reason, Paul said, "It is better to marry than to burn" (1 Cor 7). Even after 70 CE and the growing enculturation of the church in the world, the church remained a counterculture element within society. They were not servants within the culture because the cultural elite, at least until the beginning of the fourth century, refused to accept the saving message of Jesus and the church. Yet, since they served and loved one another, Christians became models of service to many lower- and middle-class members of the Empire. Sociologists of the late Roman world believe that this exemplary service allowed the small, counterculture community to survive and eventually triumph against periodic persecutions, especially at the end of the third century under Diocletian. Christians were caring for the poor and the sick, not just of their own community but also of the pagan world of which they were a part. This won over many non-Christians to their cause, at least to refusing to inflict harm on the early members of the church.

In the 1960s, the model of church as servant emerged with the wave of new social consciousness in the church. If the Protestant theologian, Dietrich Bonhoeffer, could describe Jesus as the "man for others," then surely the church could also be understood as the church for others. Modern Christians may have forgotten that all the charitable institutions of Western civilization—schools, hospitals, orphanages, and asylums, among others—all emerged from the Christian ideal of loving one another as Christ loved us (see Jn 15). This model seems especially well attuned to young people in our culture who want to do more than be passive Christians; they have heard the Gospel's call to feed the hungry and clothe the naked (see Mt 25:31–46) and want to reply accordingly. They are deeply committed to the contemporary Jesuit ideal of "faith through justice."

8.10.4 The Church as Institution. The most popular image of the Catholic

[83] DeLeers, 11. See Lori Carrell, *The Great American Sermon Survey* (Wheaton, IL: Mainstay Church Resources, 2000).

Church for four centuries, the institutional model, has been deeply ingrained into the average Catholic who grew up before Vatican II in the 1960s. In the history of ecclesiology in preceding chapters, much information about this model has been detailed, especially in the centuries since the Reformation. Unfortunately, the history of ecclesiology is usually the history of the institution, not the People of God, Body of Christ, and community of disciples. At the core of this model is the belief that Jesus himself established the institution of the church for the salvation of humankind. This is very different than affirming an institutional element within the church. All things human and societal have such an institutional element. Much of the institutional church model is a direct result of the apologetic stand of the Catholic Church in light of the Protestant Reformation in the sixteenth century. This model became what Dulles calls a paradigm, a super-model that became normative because of its ability to answer the needs of the time. For centuries, because the church was modeled on secular society, the church was considered a "perfect society" (*societas perfecta*), above history and above human imperfection.[84] The model of the church as institution, while having its roots in the marriage of church and state in the high Middle Ages, was given final and definitive form in the Tridentine church, in the implementation of the reforms conceived at the Council of Trent.

8.10.5 The Church as a Community of Disciples. In 1987, Avery Dulles added a sixth model, the church as a "community of disciples." In this model, the church is defined as those who have been called by Jesus to follow him in his mission of making all peoples his disciples. The mission of the church is to profess the fullness of faith to a secularized and sometimes faithless world; it is to follow Jesus and his values and not the values of the world. Two poles of a discipleship church exist: first, the inner pole—assembly and the centripetal phase of worship; second, the outer pole—mission and the centrifugal phase of service.

The model has certain clear advantages: it is closest to the historical Jesus who called disciples to his side; it is open to all people before distinctions are made between men and women, lay and clergy; it gives a strong sense of mission, which is important to many younger people attracted to the church. At the same time, the model has some weaknesses: it may become too countercultural in its creation of what Dulles calls a "contrast society." It may appear too elitist or too difficult for certain special people; it also tends to reduce the role of other models. Dulles wishes to avoid the objection that the church is

[84] Dulles, *Models of the Church*, 29.

based on free association and an individualistic ecclesiology, a view that would "seem to be at odds with the Catholic vision of the church as a necessary society that gives birth to its own members." He replies that discipleship depends on a prior call from Jesus or "the community of disciples in some sense prior to its own members."[85] Uniting the biblical historical view of the church as a community of disciples with the mystical view of the church as part of God's plan from all eternity appears the be the major problem with the model.

[85] Dulles, 225.

9.

THE TWENTY-FIRST CENTURY'S CLASH OF ECCLESIOLOGIES

9.1 An Overview

This final chapter is a sum of the history of ecclesiology in the previous chapters and some speculation on the church in 2022 and where its ecclesial understanding is headed. Seventy years have passed since the Second Vatican Council, called by Pope John XXIII, convened in Rome in 1962. Only septuagenarians and octogenarians have any personal memory of the Council today. While much scholarship on the theology and history of the Council has been published, some fundamental questions still remain. Was Vatican II a continuation of the theology of the Council of Trent four centuries earlier? Was it a radical departure in both the substance and style of Trent's theology and ecclesiology? Alternatively, is there some kind of median position in between these two polar opposites? Shortly after the Council in 1965, the church found itself split into three camps: first, the traditionalists, who held that Vatican II was a serious departure from the Tridentine heritage; second, progressives, who believed that the Council did not go far enough in reforming the church; third, many individuals caught in the middle, comprised of faithful Catholics who supported reforms of Vatican II and wanted them carried out in an intelligent and judicious manner.[1]

While the conservative camp pushed to restore the church to its preconciliar reality, the radical group sought to change the church more dramatically by pushing for substantive reforms in clerical discipline, a married

---

[1] McBrien, *The Remaking of the Church*, in which he describes these groups as A, B, and C Catholics.

clergy, and the ordination of women. A decade later, the Lutheran sociologist Peter Berger would describe the first camp as neoorthodox; today they would be called restorationists. For Berger, this radical group became "bargainers with modernity," surrendering little by little the mission of the church to that of the modern world. Many in this latter group gave up on the church completely, becoming secular or cultural Catholics, or losing all sense of transcendence in their lives. The conservative Hartford Appeal of 1974, signed by both Peter Berger and Avery Dulles, among others, describes these people as living in a "world without windows."[2] Even before this, Paul VI's encyclical of July 1968, *Humane Vitae*, barring all artificial contraception, sent a chill through the church of the progressives. Was Vatican II to be taken seriously or not? Were the reforms of the Council a continuation of Trent, or the beginning of a completely new church in the final century of the second millennium?

At the same time, the Protestant tradition was also changing dramatically. Mainstream Protestantism—Lutherans, Presbyterians, Methodists, the United Church of Christ, and other denominations—were losing members at a significant rate. Most Protestant churches in the United States have fewer than fifty people at every Sunday worship service. Where have all the people gone? Some join progressive Catholics in rejecting any church affiliation whatsoever. These people, in the jargon of the new millennium, fancy themselves "spiritual" but not "religious." Others join large evangelical churches, where the emphasis is on preaching a simple Gospel message and telling the people what they want to hear. Some of the radical evangelicals deny evolution, affirm the inerrancy of Scripture, and often link themselves to the political right. So-called lapsed Catholics are more likely to join an evangelical church, if they are interested in any church at all, than return to the Catholic tradition. An interesting alliance has been formed in recent years between conservative Catholic hierarchy and conservative evangelical Christians. Some see this alliance as truly unholy, but only time will tell if it is a harbinger of renewed Christianity or the death knell of noncritical and reactionary Christian attitudes.

9.2 Fast Forward Sixty Plus Years

Looking back more than a half century on the Second Vatican Council, the

---

[2] Peter Berger, "For a World with Windows," in *Against the World and For the World: The Hartford Appeal and the Future of American Religion,*" ed. Peter Berger and Richard John Neuhaus (New York: Seabury, 1976), 8–19.

question for historians, theologians, liturgists, and church ministers is simple: did Vatican II genuinely reform and renew the church or did it rupture and segment the church in a way that now must be remedied if possible?

One's interpretation of the Second Vatican Council affects one's interpretation of the church today; likewise, one's understanding of the church today will affect one's understanding of the Council sixty years after its first session. Let us explore this question of reform or rupture, renewal or segmentation, since Pope John XXIII opened the great twentieth-century Council. My thesis in what follows is this: the contemporary Catholic Church is in a conflict of ecclesiologies—between the revival of Tridentinism, or "neo-Tridentinism," visible in the policies of the two popes before Francis, and the authentic spirit of reform and renewal in the documents of Vatican II.

At the outset, I suggest as a cautionary reminder that we recall, in the words of Antoine de Saint-Exupery, we lack the perspective for those transformations that go deep. In spite of all of our current technology of instant communication and social networking, authentic vision can be found no more quickly than human knowledge and wisdom allows. In the Old Testament, God's revelation to the ancient Israelites that culminated in Jesus took almost two thousand years. God's patience should inspire a similar patience within us: sixty years allows a small vision and a little perspective, but we must be fully aware of the illusions of history and our own personal limitations. We must also remember that in evaluating the Second Vatican Council, we are also implicitly, and explicitly, too, examining the First Council of the Vatican (1869–1870) and the Council of Trent (1545–1563). These three councils comprise our understanding of the church in the modern era and of the Catholic tradition since the Reformation.

Church councils are not called by whim but in times of crisis and indecision. Both the Council of Trent and Vatican II responded to an urgent need for change in the church: reform at Trent after the split between Protestants and Catholics, and renewal at Vatican II in a time of the church's growing irrelevance in the modern world. It is true that Vatican II "followed in the footsteps" of Trent, but only in part. A different and distinct type of ecclesiology emerged from each council. The first, which hardened into a system called Tridentinism, understood the church as a *societas perfecta* or perfect society, an institution in possession of changeless divine truth in its doctrinal and moral proclamations. Vatican II's ecclesiology, in contrast to Trent's, restored a biblical and historical approach to understanding the church and doing theology, and it made a final break with the ahistorical neoscholastic era; it opened the doors of the church and admonished it to scrutinize "the signs of the times."

The documents of Vatican II, designed to renew the church and to bring *aggiornomento* to the church's self-understanding and its relationship to the world, led the church into the turbulent theological struggle among the three groups already mentioned: those who adhered to the spirit of the conciliar documents, those who wished to push reforms beyond what the documents explicitly said, and a group—in many cases the official magisterium—who embodied a restorationist or a "neo-Tridentine" attitude.

The restorationist attitude has grown stronger in the time since Vatican II, creating a visible polarization within the church. Whether this attitude will create a third millennium church ultimately more faithful to Sixtus V than to John XXIII remains to be seen. Who will populate this church is also another question: many of the older generation, those few who recall the pre-Vatican II church? A small group of young people nostalgically attached, as Philip Rieff says, to the "archaic alone as the substance of that dark patina they call faith?"[3] Likewise, the decline of mainstream Protestant churches perhaps suggests that only the Roman Catholic tradition can stand prophetically among all types of neo-fundamentalisms, therapeutic mega-churches, and the secular world closed to the Transcendent.

9.3 Two Ecclesiologies

First, the Tridentine idea of church as the "perfect society" developed during and after the implementation of the decrees of the Council of Trent; it may also be called ultramontane, because its focus is exclusively on papal and curial power. This ecclesiology reached its pinnacle at the First Council of the Vatican (1869–1870) in the decree, *Summo Pontifice*, which for the first time gave juridical power to the papacy over every diocese and bishop in the world. This document also declared the papacy infallible in matters of faith and morals. In the words of the great Dominican theologian mentioned, Yves Congar, ecclesiology at Vatican I was more properly "hierarchology" (see chapter eight), where the study of the church was reduced to the study of hierarchy. This idea of the church is embodied in the figure of Pius IX, the longest reigning pope in the church's history, and in the Pian popes that succeeded him. Under Pope Pius X, and with the support of his Spanish Secretary of State, Cardinal Raphael Merry del Val, the so-called heresy of "Modernism" led to the firing of many seminary professors. Modernism espoused the

[3] Philip Rieff, *The Triumph of the Therapeutic*, 253–54.

importance of subjective experience in doing theology; the oath against modernism, required of every priest, survived until 1967, at last a victim of Vatican II's renewal. Today, with an irony that Pius X would *not* enjoy, most theologians assert that human experience is the starting point of doing theology.[4]

Thus, the Tridentine church believed that the church was an institution established by Christ with a hierarchical structure, an unchangeable belief system, and a strict and unyielding moral code. In 1903, the Biblical commission, when asked why the death of Moses is described in the Pentateuch, replied that Moses must have appeared to tell the author about his own death! Here is *a priori* knowledge, completely closed to experience. This reflects a post-Reformation understanding of theology and church, buffeted for centuries by opposition of all sorts: the Reformation itself, Gallicanism, Rationalism, Darwinism, Marxism—in short everything associated with modernity. This idea of the church endured at Vatican II in the vocal minority that supported the conservative *original schemas*, especially of the four major constitutions—the Church, the Church in the Modern World, Divine Revelation, and the Sacred Liturgy. These schemas would ratify the Tridentine church with little or no concessions to contemporary experience and the signs of the times, in the famous phrase of *Gaudium et Spes*. This idea of the church unfortunately flourished to some degree in the papacies and curia of Pope John Paul II and Pope Benedict XVI. William E. Murnion sees the pontificates of John Paul II and Benedict XVI as a "single long pontificate" meant to "arrest and in some cases reverse the aggiornamento—the modernization of the Roman Catholic Church initiated by Vatican II."[5]

Second, the idea of the church is what may be called post-Vatican II ecclesiology. The church is not an eternal perfect society, but a pilgrim church, a sacramental church. It is a biblical and historical church, the Body of Christ and the People of God, a church where all of its members—clergy, religious, laity, men and women, are called to holiness. This church begins in the Trinitarian life of God (chapter one of *Lumen Gentium*), and is the whole People of God (chapter two of *Lumen Gentium*). These chapters precede the distinction between hierarchy and laity (chapters two, three, and four). Because this church watches the signs of the times, it is always open to change; more

[4] See Lane, *The Experience of God*, introduction and chap. 1.

[5] William E. Murnion, "Faith and Reason in Aquinas" (paper delivered at the Lonergan Workshop, Boston, 2010); cited in Thomas Gwozdz, "Catholicism and Roman Catholicism," *American Theological Inquiry* 5, no. 2 (2012), 13.

importantly, it recognizes that it has always changed. To repeat, "Theology [does] exist in history, not eternity."[6]

This Vatican II idea of the church did not begin, of course, with the Council itself. It has its foundations in the great Pauline biblical images of the church as the Body of Christ and the People of God. It flourished for more than a millennium where the church was understood as the Body of Christ (the Eucharist was called the mystical Body of Christ until an eleventh-century heretic, Berengar of Tours, when "mystical" was applied to the church instead). In the twelfth and thirteenth centuries, political, social, philosophical, and theological changes took place that narrowed the church's understanding of itself into a social structural and institutional reality. It is no surprise, then, that the first formal ecclesiologies that appear at the beginning of the fourteenth century were not about the mystery of the church but a defense of the church's political authority and papal power. One might argue persuasively that this defensive definition, intensified and set in stone by the Reformation, survived until the mid-twentieth century. Not until Vatican II did the church reflect upon itself comprehensively as a mystery and, in Avery Dulles's words, as a "divine self-gift."

The changing ecclesiology of Vatican has its immediate origins in the theological experience of the First World War. Three important theological movements took place: the biblical movement, the liturgical revival, and the return to the theological sources in the Fathers of the Church (see chapter eight). Catholic biblical scholarship is now on a par with Protestant biblical scholarship. The liturgical movement, associated with the Benedictine Abbey at Maria Laach and the name of Dom Odo Casel, influenced the Constitution on the Sacred Liturgy that emphasizes the participation of the Christian in Christ's death and resurrection. Joseph Jungmann, a Jesuit, was also an important name in pre-Vatican II biblical scholarship. Finally, the return to the writings of the Fathers of the Church as a rich source of theology stood in sharp contrast to the static and neoscholastic theology of the Tridentine church. People like Karl Adam, Romano Guardini, Emile Mersch, Yves de Montcheuil, Henri de Lubac, Yves Congar, Jean Danielou, and Karl Rahner, among others, were the theologians who changed theology after the Great War and were the precursors of Vatican II. All these theologians influenced the bishops who gathered in Rome in 1962. The papacy itself, with Pius XII's two encyclicals, *Mystici Corporis* (1943) and *Mediator Dei* (1947), was also a contributing factor in the creation of Vatican II's idea of the church.

---

[6] Schoonenberg, *Man and Sin*, 192.

9.4 The Clash at the Council

These two ideas of the church, never mutually exclusive, were embodied at Vatican II. The minority Tridentine ecclesiology's best-known supporter was Alfredo Cardinal Ottaviani, the head of the Holy Office from 1953 to 1966, and then the reorganized Congregation for the Doctrine of the Faith from 1966 to 1968. Perhaps the best-known name associated with the majority progressives was Augustine Cardinal Bea, a noted German Scripture scholar, Pius XII's confessor, and head of the Secretariat for Promoting Christian Unity. Pope Paul VI kept major issues off the agenda of the Council, believing them too sensitive and potentially explosive: clerical celibacy, birth control, and the reform of the Roman Curia. To this list, one must add a crucial item that the Council fathers also did not consider—the reform of the papacy itself. The Council of Trent sought to reform the church "in head and members" and saved it from self-destruction. The reforms were many: education of the clergy with the creation of seminaries; the proper role of bishops as shepherds of their own diocese (recall that of the twenty-two dioceses in France in Luther's time, seventeen bishops were living in Rome permanently, enjoying the Renaissance); the pastoral care of the laity or the *cura animarum*, the care of souls, so neglected in the fourteenth and fifteenth centuries. It was unable to consider the papacy itself because the pope was needed to implement the reforms.

At Vatican II, the progressives clearly won the day in both style and substance. However, the minority did not give up, and have not given up sixty years after the Council. Several significant changes were present in the documents of Vatican II. *First*, and perhaps the most important and comprehensive, was an awareness by the majority of the historicity of the church. As Joseph Komonchak writes:

> There is no point at which Vatican II departs from any dogmatic teaching of the Council of Trent, but at Vatican II, Trent and its problematic ceased to serve as the supreme touchstone of faith. The tradition was no longer read in the light of Trent; Trent was read in the light of the tradition. This is visible in what Vatican II has to say about the common priesthood of the faithful, the eucharist, and the ministerial priesthood: the teaching of Trent is neither denied nor passed over in

silence; it is integrated into a larger whole.[7]

While Vatican II was faithful to Trent, the church's entire worldview changed. Trent was no longer the static and ahistorical norm of the entire tradition, but one aspect, albeit a very important one, in a living historical tradition. The conservatives at Vatican II refused to accept this shift; likewise, it appears that Pope John Paul II and Benedict XVI have sought to return the church's ecclesiology to the ultramontane idea of the church before John XXIII's call for aggiornamento.

The *second* important change involved the style of the Council. As distinguished church historian John O'Malley writes: "[Trent and Vatican II] were different cultural entities. In this regard, Vatican II was not only unlike Trent but unlike any council that preceded it." He distinguishes between two traditions in the church that express themselves in distinctive styles of discourse: the legislative-judicial and the poetic-rhetorical. These traditions create "two styles of being Christian, two styles, therefore, of spirituality, and, thus, two styles of church." The poetic-rhetorical tradition emerged at Vatican II in sharp contrast to the juridical approach. As O'Malley says, "For the first time, a council adopted in a consistent and comprehensive way for its enactments the poetic-rhetorical mode of discourse."[8] It is difficult to underestimate the importance of this change of styles since virtually all of the implementations of the Tridentine teaching were in the legislative-juridical style, a style that lends itself easily to hierarchical power and papal authority.

9.5 A Clash of Ecclesiologies Today

The issues facing the Catholic church today in 2022 are, in many respects, the same issues that it has faced since the Reformation and the Council of Trent. There is a conflict of worldviews, of ways of doing theology, of understanding authority, of being church and being responsible for church. In the period before the Vatican II and immediately after the Council, theology was very focused on the church and its nature and mission in the world. More recently, other issues interested theologians—rethinking Christology, the question of

---

[7] Joseph Komonchak, "The Council of Trent at the Second Vatican Council," in *From Trent to Vatican II: Historical and Theological Investigations*, ed. Raymond F. Bulman and Frederick J. Parrella (New York: Oxford University Press, 2006), 74.

[8] John W. O'Malley, "Trent and Vatican II: Two Styles of Church," in *From Trent to Vatican II: Historical and Theological Investigations*, ed. Raymond F. Bulman and Frederick J. Parrella (New York: Oxford University Press, 2006), 301–20.

God, the meaning of faith in a secular world, social and political questions, individual moral questions, and medical ethics. Ecclesiology was always implicit in both the work of theologians and in the statements of the Magisterium—and sometimes this ecclesiology was more than just implicit.

The two ideas of the church or two ecclesiologies that we have considered remain very much the same, from the Reformation through Trent, the two Councils of the Vatican, and now into the third decade of this third millennium. *First*, the minority at the Vatican II continues to espouse the legislative–juridical understanding of church; they wish to return to the Tridentine/ultramontane church that flourished, with minor exceptions, before Vatican II. While Pope John XXIII and Pope Paul VI embodied the spirit of reform at Vatican II, Pope John Paul II and Benedict the XVI did not. For these popes, power and authority is centered in Rome and in the Roman Curia. (It is interesting to note that when the sex abuse scandals emerged in 2002, the American bishops rushed to Rome for advice and direction—much to the amusement of the European hierarchy.) Many Catholics understand the pope to be not unlike an all-powerful chief executive officer of a major world religious corporation rather than the Bishop of Rome and the Servant of the Servants of God. This understanding of the papacy is relatively new, beginning with Pope Pius IX in the nineteenth century, and was a direct result of his pontificate. Indeed, Pius IX was the first "world pope." The hierarchical ecclesiology of Pio Nono and its Vatican-centered adherents today understand Vatican II as a rupture in an eternal pattern, not genuine reform and renewal.

On the other hand, the idea of the church to emerge from Vatican II understands the church in biblical and historical categories. While the wording of the conciliar documents themselves was often a compromise between the conservatives and the liberals at the Council, the fundamental thrust of Vatican II's documents was reform and renewal. The majority of Catholic theologians in the past half century are theologians in the spirit of Vatican II, and they do theology according to this spirit. The majority of American Catholics, raised with the reform and renewal of Vatican II, no longer see the church as an institution but as community, sacrament, and servant. Of course, there are some who like the Tridentine Mass in Latin; virtually all of these people, of course, do not know Latin themselves! The major confrontations between Catholic theologians and church authority since the Council are the result of two different ecclesiologies, two different ways of doing theology.

In a recent article, theologian Thomas Gwordz suggests that the Tridentine church, hardened by its anti-world, anti-modern position, fundamentally changed the ancient meaning of the term "Catholic," an openness to the universal in knowledge and a quest for truth and transcendence, into its virtual opposite, the Roman Catholic Church. As he says, "It is unfortunate that the term 'Catholic' was swallowed up by its association with the institution of Roman Catholicism."[9] As Gwozdz writes:

> We do not yet know the full meaning of what it means to be Catholic. However, Roman Catholicism of the nineteenth century seemed to claim that it did. Given the fact the Catholic Church has always had a tradition and openness, the worst kind of Catholic bias would be enunciated as follows: "Since we have the truth, there is nothing to learn that could change what we already know."

This is reminiscent of the pre-Vatican II Church, a Church that no longer looks forward, but backwards, a Church theologically certain of itself and its teachings. It was this Roman Catholicism or Tridentine Church that was challenged by the Second Vatican Council. Yves Congar argued that the great achievement of Vatican II was a departure from the Tridentine system.

Thus, Vatican II called into question the logic of modern Roman Catholicism in three basic ways: first, a more positive view of modern culture; second, a reform of Church worship, devotion, and practice; third, encouragement of local Catholic churches to achieve cultural diversity within the one Catholic Church.[10] In essence, the Council moved the church away from a Catholicism that was static, backward looking, dogmatic, authoritative, and centralized, to an open, forward-looking, decentralized ecumenical church. This was a church in line with its name, "catholicity," a dynamic church, open to search for what is authentically true and good in all things; a church aware that it is an eschatological church that remains a "pilgrim church." The Catholic Church has always had the mark of "catholicity," or universality, an intellectual tradition of discerning truths and values in economics, politics, culture, the arts, science, humanities, and religion. It was always open to further insights and development. According to Komonchack, Karl Rahner claimed that the Second Vatican Council was "the beginning of a tentative approach by the Church to the discovery and official realization of itself as a world-Church." This was a dramatic shift from a Eurocentric church to a church open to other cultures. As such, Rahner felt that the Council contained a

---

[9] Thomas Gwozdz, "Catholicism and Roman Catholicism," *American Theological Inquiry* 5, no. 2 (2012), 9–15.

[10] Joseph A. Komonchak, "Modernity and the Construction of Roman Catholicism," in Christianesimo nella Storia 18 (1997), 384.

theological will to change church tradition and break from a Eurocentric Christianity, a break with the Roman Catholicism of the nineteenth century to a new multicultural ecumenical age.[11] Is William E. Murnion correct that the pontificates of John Paul II and Benedict XVI are a "single long pontificate," meant to "arrest and in some cases reverse the aggiornamento—the modernization of the Roman Catholic Church initiated by Vatican II?"[12] Evidence of this clinging to the past is John Paul's singling out Aquinas as the theological exemplar for reconciling faith and reason. Murnion claims that this "exclusive endorsement of Aquinas for both his systematic and his moral theology reversed the approach of Vatican II, which, while giving a ritual endorsement to Aquinas, freed Catholic philosophers and theologians to explore the entire universe of thinkers, ancient, medieval, and modern, and develop their own independent philosophies."[13] It seems that John Paul II explicitly intended to revive and continue the Thomism sparked by Leo XIII's encyclical *Aeterni Patris*. In line with the practice of nineteenth century Roman Catholicism, Cardinal Ratzinger as Prefect of the Congregation of the Doctrine of the Faith enforced orthodoxy by silencing or otherwise disciplining many Catholic theologians and philosophers, generally in secret and with peremptory decrees.[14] Both John Paul and Benedict have depicted the modern world "as a reign of secularism—a crisis to which they call the Catholic Church to oppose with the rule of faith."[15] They have also "described ecumenical relations and inter-religious dialogue, not as valuable endeavors in and of themselves, but simply a tactic in the Church's mission of universal evangelization."[16] This was the task of John Paul II's encyclical *Redemptor Hominis*. In short, the medium of the Kingdom of God "subsisted" in the Roman Catholic Church. Other Christian churches were simply "deficient as churches."[17] In this way, the Roman Catholic Church is the sole representative of a complete and unblemished Christianity.

---

[11] Joseph A. Komonchak, "Interpreting Vatican II" (paper delivered at the Lonergan Workshop in Boston, 2011).

[12] William E. Murnion, "Faith and Reason in Aquinas" (paper delivered at the Lonergan Workshop, Boston, 2010), 4.

[13] Murnion, 5.

[14] Murnion, 5.

[15] Murnion, 6.

[16] Murnion, 5.

[17] Murnion, 6.

9.6 The Future of the Church

Where does the church go from here? Both conservatives and liberals today seem more militant. In Pope Benedict's pontificate, he appeared to accept the idea of a much leaner but fiercely loyal church. In response, many young people vote with their feet by no longer attending the liturgy or identifying themselves as Catholic. They are sometimes part of the SBNR generation, those that claim to be spiritual but not religious. A significant percentage of young people become NONES, uncommitted to any religious tradition.[18] Many religious institutions are not meeting the spiritual needs of high school, college, and post-college Americans. Mainline Protestant churches have been in decline for some time. Catholicism is doing better because of its stronger sense of authority and a traditional communal culture. Only mega-churches are thriving, because they tell people what they want to hear and give them a strong sense of security. But even their growth has been leveling off.

What will be the outcome of this present clash of ecclesiologies? Let us consider both the short-term and long-term possibilities. I believe that history is on the side of the reforms of the Second Vatican Council and the liberal agenda that followed it. As J. M. R. Tillard asked almost forty years ago, "Have we received the documents of Vatican II?" "Receive" is a technical theological term which means integrated into the life of the church.[19] His answer was clear: some documents have been received, some have been partially received, and some have not been received at all and never will be received. The theology of the major constitutions cannot be subject to a return to a Tridentine perspective: thus, the church is the People of God; the church must dialogue with the contemporary world and recognize the primary Catholic principle that "grace perfects nature" in all things; finally, the liturgy is a true celebration of death and resurrection written deeply in the human heart. Inevitably, reform and renewal will continue.

In the short term, however, the picture is of some concern. The church in the United States, like American politics, is intensely polarized. Church authority's adamant stand against discussing priestly celibacy and the ordination of women does not bode well. Sadly, in the United States media, church authority gets all the press on questions such as birth control, abortion, and gay and lesbian rights. The hierarchy's occasional and convenient alliance with

[18] See Ryan P. Burge, *The Nones: Where They Came From, Who They Are, and Where They Are Going* (Minneapolis: Fortress Press, 2021).

[19] J. M. R. Tillard, "Vatican II: Did We Receive It?" *One in Christ* 21 (1985): 276–83.

Evangelical or fundamentalist Christians only adds to the difficulty and ambiguity. "Catholic" is too often understood in the popular mind to mean to be "against something." While the Catholic League of New York defends the church against anti-Catholic incidents, it does not represent the majority of Catholic laity in the United States. Catholic politicians, such as Steve Bannon and Ron DeSantis, often take a very right-wing political positions *against* the official church. These people are less Catholic than the average Catholic in the pews. Often forgotten is the broad social justice agenda of the church, its rejection of the death penalty, its fight for immigration rights, its work for the homeless, and other vital social issues. American Catholics should be reminded by the hierarchy and authentic Catholic politicians and educators of the other and more inclusive side of the Catholic agenda.

In contrast, progressive Catholics, on the boundary of remaining Catholic, or Catholic in name only and disassociated from the community—all these people see the world differently. These Catholics have a new advocate and hero in Pope Francis. From 1846 to 2013, the papacy was almost exclusively in conservative hands. Francis's modesty and humility have made him a popular figure around the world. Inside the church, however, his reforms have infuriated conservatives and sparked a revolt against many of his positions. He has significantly expanded the College of Cardinals, naming twenty-one new Cardinals (sixteen are under eighty and eligible to vote for the next pope). In America, some politically conservative Catholics have long criticized Pope Francis for being pro-migrants, anti-capitalist and less rigid on doctrine than his two predecessors. Perhaps his stance on the LGBTQ community is most infuriating to reactionary Catholics in the United States. The spirit of Pope Francis, not any archconservative and anachronistic faction, is the future of the church and its papacy.

I am certain that the church in the centuries to come will survive but perhaps in a dramatically different form. For the first three centuries, it was part of the counterculture, unassociated with power; perhaps a similar social structure awaits the church in the future. The Holy Spirit is always at work everywhere, in ways we do not understand and cannot fathom. My own opinion is this: Only if the documents of Vatican II are authentically "received," that is, accepted into the life of the Church, allowed to flourish, and to develop in the context of what Karl Rahner called a "world church," will the church, in deed and not merely in words, be the "sacrament of the world's salvation."

As a final word, allow me to quote the words of Lutheran theologian Paul Tillich (see chapter eight) who possessed a remarkable appreciation of the Catholic tradition. This admiration inspired him to describe Catholicism in 1929, when the Catholicism of Vatican II and this third millennium was as unimaginable to his world as persons landing on the moon. His words should be repeated today, almost a century later, to remind us of the living and changing tradition of the great and boundless Catholic Church, not merely its institutional form.

> The Catholic Church…has manifestly been able to preserve a genuine substance that continues to exist, although it is encased within an ever-hardening crust. But whenever the hardness and crust are broken through and the substance becomes visible, it exercises a peculiar fascination; then we see what was once the life substance and inheritance of all of us and what we have now lost, and a deep yearning awakens in us for the departed youth of our culture.[20]

[20] Paul Tillich "The Protestant Message and the Man of Today," in *The Protestant Era*, 194.

INDEX